Ernest J. Gaines: Conversations

Literary Conversations Series
Monika Gehlawat
General Editor

Books by Ernest J. Gaines

Catherine Carmier, Atheneum, 1964
Of Love and Dust, Dial Press, 1967
Bloodline, Dial Press, 1968
The Autobiography of Miss Jane Pittman, Dial Press, 1971
A Long Day in November (children's book), Dial Press, 1971
In My Father's House, Knopf, 1978
A Gathering of Old Men, Knopf, 1983
A Lesson Before Dying, Knopf, 1993
Mozart and Leadbelly: Stories and Essays, Knopf, 2005
The Tragedy of Brady Sims, Vintage Books, 2017

Ernest J. Gaines: Conversations

Edited by Marcia Gaudet

University Press of Mississippi / Jackson

The University Press of Mississippi is the scholarly publishing agency of
the Mississippi Institutions of Higher Learning: Alcorn State University,
Delta State University, Jackson State University, Mississippi State University,
Mississippi University for Women, Mississippi Valley State University,
University of Mississippi, and University of Southern Mississippi.

www.upress.state.ms.us

The University Press of Mississippi is a member
of the Association of University Presses.

First printing 2019
∞

Library of Congress Cataloging-in-Publication Data

Names: Gaines, Ernest J., 1933– interviewee. | Gaudet, Marcia G., editor.
Title: Ernest J. Gaines : conversations / edited by Marcia Gaudet.
Description: Jackson : University Press of Mississippi,
[2019] | Series: Literary conversations series |
Identifiers: LCCN 2018045736 (print) | LCCN 2018046556 (ebook) | ISBN
9781496822192 (epub single) | ISBN 9781496822208 (epub institutional) | ISBN
9781496822215 (pdf single) | ISBN 9781496822222 (pdf institutional) | ISBN
9781496822178 (cloth : alk. paper) | ISBN 9781496822185 (pbk. : alk. paper)
Subjects: LCSH: Gaines, Ernest J., 1933-—Interviews. | Authors, American—
Louisiana—20th century—Interviews. | LCGFT: Interviews.
Classification: LCC PS3557.A355 (ebook) | LCC PS3557.
A355 A5 2019 (print) | DDC 813/.54—dc23
LC record available at https://lccn.loc.gov/2018045736

British Library Cataloging-in-Publication Data available

Contents

Introduction

Ernest J. Gaines has been publishing fiction for over sixty years, from his first short story publications in his college literary magazine in 1956 to his latest book in 2017. The author of ten books, including *The Autobiography of Miss Jane Pittman* and *A Lesson Before Dying*, he is now one of the most respected and beloved living American writers.

In the 1995 publication *Conversations with Ernest Gaines*, editor John Lowe says in his introduction, "we seem to be on the verge of a veritable Gaines goldrush." The twenty-three plus years of Gaines studies following this publication show that Lowe's prediction was accurate. Since 1995, Gaines's 1993 novel, *A Lesson Before Dying*, has reached over two million copies in sales. In 2005, he published *Mozart and Leadbelly: Stories and Essays*. Gaines's short novel *The Tragedy of Brady Sims* was published in August 2017. The scholarship on Gaines has continued with 260 listings on Gaines (137 since 1995) in the *MLA Bibliography* and thirteen books published on Gaines. Interviews with Gaines have continued as well, particularly important because of all the conversations in the 1995 volume, only one deals significantly with *A Lesson Before Dying*—Lowe's 1994 interview. Because of the importance of Gaines and his work in the literary canon, a new volume of his interviews is warranted. *Ernest J. Gaines: Conversations* brings together, for the first time, the past twenty-four years of Gaines's conversations about his writing, his life, and his perceptions of the world around him.

This volume brings together the significant and valuable interviews with Gaines that discuss *A Lesson Before Dying*, as well as Gaines's 2005 publication, *Mozart and Leadbelly: Stories and Essays*. It includes as well an interview with the editor on *The Tragedy of Brady Sims*. The interviews with Gaines since 1994 provide a retrospective of his work from the viewpoint of a senior writer, now eighty-five years old. These include the first interviews conducted at Gaines's home on False River, built on land that was part of River Lake Plantation and purchased from one of the heirs. It also gives an important international perspective on Gaines and his work—five of the interviews were conducted by international scholars.

The earliest published interview following the 1995 *Conversations with Ernest Gaines* is French journalist Bernard Magnier's "Interview with Ernest J. Gaines," published in the April 1995 edition of the *UNESCO Courier*. In this interview, Gaines talks about regionalism and the liability of labels for writers. He says, "All the great writers are regionalists. Faulkner wrote about Mississippi, Homer about Greece, Balzac about Paris, and Shakespeare about a kind of England. But that doesn't mean they're not universal" (6). He also discusses how a conflict serves as an impetus for narrative fiction, as well as his ideas about Africa and *négritude*.

Gaines and his wife, Dianne, lived in France for a year during 1996. He was on leave from his position as writer-in-residence at University of Louisiana at Lafayette, and he taught creative writing at University of Rennes. The next two interviews were conducted in Europe, and Gaines discusses the experience of living and teaching in France as well as the reception of his novels in Europe. Raphaël Lambert and Claude Julien interviewed Gaines in 1996 in Rennes. The interview focuses on *A Gathering of Old Men,* but it includes several of Gaines's other works. Wolfgang Lepschy's 1996 interview with Gaines was conducted at University of Bonn, in Bonn, Germany, where Gaines had presented a reading from his novel *A Lesson Before Dying.* He talks about his works in translation, the influences of European writers on his work, and the European perspective.

Among the many things Gaines discusses in his interviews are the recurrent themes in his works: the search for manhood, the importance of personal responsibility and standing with dignity, and the problems of fathers and sons in his fictional world, all firmly grounded in a deep sense of place. He addresses his role as teacher and mentor, the importance of strong women in his life, and the influence of spirituality, religion, and music on his work. He also talks about storytelling, the nature of narrative, writing as a journey, and how he sees himself as a storyteller.

In Allen Gee's 1998 interview, Gaines examines the development of his writing style and his writing process. He discusses, as well, the critical influence of an author's childhood on his writing and the force of strong women in his life. In the Levasseur and Rabalais interview in 1998, Gaines considers how he sees his responsibilities as a teacher of creative writing. He also talks about his use of dialogue and voice in writing *A Gathering of Old Men, Of Love and Dust, Catherine Carmier,* and *A Lesson Before Dying,* including Jefferson's notebook. Marcia Gaudet questions Gaines about the influence of religion and belief in her 1999 interview for *Louisiana Literature.* Gaines discusses the nuances of religion in his works, in the African American culture, and in his own life.

Rose Anne Brister's 2001 interview gives a wonderful retrospective of Gaines's writing up to that time. Gaines focuses on sense of place and the southern pastoral, as well as the future of southern literature. Gaines talks about writing *A Lesson Before Dying*, its selection for the Oprah Winfrey Book Club, and his response to meeting Oprah. Dale Brown's 2001 interview addresses a range of questions, including how Gaines deals with the celebrity of being an acclaimed writer. It focuses, in particular, on how issues of religion, faith, and doubt affect his development of characters within the rural Louisiana culture of Gaines's work. Marcia Gaudet and Darrell Bourque's 2002 conversation with Gaines is really a discussion of art forms among three colleagues and friends. Gaines expands upon how visual art and music, in particular, have influenced his work.

In the 2005 interview with Wiley Cash, a former Gaines student and a bestselling author himself, Gaines considers his retirement and his return to the land that was part of the plantation where he grew up. It includes a discussion about Hurricane Katrina and its effect on Gaines's family, as well as New Orleans and its culture. Gaines also discusses *Catherine Carmier, A Lesson Before Dying*, and *Mozart & Leadbelly*. Anne Gray Brown interviews Gaines in 2006 about writing as a process of discovery and the influence of place on his fiction. He then discusses his novel *A Lesson Before Dying*, particularly focusing on Jefferson's diary and his process of coming to this form of having Jefferson express his thoughts.

Gaudet and Richard's 2007 interview "Working from Home" was a celebration of Gaines's return to living on the plantation land where he was born. Gaines talks about his friendship with Wendell Berry and his education as a writer. He also expresses his appreciation of the Ernest J. Gaines Award for Literary Excellence established by the Baton Rouge Area Foundation and the importance of providing young writers with the chance to work.

Among the many things discussed in Dominique Audiat's 2008 interview, Gaines explains how his own experiences as an African American led to his becoming the writer he is. He also talks about the meaning of the book title *Mozart and Leadbelly*, as well as the essays and stories in the book. Audiat's 2009 interview with Gaines focuses on comparisons of Gaines's *The Autobiography of Miss Jane Pittman* and President Barack Obama's *Dreams from My Father*. It examines race in America and how Obama's election as President has affected discussions of the black experience. Audiat was a doctoral student at the Sorbonne at the time of the interviews, giving an updated perspective on Gaines's international influence.

Several articles and interviews not in this volume include Cindy Urrea's "Reflections of a Serious Writer," R. Reese Fuller's "Going Home," and Bob

Edwards's "Fighting Illiteracy with *A Lesson Before Dying*" on NPR's *Morning Edition*. In Katharine Q. Seelye's 2010 *New York Times* piece Gaines says he has "put down" his pen. Instead of writing, he says, his goal is to preserve the cemetery where his ancestors are buried and the church from the plantation quarters where he grew up. He also relates this effort to the stories his people provided for him as a writer. While Gaines has deliberately cut back on his interviews and appearances, at eighty-five, he continues to write. He continues to write because, as he has said many times over the years, he has not yet finished with "this Louisiana thing that drives me." There are still things to be said.

In Melanie Warner Spencer's 2016 "Literary Legend" interview essay published in *Louisiana Life*, Gaines "reflects on his hopes and passions." He also talks about *A Lesson Before Dying* and the continuing problems of racism in the United States. In a brief interview with Rick Fahle (of PBS's Book View Now) on *The Tragedy of Brady Sims* at the 2017 National Book Festival in Washington, DC, Gaines said (when asked how things have changed for blacks today compared to the past when white men wearing hoods threatened them): "People talk about change, change, change, but I don't think there has been that much change. The reason why you don't have the hood today is because the law says you shouldn't have the hood. But the character who was under that hood is still out there today. He just stopped wearing the hood. So I don't know how people have changed. I really don't know *if* they have changed. Situations have changed."

Marcia Gaudet's previously unpublished interview focuses on Gaines's 2017 short novel, *The Tragedy of Brady Sims.* Once again, Gaines has written about concerns and themes that persist—race and power, the challenges of black manhood in an unjust society, the need to understand how good and evil coexist in the world and in the individual, the elusive nature of truth, and the role of humor in enabling survival. He addresses these concerns as well as his work-in-progress, a novella tentatively titled "The Daughters of the Creole Lady." The interview includes Gaines's retrospective thoughts on his life and writing career.

Ernest Gaines's importance as a writer is evident by the continued interest of scholars and readers in his work. This new volume of interviews with Gaines brings together the writer's own thoughts and words over the last twenty-four years about his life, his work, and his literary legacy.

MG

Chronology

1933   Ernest James Gaines is born on January 15, in Oscar, Louisiana, to Adrean Jefferson and Manuel Gaines. Later attends the plantation school on River Lake Plantation and then St. Augustine School in New Roads. After his parents' divorce, he and his siblings are raised primarily by his great-aunt, Miss Augusteen Jefferson.

1948   Goes to California to join his mother and stepfather, Adrean and Raphael Colar, and to attend high school.

1953   Graduates from Vallejo Junior College. Then serves in the United States Army.

1957   Graduates from San Francisco State College. His short stories, "The Turtles" and "The Boy in the Double-Breasted Suit," are published in the college journal *Transfer* in 1956.

1958   Wins a Wallace Stegner Fellowship to study creative writing at Stanford University.

1964   His first novel, *Catherine Carmier*, is published.

1967   *Of Love and Dust* is published.

1968   *Bloodline* is published.

1971   *The Autobiography of Miss Jane Pittman* is published. It is nominated for a Pulitzer Prize. *A Long Day in November* is published as a young adult book.

1974   The television movie *The Autobiography of Miss Jane Pittman*, starring Cicely Tyson, brings added attention to the novel and later wins nine Emmy Awards.

1978   *In My Father's House* is published.

1981   Begins teaching creative writing at University of Southwestern Louisiana (now University of Louisiana at Lafayette). Later becomes writer-in-residence.

1983   *A Gathering of Old Men* is published. It is later made into a television film starring Louis Gossett Jr., who wins an Emmy Award for his performance.

1993   *A Lesson Before Dying* is published. Marries Dianne Saulney in May. Receives a John D. and Catherine T. MacArthur Foundation Fellowship. Wins the National Book Critics Circle Award for *A Lesson Before Dying.*

1995   Receives honorary doctorates from Tulane University, Loyola University, and Sewanee University.

1996   Takes leave from University of Southwestern Louisiana (now University of Louisiana Lafayette) and spends year in France teaching creative writing at University of Rennes. Awarded the honor of *Chevalier de l'Ordre des Arts et des Lettres* in Paris.

1997   Returns as writer-in-residence at USL. Works with wife, Dianne, and others to establish the non-profit Mount Zion River Lake Cemetery Association, and serves as president. Oprah Winfrey chooses *A Lesson Before Dying* as an Oprah Winfrey Book Club selection.

1998   Inducted into the American Academy of Arts & Letters. Receives honorary doctorate from Dillard University. First annual Mount Zion River Lake Cemetery Beautification Day on Saturday before La Toussaint (All Saints Day).

1999   The movie *A Lesson Before Dying* premieres in New Orleans, starring Don Cheadle, Mekhi Phifer, Cicely Tyson, and Irma P. Hall. Awarded Acadiana Arts Council Lifetime Achievement Award and receives Honorary Doctor of Letters, University of Miami.

2000   *A Lesson Before Dying* wins Emmy for best movie made for television. Receives Honorary Doctor of Letters from three institutions: Elmira College, Colgate College, and Centenary College. Receives the Governor's Arts Awards Lifetime Achievement Award (Louisiana), National Governors Association Award for Lifetime Contribution to the Arts, Louisiana Center for the Book Writer of the Year Award. National Humanities Medal presented to Gaines by President Bill Clinton.

2001   Romulus Linney adapts *A Lesson Before Dying* into a play, which is performed at theaters and universities throughout the country. "Old Jack" published in *Callaloo*. Chapter Three from *The Man Who Whipped Children* published in *Callaloo*.

2002   Presents Baylor University Ferguson-Clark Author Lecture.

2004   Nominated for Nobel Prize in Literature. *A Lesson Before Dying* is a One Book, One Community Selection. Retires from University of Louisiana at Lafayette and becomes writer-in-residence emeritus.

2005   "Christ Walked Down Market Street" published in *Callaloo*. *Mozart and Leadbelly: Stories and Essays* published (Knopf).

2006   *A Lesson Before Dying* becomes a National Endowment for the Arts Big Read Selection. Presents Tougaloo College Presidential Lecture. "Where Have You Gone, New Orleans?" published in *National Geographic.*

2007   The Ernest J. Gaines Award for Literary Excellence established by Baton Rouge Area Foundation. Receives honorary doctorate from University of North Carolina at Asheville. "My Uncle and the Fat Lady" published in *Callaloo.*

2008   The Louisiana Board of Regents approves the Ernest J. Gaines Center at University of Louisiana at Lafayette. Receives honorary doctorates from University of Louisiana at Lafayette and Emory University. "Writing on Writing: Louisiana Bound" published in *Oxford American.*

2009   *"This Louisiana Thing That Drives Me": The Legacy of Ernest J. Gaines* published, with introduction by Gaines. *"An Obsession of Mine": The Legacy of Ernest J. Gaines* documentary film premieres.

2010   Receives Aspen Prize for Literature, Aspen Writers Foundation. The Ernest J. Gaines Center has its formal opening on October 31.

2011   Receives the Cleanth Brooks Award for Lifetime Achievement from Fellowship of Southern Writers. Receives honorary doctorate from University of North Carolina at Chapel Hill.

2012   Receives Sidney Lanier Prize for Southern Literature. Irvin Mayfield's original jazz tribute to Ernest J. Gaines, "Dirt, Dust, and Trees," premieres in New Orleans, with the New Orleans Jazz Orchestra. Receives Faulkner Society ALIHOT (A Legend in His/Her Own Time) Award, New Orleans.

2013   Receives the National Medal of the Arts for 2012, presented by President Barack Obama on July 10.

2014   Receives Celebration of Black Writing Lifetime Achievement Award in Philadelphia on May 30.

2015   Receives (with wife, Dianne) the Foundation for Historical Louisiana award for preservation of the church and cemetery at River Lake Plantation.

2016   Receives the North Star Award, Zora Heale Hurston/Richard Wright Foundation Legacy Award for career accomplishment and inspiration to the writing community on October 21.

2017   *The Tragedy of Brady Sims* (earlier titled *The Man Who Whipped Children*) published.

Ernest J. Gaines: Conversations

Interview with Ernest J. Gaines

Bernard Magnier / 1994

Reprinted from the *UNESCO Courier*, April 1995, interview with Ernest J. Gaines by Bernard Magnier. Reprinted with permission.

Ernest J. Gaines (born 1933) grew up on a Louisiana plantation where, at the age of nine, he started work as a potato picker, earning fifty cents a day. When he was fifteen he joined his mother in California, where he began to study and discovered a passion for reading. Disappointed to find in books nothing about the world he knew, he decided to start writing himself. His first short stories were published in 1956 and were followed by novels including *Of Love and Dust* (1967) and *The Autobiography of Miss Jane Pittman* (1971), which brought him to the attention of a wide American public. Considered a major "southern novelist," in 1994 he received the US National Book Critics Circle Award for *A Lesson Before Dying*.

Bernard Magnier: Tell us something about your childhood and family background.

Ernest J. Gaines: For more than a century my family lived on a sugarcane plantation in Louisiana, and I am the product of a mixture of Africans, Indians, and whites. That's all I know about my ancestors. I don't know which African country or which Indian tribe they came from.

So I was born on the plantation where my parents worked, and that was where I first went to school. Later I attended school at New Roads, a nearby town that I call Bayonne in my books, until I was fifteen. Then my parents separated. My mother went to live in California, and I followed her there to continue my studies. It was then that I became interested in writing and started to frequent public libraries, which in California were open to everyone, not just whites.

BM: What were the first books you read, the ones that most influenced you?

EJG: I liked to read fiction. There were no black writers and so I started by reading southern writers. But I didn't think much of the demeaning way they spoke of blacks. I turned to European writers, particularly the Russians—Gogol, Turgenev, and Chekhov—who described peasant life in a rich and interesting way. My first novel, *Catherine Carmier*, was inspired by Turgenev's *Fathers and Sons*. Later I discovered Maupassant and Flaubert.

BM: Did you take these writers as your models?
EJG: All these European writers only half satisfied me because they only talked about their own people, and I couldn't find myself in their work. I wanted to talk about my people, so when I was around sixteen or seventeen years old I started to write.

When I was twenty, after I had done my military service, I went to college, where I studied creative writing and English literature. It was there that I discovered Hemingway, Steinbeck, Joyce, and others. But none of these great novelists had any particular influence on me. As someone once said, to take from one person is plagiarism but to take from everybody is genius!

BM: What was your first published work?
EJG: A short story called "The Turtles," which appeared in 1956 in a college literary review in San Francisco. The turtles were a kind of challenge for two young fishermen. Both of them are taken by their fathers to a young lady to initiate them to sex. The little boy who is afraid of the turtle is also afraid of the girl. The little boy who's brave enough to fish and catch the turtles obeys the father. I am very proud of this short story. It has just been republished by the journal of the university where I teach now. Thirty-five years later!

BM: When did you turn to writing novels?
EJG: A literary agent read "The Turtles" and liked it. She contacted my professor, and she encouraged me to write my first novel. I had already written what I thought was a novel when I was sixteen years old. I sent it to a publisher, who turned it down and sent it back to me. I threw it on the fire. Ten years later I went back to this novel, which took me five years to finish and gave me a lot of trouble. But all the time I was learning how to write. After it had been substantially rewritten a dozen or more times and returned to me seven times by the publisher, it was finally accepted. That was how *Catherine Carmier* came to be published by Atheneum. Thirty-five hundred copies were printed, and I doubt even twenty-five hundred were sold. The rest were remaindered at twenty-five cents. If you could get your hand on an original copy today, you'd have to pay more than a hundred dollars for it.

BM: In the United States you are thought of as a "southern writer." Do you think that label accurately describes a literary category or is it too narrow?

EJG: It's too narrow. I have been categorized "a black writer," "a southern writer," "a Californian writer" because I lived in California, "a Louisiana writer" because I wrote about Louisiana . . . I don't feel I fit into any of those categories. I just try to be a decent writer.

BM: And yet almost all your novels are set in a small area, Bayonne Parish . . .

EJG: All the great writers are regionalists. Faulkner wrote about Mississippi, Homer about Greece, Balzac about Paris, Shakespeare about a kind of England. But that doesn't mean they're not universal. People write about what they know best, and readers respond to that wherever they happen to live. *The Autobiography of Miss Jane Pittman* has been translated into several languages, and readers of all races have written to me and said they felt that the old lady was somebody they recognized.

BM: In a way, isn't your Bayonne Parish the Louisiana equivalent of Faulkner's Yoknapatawpha County in Mississippi?

EJG: I did get the inspiration for the parish of Bayonne from Faulkner's mythical Yoknapatawpha County and the use of the multiple point-of-view in the novel. But Faulkner himself was influenced by Sherwood Anderson, whom he knew, and by James Joyce's writing about Dublin. So just as Faulkner inherited from them, I inherited from Faulkner. It's a continuing process.

I certainly feel close to Faulkner. We both belong to the South. We write about the same things—life in small towns, the everyday struggles of poor people, the influence of big landowners on small farmers, race problems. And Mississippi isn't far from Louisiana.

BM: In your novels a breaking point often occurs as a result of a love affair, as if this kind of relationship is a crucible for all kinds of taboos and conflicts.

EJG: That is true of some of my novels, but not all. *A Lesson Before Dying* is the story of an uneducated young black condemned to death for a crime he did not commit and a black schoolteacher who restores his dignity before he dies. Love relationships are not the only situations that breed conflict; it is constant. The major conflict in my work is when the black male attempts to go beyond the line that is drawn for him. But you've also got conflict between young and old, between desire to go back to the place where you were born or to stay where you are, between religious feeling and atheism. . . . There has to be a conflict before there can be a story and before the story reveals racial tension.

BM: Early in their careers, the French-speaking writers of black Africa and the Caribbean gathered beneath the banner of the négritude movement to assert black cultural values. Do you think this movement is still relevant?

EJG: Yes, I do. Even if I don't belong to this school or to any other school, I accept that this idea of négritude, put forward by writers who express themselves in French, can provide young writers with the bearings that are so lacking. In my own little sphere I do the same thing as these African and West Indian writers. I try to describe the daily lives of African Americans as well as I can. I think I'm doing the same thing as they are without putting myself in a box.

BM: What are your feelings about Africa?

EJG: I have never been there. I feel very close to Africa because of my origins but also because every human being ought to feel concerned about the very serious things that are happening there. I sympathize with the sorrows of Africa because they are similar to those we experienced in the South forty-odd years ago. But there are problems in the rest of the world, too. I like African literature and music just as I like those that come to us from Europe and the Americas. My culture is, perhaps above all, Western.

BM: Do you read African writers?

EJG: A little. Not nearly as much as I should!

BM: Do you feel that there is a black cultural community in the United States?

EJG: I don't think there is any kind of school of black culture in the United States today. The expression "black community" is very vague. Is there a white community? I don't know. Nevertheless, black writers tackle the problems they know well but with different approaches. Toni Morrison, Alice Walker, Maya Angelou, and I share common preoccupations.

BM: These days there are plenty of meetings, anthologies, book series, and critical works on black African and Afro-American literature and so on. Do you think it's ludicrous to lump together writers from the United States, the Caribbean, and Africa because they are black?

EJG: No, not at all! I approve of this kind of thing. It is important for us black writers to meet and talk because our works are not taught as much in colleges as those of whites. All the same I don't spend too much time at those gatherings; I prefer staying at home and writing.

BM: Louisiana is presented in your work as a land of conflict but also as a place of meetings, peace, and compromise. In spite of "the sound and the fury," your writing seems more serene than that of other black writers.

EJG: I write from my own viewpoint. I don't see the world as Jimmy Baldwin or Richard Wright did. I may not have suffered racism as directly as either one of those men did, and I haven't lived in large cities as they did—in Harlem or Chicago's south side—but we have fought for the same causes. I went to California when I was very young to a decent, small town where I was completely integrated into the school. There were people of all backgrounds. There were whites, Hispanics, Native Americans, and Asians.

That doesn't stop me from writing about serious subjects. In *A Lesson Before Dying* an innocent person is sent to the electric chair. I was criticized for *The Autobiography of Miss Jane Pittman* because at the time of the civil rights struggle the life of a woman aged 110 was not a topical subject! For me it was primarily a piece of literary work, sure, but I also described in this book terrible events that were not unconnected with what was going on. I'm doing what the others are doing, just more quietly.

BM: Do you think that things have changed in North America in this respect?

EJG: There have been some changes in the last forty years, but I don't feel that writers and artists have changed very much in their choice of subjects. The change has not been substantial enough to halt the struggle against racism. The race problem still exists—that's why I have been writing about it for forty years. On the other hand, the work of black writers is certainly far more widely accepted now. Today I am accepted on the same footing as others, and that would have been impossible thirty years ago.

BM: Have things changed in everyday life?

EJG: Some people have changed, especially in educated circles. The situation has changed for some people, progress has been made. People have accepted black people's participation in public life. Times have changed from the days when Nat King Cole had his show cancelled simply because he held a white female's hand up on the stage at the end of a show when the credits were going on. But so many serious problems are still unsolved—education and unemployment, for example. There's still a long way to go.

A Gathering of Old Men:
An Interview with Ernest J. Gaines

Raphaël Lambert and Claude Julien / 1996

From Revue d'Etudes Anglophone 2 (1997): 55–71.

Raphaël Lambert is a doctoral student at *Orléans-Tours*. Claude Julien is professor of American literature at University of Tours. He revised the manuscript after an encounter with Ernest Gaines who recently visited France at the invitation of the "*Fondation* William Faulkner." The original interview took place in Rennes on May 23, 1996.

Ernest James Gaines was born in 1933 in Oscar (Pointe Coupée Parish), Louisiana, in a family of agricultural workers. At fifteen, after his parents' divorce, he left to live in California. His short stories and novels, however, are rooted in the land of his childhood. This flat country, marked off by bayous and screens of trees that border them, is isolated between an oxbow lake and the Mississippi. Gaines portrays the difficult coexistence among the inhabitants of this closed community which he "peoples" with native whites, Cajuns and, at the bottom of the social scale, blacks.

Nothing would seem to have destined Gaines to become a writer, unless it was the attentive ear he lent to the stories he heard at evening gatherings at his aunt's. Storytelling, supposedly an African tradition, is perhaps, more fundamentally, a distinctive feature of all rural cultures. In any case, Gaines's writing is characterized by a deceiving simplicity: his laconic dialogues, for instance, are much more meaningful than they at first appear. This minimalist way of composition makes use of simple situations, simple people, simple words. Such *ordinary* writing amounts to a sort of asceticism, and one could say that, in the work of Gaines, simplicity is sophistication.

Gaines is one of the founders of the "quest for the past" in African American fiction, this search for a painful history which must be weighed and understood in order to exorcise its present effects: such, for example, is the case of *Bloodline*, a collection of short stories published in 1968, whose very title evokes the call of blood, the memory of kinship. Gaines achieved success suddenly with *The Autobiography of Miss Jane Pittman* (1971), a book relating the life of a hundred-year-old woman who, in 1965, defies the segregation laws by drinking from a fountain reserved for whites in front of a courthouse. Miss Jane is so "real" that at the time many people believed the book was based on a true story, and the author was asked if he would lend out a copy of the tape recording. Gaines's most recent novel, *A Lesson Before Dying* (1993), is a beautiful story with a solemn, meditative dimension.

The interview conducted by Raphaël Lambert focuses on *A Gathering of Old Men* (1983), a novel in which Gaines describes the courageous revolt (at a rather late stage in their lives) of a small group of men deprived of "their" lands by the white owners who try to deny the past by renting the farmlands to Cajuns.

Raphaël Lambert and Claude Julien: I wanted to ask you first about the question of "manhood," which is at the center of *A Gathering of Old Men*. Has today's American society finally granted manhood to black males?
Ernest J. Gaines: I think this is something that we, as black men, will have to struggle for and fight for as long as we're in . . . In America, in the United States, there are people who cannot accept the fact that we are already on an equal level with them; then there are those who can. They can see us as men in certain professions . . . When it comes to the athletes, you know, we are as much men as anybody else out on that playing ground, with baseball, football, basketball, the fighting in the ring, and things like that. Everyone can see that!

But when it comes to being representative—representing your people, your town, your parish, or your state, then they feel that you're not qualified for this sort of thing. So this is a struggle that we're going to have to put up with and continue to fight for the rest of our . . . of my lifetime, I'm sure. I would say that it will be there for quite a while to come.

Lambert and Julien: So you think Du Bois's concept of "double consciousness" still exists?
Gaines: Oh, yes. I agree.

Lambert and Julien: What is the difference between people like Munford Bazille in "Three Men," Billy in *In My Father's House*, Copper in "Bloodline," and people like Johnny Paul, Rufe, Dirty Red, etc. in *A Gathering of Old Men*?

Gaines: You give me too many characters to work with here. You'll have to choose one character and see what I can do with that one. OK, choose two characters. I need two characters you'd like to bring up, and then we'll try to work with that.

Lambert and Julien: Let's say Billy in *In My Father's House*, who is this young activist, and let's take Johnny Paul in *A Gathering of Old Men*. My concern is with what they embody. Billy seems to be the nonconstructive angry type while Johnny Paul and all his friends introduce militant behavior that will have a long-lasting impact.

Gaines: Well, I think you find both of those situations there. Both of them are there. I just hope that the Johnny Paul type will continue to struggle. I know that men like Billy will continue to exist because of this anger that they cannot control. And when you have this kind of anger and cannot direct it towards the thing that makes you angry, then you withdraw. I mean, you turn it within or upon yourself, upon your own community.

That's the sense in which, at least, Billy says it. As with Johnny Paul . . . There *are* very strong men like Johnny Paul. Not that they are standing up with guns to shoot something up, to shoot out in the street or anything like that, but they are men who believe in using some other approach to accomplish what they'd like to accomplish. Not with a gun because there is no way to win with a gun. Billy does not care whether he lives or dies, you know, because of his anger. He's reached a point that it doesn't matter to him anymore. Johnny Paul is a guy, a more patient guy who says, "OK, maybe things will change a little bit if we keep working." That's the difference between those two characters who, besides, do not function in the same fictional contexts.

Lambert and Julien: In a loose way, *A Gathering of Old Men* can be regarded as your first protest novel, but at the same time, the protagonists are like one-day militants. They act for themselves, for their own salvation rather than for the cause of the entire community; their action is restricted to their own little area. They don't expect it to gain any political or national significance. They are very old and their rebellion takes place about twenty years after the sixties. But it is a success . . . Is all this a kind of wry answer to your detractors in the past?[1]

Gaines: Well no, it was not that. I just feel that what I was trying to do in *A Gathering of Old Men* was to show that all men—of any race, any nation, any whatever—who are oppressed do have that desire to stand. If it's only for once, they do have that desire to stand up. And that is about the only thing that I was trying to do with that story. I've heard many stories told by old men, by some young men about how wonderful my great-grandfather was because he stood up one day to a bad white man. But they're always talking about something like that happening a long time ago. They cannot put their hands on anything that happened only within the last year, or two years ago. They cannot do that. So they're living . . . it's all of it a false life. They are living a lie really because that probably never did happen. But it is something that . . . it's a story that has to be told in a family to keep people sane, to keep people going. In the case of *A Gathering of Old Men*, I wanted a situation that would bring these men together for the first time in their lives. I was not mocking the sixties; I was not mocking that at all. This is just what I put in these old men: I heard a story from my stepfather about him and some friends, cousins, and brothers who got together one day into a group against someone supposed to be coming down there to shoot up a place for some reason or another. They'd come together just as a group, but nothing, of course, nothing like that story ever happened to them. They were just there, they were ready, they were not old, they were just sitting inside our house if anything came by, if anything happened, like this: "We will be ready. If anybody come here and shoot up this place, we will be ready." Maybe I had that in mind when I was writing the novel.

But it's not all men, and the whites can have a different approach to the same thing. And you'll find in different books, stories by whites, how to relive a day, try to relive like an old athlete tries to relive that day when he dropped the football, when he struck out in the baseball base: "I could live that day all over again. What I should have done that day was to keep my eyes on this ball just a little bit longer, hold the bat a little bit higher; I would have gotten this."

So what I did was just get a situation, the strongest situation I could think of, which would be a murder situation, and a group of old men who would never ever have stood up, not only to hit a baseball or throw the ball right or to catch a ball, but who never stood up to all this brutality which they've suffered for all these years. And then I created this situation where they knew someone who would stand. They knew that one person—mad—who would stand. They are old men! And they have nothing to lose now. They are not afraid of anything anymore. They might die tomorrow, so what? Most of them don't have wives, don't have anybody else to live for. "So if I died . . . So what if I died?" I think it is a common thing among men, old men. It is a universal thing: "I would like to stand up." And those who have been suppressed . . . You occasionally find incidents where they just stand up.

Lambert and Julien: In all your novels and short stories, you've been very careful to avoid caricature, and I guess that's part of your will to tell the truth, to show things and people as they are. For instance, Fix, who is known to be cruel, is also very touching with his grandson on his knees. Similarly, Mapes, known to be a brute, obviously shows respect—as much as the other black men do—for Mathu. Now, I wondered about people like Luke Will and Deputy Griffin. The story takes place not so long ago in 1979. Could you tell me whether those characters are caricatures? And if not, do you think that today, seventeen years later, that kind of behavior and overt racism could possibly happen in rural Louisiana?

Gaines: Yes, it could. A simple yes. I was telling a student a few minutes ago that about ten years ago . . . or maybe six years ago, 65 percent of the citizens, white people of the State of Louisiana, voted a Ku Klux Klansman to be governor of the state. That's David Duke. So there are people out there who would go for that, who would like to see this Klansman as our governor. We have a very conservative governor there, in the State of Louisiana, right now. And, so, that Luke Will mentality is out there; and that little Deputy Griffin, he is still there. Recently, my brother's wife was called for jury duty, but my brother was ill that day. So, his wife did not go to jury duty but did not call them. So they sent a deputy out there, and he said, "What the hell is wrong with you niggers? I mean, now you can serve on juries, and you don't want to do it!"

Lambert and Julien: Did he actually use that word "nigger"?

Gaines: Yes. He used that word. And he said, "If it was just up to me"—he was a deputy, like Griffin—"if it was just up to me, if I was sheriff I'd drag you back there to make you serve for jury duty." This happened in 1995. My brother told me about it. My brother told my wife and me about this insane incident. So those people do exist.

Lambert and Julien: Do you see in Luke Will and his friends a modern extension of Albert Cluveau (the Cajun who murders Ned in *The Autobiography of Miss Jane Pittman*)?

Gaines: Oh! Yes, yes. You can see what's happening in different parts of the United States: these militant groups, these ones who blew up the FBI building in Oklahoma City. I mean that's the same kind of guys. They are a group of brutes who will try to change the government their way, try to run the government their way. They're the same people. They are the same.

Lambert and Julien: History and the remembrance of the past is at the center of much of your work. In *A Gathering of Old Men* for instance, the old men stand up against their past lives. Thus, could the scene in the old cemetery be looked upon as a kind of a ceremonial in which the warriors pay tribute to their forefathers before the battle?

Gaines: Absolutely. Absolutely yes. I was discussing the same point with a student not so long ago.

Lambert and Julien: You have mentioned storytelling as part of your childhood background, a folk heritage you claim as your own. You said once that you'd rather have your stories told in a loud voice rather than written to be read alone silently. To what extent do you consider writing a distortion of this urge to tell stories aloud?

Gaines: Because you cannot get your point over any other way, you have to *write* them. But as I said in that story, I'd rather be able to read to a group of people. And what I'd like to do really is to record my stories and sell the tapes. I would like to do things like that. Most of my books have been recorded. Not by me. They would always get someone else to do it; they'd ask an actor to read the thing. But I still felt the same way: that I'd much prefer reading or talking to a group of students if I could get them to support me. I'd rather do that than have them read from the page. Well, I'd write it, but I'd read it out to them, you know. Because I think what I try to do is write from a storyteller's voice.[2] I'm telling you a story about something that happened. And I think this is what I try to emphasize to my students, there must be a story. There must be a beginning, a middle, and an ending. I want to see characters developing in these stories, which we are not getting very much of anymore. I still believe in the traditional storytelling. But you said something about distortion of . . .

Lambert and Julien: Well, yes. Doesn't the need to write distort the storytelling intention and voice?

Gaines: Well, I never thought of it as being distorted. I just feel that I try as well as I possibly can to repeat what I hear. And the sounds of the voice on the paper, I try to do it without using too much dialect, you know. So you can understand it.

Lambert and Julien: Talking about storytelling and tradition, I have spotted in *A Gathering of Old Men* some small events and attitudes which, I think, have something to do with the culture of Afro-American people. Could you comment upon them so I may gauge the relevance of my insight. In the cemetery, for instance, Dirty Red makes a remark that I personally find very strange, "Graveyard pecans always taste good to me." Does it mean that dead bodies have sown ideas and that your forefathers, in a way, nourish you with their strength and their will?

Gaines: Well, others have chosen that as the meaning of that line. I have just felt that Dirty Red is the kind of guy who would say almost anything. And, you see, if he was eating pecans on a roadside, he'd say, "You know, those pecans really taste good, you know." I don't know that he'd say, "They're better than any other pecans." I don't know that he'd say that they are better. I have eaten pecans in the graveyard. The first time I took my wife back to this old place, she and I went back there in the fall, September or October. There were pecans on the ground, and I broke them. They were ripe enough to break them with my hands, squeezing them. And we ate the pecans, and they were very, very good. Very good. So when Dirty Red says something like that, I'm saying the same thing. They're good, and we always had pecan trees in that cemetery. And our forefathers are there . . . their very lives that they gave to the ground made the ground richer.

Lambert and Julien: This also reminds me of the passage in the Bible, the Valley of Dry Bones that comes up in Ned's sermon . . .

Gaines: In *Pittman*, yes, yes.

Lambert and Julien: You know, they will rise again.

Gaines: Yes, yes. Absolutely.

Lambert and Julien: And again, I am thinking about another remark Dirty Red makes when touching Big Charlie's corpse, hoping that ". . . some of that stuff he has found back there in the swamps might rub off of me." Does this event, which already occurs in *The Autobiography of Miss Jane Pittman* with Ned's body, suggest some link between those people and nature? And what kind of link?

Gaines: Those are men, those are brave men who have shown great courage. "By touching Ned, maybe this will give me some courage as well." This is what I had in mind. These men have shown this great courage, both Ned in *The Autobiography of Miss Jane Pittman* and Charlie in *A Gathering of Old Men.*

Lambert and Julien: And what about Miss Merle feeding everybody, creating a situation where death and life are, in a way, side by side in a kind of rather joyful celebration?

Gaines: Well, for one thing, they were hungry! So we needed some food in there. And another thing, I wanted to show a certain side of the South—not only trying to continue the patriarchal society, but a person like Miss Merle who knows the basic needs of people. So it is she who would bring food to them and who gives the food and, at a time when this other thing is going on, there is still this: "You guys can be out there and play killers and all this sort of thing, but basically, you're hungry as well." And this is what I wanted to do. I just wanted to bring this good person to see beyond this—well—this insanity that is going to happen and to bring food. That's all I wanted with her.

Lambert and Julien: Also, it is interesting to notice—while Reverend Jameson is trying to convince them not to carry out their plans—how "a pecan dropped from that tree in the backyard, fell on the tin roof, and tumbled to the ground." This is just a detail, and it could be interpreted as a means to accentuate the silence or what we could call a collective rejection of the churchman's prayer. But it also made me think of the "goober"[3] thing in Louisiana. I've read that in the South—and I'm told this comes from an old African tradition—peanut shells spread in front of someone's door are the sign that something terrible is going to happen to that person. Did you include that on purpose?

Gaines: I don't know that . . . I don't know that. But the pecan falling off this roof. What I was trying to do was the silence, work with the silence. And the other thing I wanted to suggest was the time it took the pecan to tumble from the roof down to the ground because what we're doing here . . . Everything takes place in one day. Although there are flashbacks, all the action takes place in one day, and I just wanted someone to concentrate on that small movement of time for that moment. And that of course broke the silence for a moment. But that small movement of time is what I was trying to concentrate on.

Lambert and Julien: My research focuses on orality, trying to show how this orality is much more than pleasure or entertainment for those people from the "quarters"—that it is deeply rooted in their minds and part of their daily lives. I've tried to show that it implies and shapes some behaviors and even some situations.

Gaines: Yes, yes.

Lambert and Julien: Would you agree with that idea, that everything goes together, orality and the situation, that, in a way, everything is connected?
Gaines: Well, yeah. Give me an example.

Lambert and Julien: I'm thinking of the dialogue between Johnny Paul and Mapes (the "I see / No, you don't see" game) which comes from the fact that they look at life in a totally different manner.
Gaines: Right. Right. Since you've explained it now I agree with you. OK. Yes, I know the scene you're talking about. Whenever I read *A Gathering of Old Men*, I would always read that particular scene. I wanted a rhetoric, and I wanted a certain rhythmic, a way of distinguishing his voice from others' voices. And at the same time letting Mapes know that, although Mapes thinks he know blacks—and that's another thing that a lot of southern whites think, "I know those blacks over there. I know exactly what they would do. I know exactly how they act. I know exactly what they want in life, you know. I know all of this." And Johnny Paul is convincing him, or trying to convince him, by telling him that "No, you don't know because you can't see anything. You don't know what we're talking about. You don't know why we're standing here at this moment. You don't know why we have these guns. You don't know why this poor old black man is standing here." This is what he is saying to him, "You don't know because you don't know about the flowers over here, you don't know about the old people sitting over here, you can't just drive into the area and see the people one time and think you know these things. You don't know anything about it."

I've been in Rennes now for nearly four months, but I don't know Rennes. This is what he's saying. You have just lived here for a moment; you don't know what you're looking at. I can't go back to the United States and write a big story about, a novel on the Rennes character or the Breton character. I cannot do that. I don't know enough. And this is what he is trying to tell Mapes, although Mapes has been living there all of his life as well. But Mapes has not shared those little moments, that pecan falling there before. He has probably never noticed a pecan falling like that before. So, what Johnny Paul is saying is that "You may have come down here before. You may have arrested me before. You may have done so many other things before, but you don't know the basic things. You don't know the little everyday things. You don't know me."

Lambert and Julien: . . . You're not part of my club.
Gaines: No, no. That's right. "You are not part of the club. You don't really know me; you just don't live here. You have to live here seventy years to

know what I'm talking about now." He didn't know, like Candy. Neither did Lou Dimes. Nobody knew these guys like they knew themselves. But maybe, even they didn't know they had that kind of courage until that day as well, you know.

Lambert and Julien: The way you use "silence" for an effect has drawn my attention. For instance, after Gable has told about the killing of his son, Rufe notices that everything "was quiet" and that "the only thing that moved was the shadow from the house. It covered the yard now." Can you tell me how you create those silences, when, and why?

Gaines: There was a break so that people could remember, could reflect on what this man had said. It's almost a reminder of why I'm here, because of these things. So that's a break for reflecting.

Lambert and Julien: There is also Aunt Glo looking at Snookum in such a way that it is enough to make him understand her orders. Nothing much is said about this way of looking, but the reader actually doesn't need extra comments to understand—and neither does Snookum—what he should or shouldn't do. Can you comment upon this way of making things very clear with a restricted number of words?

Gaines: I was raised by someone who used *very* few words. My aunt who raised me was a cripple who crawled over the floor all of her life, and she used few words to tell you anything. But, then that was characteristic of a great many of the older people in the South at that particular time. They had communication without words all the time. And yet I don't know anyone else but maybe these people here in France who can talk more than they did because they would gather at my aunt's place all the time and just talk and talk all the time. But then, there would be those long breaks of silence. Just long breaks of silence when nothing was being said. There is still that kind of communication going on. And when the old people spoke to a child, the child understood with one word or one phrase—whatever—and just would break that whole silence and the child understood very well. [*Chuckle*] Look, I think you have read those books very well; I mean bringing up such points as silence is important to me.

Lambert and Julien: Thank you. The fact that you use a lot of dialogues helps to avoid long descriptions. But it also compels you to say a lot without actually stating things, since you let your characters express themselves in their own words. Could you comment on the advantages and drawbacks of this technique?

Gaines: The reason why I do that is because I, as a writer, try to avoid interfering with the story. I let the story tell itself, let it go on. Dialogues are one way to achieve this. I'm searching for a certain kind of way of telling in a dialogue who the character is.

Lambert and Julien: Do you sometimes regret not being able to say "this is how it is" because characters are talking to each other and you don't want to interfere?

Gaines: I do not wish to interfere with dialogues. Never. I think that through dialogues, you can get much description without describing. Once you start to describe, you slow up the progression of the story.[4] If the people can convince you that the story is progressing through dialogues, then that's the approach to use. Another reason why I use more dialogue than I do descriptive passages is because I'm better at dialogues than I am at the other. I prefer using dialogue to tell you something. I prefer . . . I forget who it is who saw these men beating his brother . . .

Lambert and Julien: That's Tucker's brother, Silas.

Gaines: Yes, right. You get a stronger feeling by hearing a voice telling you this than if the writer came in and tried to tell it omnisciently or just have someone narrate it. So let the character tell you these things. You feel closer to him. And this is one of the reasons I definitely depend on dialogues more than I do on descriptive passages.

Lambert and Julien: *A Gathering of Old Men* is mostly dialogue: one gets the first-person point of view and a lot of polyphony besides. There are fifteen different narrators, male and female, white and black, children, adults and old people. What is your purpose in writing a polyphonic novel?

Gaines: I needed to show different opinions, a different approach to the same story. I thought that just one character could not tell this entire story. I tried to tell the story by Lou Dimes, and then I realized Lou Dimes could not tell the story because so much of it is internal. For example, Lou Dimes cannot tell the way Snookum feels. Lou Dimes was not there at the moment, so he cannot see Snookum running across the street—spanking his butt the way you whip a horse to make it run faster. Lou Dimes cannot hear Janey in that house when she is going up and down those stairs talking to herself. Lou Dimes can't hear that. And no one else could hear that. But Janey herself could bring it in, and I wanted that rhythm. I wanted that religious, that old polite woman calling on God and sort of praying in church; I wanted that. And the only way to get that is to have her do it, and yet she could not tell the entire story because she's not there all the time. She's not in the quarters. She's still at the house, the Big House. She can't go to Fix's place. So Janey can't tell the story. Candy can't tell the story either because Candy cannot be involved. She cannot be in the area with every one; she cannot be in that room. When they leave, when they turn her out, when Mathu says, "No, I'll go with them," Candy cannot be there. So Candy cannot tell the story. So, this is why I had to use the multiple point of view. I wanted the multiple point of view because I wanted voices, I wanted that Louisiana voice in there, throughout. From the religious Janey's to Snookum's, to Griffin's way of talking, Lou Dimes's way of speaking, the guy who goes with Gilbert—T.V.—T.V.'s way of speaking about things. I wanted all of these kinds of voices going . . . This is why I had to use this multiple point of view. I could not do it only with the omniscient point of view because I could not have used all the internal voices had I done it from the writer's point of view. I could not get all these internal voices, and I wanted those voices in it.[5]

Lambert and Julien: How come all the main characters, Mathu, Mapes, Candy, are silenced?

Gaines: [*Laughs*] OK. I can't get away with this. I felt that Mathu could not speak without giving away the story because Mathu knows what has happened. This is a mystery; *A Gathering of Old Men* is a mystery. You aren't supposed to know that Charlie did this. As a matter of fact, quite a few people don't believe Charlie did it. Obviously they think Mathu did this. Mathu is the one who killed the guy. Charlie ran. And at one time I had *that* as an idea: let Mathu do it and Charlie run—but then Charlie comes back . . . And "Pity!" you know, "Well I can't run for miles and let him take this; he did it. But I can't let him suffer alone, so I'll go back and claim that I did it." So I didn't want Mathu to narrate, and I reached the point with Mapes . . . Mapes is telling it at one time. But when I sent the story to New York—no, before I sent the story to New York, for publication, I thought why not just have Mapes show up rather than have him starting all the way back in the courthouse. I mean it's not so important that this all starts all the way back at the courthouse. I don't want too many people . . . Lou Dimes starts at the newspaper place. I said (to myself), "That's OK. One person did that, but you can't have all of them do the same. Just have them appear on the scene." And that's enough. Mapes hears the news. And that's how he gets there of course. But it was not necessary for Mapes to narrate because others were narrating it for him. Not that this is an explanation to you . . . because there's always this same question: Why not Candy? Why not Mapes? And why not Mathu? And I say, "Well, why Candy? . . . Why Candy?" I get Candy's action and Candy's voice by other things. I get Candy, really. And I get Mathu by everyone talking about Mathu. Mathu is the central person here. The one everybody talks about . . .

Lambert and Julien: . . . but they don't have the responsibility of a chapter; they're not the narrators . . .
Gaines: . . . No, no, no. When I was writing the story . . . It was not until after I finished writing the story that I realized that Candy and Mathu, Mapes, weren't absolutely necessary to have been included (as narrators). I'd never thought about it. I've written a chapter of Mapes's. I've done Mapes that way. But I cut it out; as I said, I didn't think it was necessary for him to start, for that chapter to start back at the courthouse, and then come up to the quarters. I don't think that was absolutely necessary.

Lambert and Julien: I also wanted to bring up the influence of jazz, blues, rural blues in your writing. You have already explained to a lot of people how all this has influenced you. But regarding *A Gathering of Old Men*, I'm thinking about Big Charlie's speech at Mathu's house when he sounds like a preacher delivering a sermon. Are there other striking musical references in the novel? I was thinking of Jan . . .
Gaines: Oh yes, Janey . . . It's like a sort of a call-and-response in a church; that's what Janey is caught in.

Lambert and Julien: What about improvisational skills of the old men talking? Don't they also sound like jazz improvisations?
Gaines: Yes, yes. And of course there is the rhythm of Johnny Paul when he says ". . . you don't see, you don't see what I see," et cetera.

Lambert and Julien: It's like the chorus and antiphonal rite. I've read in an interview that you gave about "The Sky Is Gray" a statement showing your conscious use of jazz and blues. You said that, in this story, like a jazzman, you were trying to "play around the note" . . .
Gaines: Yes, yes. If I remember right, I may have mentioned Lester Young or somebody like that . . .

Lambert and Julien: You did. Your point was that the situation you put James and his mother in would make the reader understand discrimination that was going on at the time; and then, instead of putting them uptown you have them go back of town, deep in the black area. And then, from that, the reader understands that they cannot go to the white area. He understands everything, the whole situation. Is there not a similar technique at work in *A Gathering of Old Men*? Actually, I was thinking of Johnny Paul's way of describing things. He doesn't say, "Look there's nothing"; he says, "Oh, there's something but you don't see it."

Gaines: Yes, yes, yes. It's the same thing.

Lambert and Julien: Are there other examples like that in *A Gathering* . . .

Gaines: I think Miss Merle brings that technique up at one time, when she's there feeding them, she tells Mapes . . . She says, "You see that sun, uh?" "You see what the shade is like?" She doesn't say, "Listen, those guys are goin' to be coming over here with those guns, and those guys are going to blow up this whole place, if you don't get Mathu to that jail." She doesn't say that to him but instead, "You see that sun, you see them shadows moving?" What she's saying is that it's getting later and later and later. This is what she means, "You see that shadow moving, there?" Things, little things like that. So, when you've already established this kind of statement, you've already established your point. You don't have to keep hammering on this sort of thing. This is why in so many of my books (well, not so many of my books: I haven't written that many), but in *A Gathering of Old Men* as well as *A Lesson Before Dying*, the murder has already been committed. Everything's been done, put *down* in the first chapter. And then you begin to see the result of it. So you just establish it there . . . which is sort of off camera, off stage, and then you discuss it. The novel, I think you made that point in your opening comment, the novel is to show the result of what happened here. And I was trying to do that in "The Sky Is Gray." I don't have to have this mother and child go into a white restaurant . . . and be thrown out and called "nigger" or whatever, you know. You don't need that sort of thing. All I needed to do there was to show that, once they've come out of that dentist office, there's no place for them to go, there's no place for them to go at all. And the mother insists on "keep your eyes in front," meaning "this is white people's business." But she doesn't have to say that; that's cliché. That's been said by every southern writer, every black writer, every white writer of the South. They've all said those things. I don't have to say that. And I said, "OK, I don't have to say that; but what can I say to show this racism, to show this segregation?" Have them stand in the cold, wanting to get warm. They cannot go in the place. And so, I just have them stand there. The little boy stands there and looks at the mannequins, and he says, "I'm gonna buy my mamma a red coat when I pick cotton; I'm gonna buy my mamma a red coat." And this gives the feeling of this child, feeling for his mother. And then of course, they have to go back uptown to catch this bus. Well, she also goes into this hardware store pretending to look at ax handles, and that's only to warm the kid. But we don't have to say that. Once she has stopped this kid by the heater, she just walks in. You must understand the idea. That's why I say you don't have to hammer at this thing, but you can play around it. And that's what a great jazz musician does. Once they've made their statement—John Coltrane, Charlie Parker, Lester Young—they can do all kinds of little frills, of little things. And then, you still get that feeling of that sound that they are trying to give you, which they do give you. Louis Armstrong had that with his singing and so did Billie Holiday . . . They would make their statement and start jazzing it up, making all kinds of sounds with their mouths. But you know what they are doing; you know exactly what they're doing. I am very much influenced by music. I love music. I love the rural blues. The jazz music, the spirituals—classical music of course I listen to. My wife and I listen to music all the time.

Lambert and Julien: I have one last question: it's still about all of this but more specifically about *A Gathering of Old Men*: I'm thinking about this concept of a wall. When Lou Dimes arrives at Mathu's place, he sees a wall of old men. Then you have T.V. Sully, who (at Mathu's place) sees a wall of old men. Then you have Charlie: he says, "I've been running everywhere, and it's like a wall everywhere. I couldn't get out of here!" What is the idea behind all this?

Gaines: I know Charlie's meaning for "the wall," and that is an undeveloped consciousness, which he's not aware of, something developing in him that he's not aware of. That's his "wall." I mean, "No matter where I go, there's something standing before me; I can't go anywhere . . ." And before he realizes, before he falls down and starts eating this dirt, and hears a voice . . . that was the voice he recognizes, the wall before he could not recognize. He was unconscious of it; he was conscious he was walled in, but he was not conscious what the meaning of the wall was. Whereas with the voice, now he becomes conscious, conscious of the meaning of the voice: "come back, come back, come back."

I think Lou Dimes—the way Lou is seeing it: "I see a wall of old men there," he must mean that: "I've never seen that many old men standing like that before." Although he had probably seen men in the fields working like that; but he's never seen this sort of stand before. I think this is what he's talking about.

And I would think that T.V. Sullivan must have felt the same way. He's never seen anything like that. He's probably seen guys on a football field, but he could never have even imagined that, you know. As he says, "It seems that I'm in the Twilight Zone." I mean, this is impossible, "I can't even imagine these things; I can't imagine these things." But Charlie's wall is that maybe he's becoming consciously aware of not being able to escape responsibility, and that's what that wall was: he will not escape this. He's not conscious, he doesn't know the meaning of it, et cetera. And then, when he falls and, I think he's eating dirt (I can't remember all of these things about the story), he hears a voice that says, "Come back, come back." And then of course he has to come back. And he does come back. That's the meaning of the wall, yes.

Lambert and Julien: And then, my very last question as a conclusion: what is your next book going to be about?

Gaines: Oh that! I never talk about something that I haven't started writing on yet. But I'll tell you this: it's gonna be about Louisiana. And there's gonna be a murder, and this sheriff, after he diagnoses murder, he tells the people, "You go tell him . . ." (I think Mapes is gonna be in there, and there'll be a flashback to Mapes and this man.) "You go tell him you'll come and get me in an hour—come and get me in an hour—. Don't anybody else come in with me *because the other guy has a gun.* So come and get me in an hour." And the people report to Mapes, to the sheriff: she says, "Come and get him in an hour!" "What the hell he thinks he is?" "He thinks he is going to shoot somebody and you don't . . ." And Mapes says, "Yes Madam. Yeah, I'm giving him an hour." And the point of the story is: why does he give him that hour? Why that hour? And then you begin to understand . . . why that hour . . . but the whole novel revolves around that: why that particular hour? And why did Mapes say "Yes" to this? This is what it is about. But the story is much larger than that. The story is not about this hour. The flashbacks will take in much more . . . The starting point is: why does Mapes give him an hour? That's the starting point. But the story will also cover years and years and years . . . But the starting point is: why would he give him an hour?

Lambert and Julien: Time is very important in your work. Not only in this next book. I've noticed time is always a shaping element.

Gaines: Well, I don't know how important time is because *Miss Jane Pittman* covers a hundred years in time, and *A Gathering of Old Men* covers one day.

Most of my books cover all kinds of periods of time. *A Lesson Before Dying* covers, I think, four or five months. Others two or three weeks of time . . . So I really don't concentrate too much on time. I say, "OK, this book has to take place within a certain time . . ." Although I have been influenced by Greek tragedy, and sometimes I'd like to write a story, a novel which takes place *only* within those twenty-four hours without any flashbacks at all, as I did in two or three of my short stories: "A Long Day in November," "The Sky Is Gray," "Bloodline" . . . The last one is "Just Like a Tree" . . .

Lambert and Julien: Thank you very much.

Notes

1. The interviewer was alluding to the criticism Gaines had to face (in the late sixties and early seventies) from activists who contended his fiction was not militant enough.

2. When Gaines read chapters 1 and 23 from *A Lesson Before Dying* in Paris at a *Cercle d'Etudes Afro-Américaines* meeting on December 14, 1996, it was obvious to his audience that reading was in fact retelling a story: when a word substituted for another here and there, it captured a dynamics that pertained to oral delivery at that precise moment.

3. "Goober" is a local word for "peanut."

4. In Paris, Gaines discussed descriptions in his latest novel, stating that descriptions must be short and that they are best used as props supporting the "needed mood." He illustrated this point with an allusion to chapter 19 in *A Lesson Before Dying* where the smoke is shown drifting from the deserted quarters over the cemetery and on to the marsh, while unseen people keep indoors against the cold Christmas wind. But Gaines added that is mostly side fact supporting the main stream of the story.

5. In Paris, Gaines pointed out that this was a difficulty he had run against while writing *In My Father's House* (1978), which he changed and worked on over a period of five or six years, using every possible character as a narrator but that neither was fully satisfactory.

A MELUS Interview: Ernest J. Gaines

Wolfgang Lepschy / 1996

From *MELUS* 24:1 (1999): 197–208. © 1999 Oxford University Press. Reprinted with permission of Oxford University Press.

The following conversation with the writer was conducted on October 22, 1996. The conversation took place at the University of Bonn (Germany) prior to Ernest Gaines's public reading from *A Lesson Before Dying*.

Interviewer: You've been in Europe now since February. What are your impressions about Europe, especially France? How do people react to your works?

Gaines: I have been to France before. I was there in '92, and I spent some time in Angers as well as in Paris. I came back in '94 when *A Lesson Before Dying* was published in France, and I had this tremendous reception. And, of course, I taught creative writing at the University of Rennes this past spring. It was the first time that a creative writing class had been taught for a complete semester in France. My work has been received very well in France. The sale of the books has been good, and I suppose I've been interviewed more in France during the last year than I have been in the States in the last four or five years. But, at the same time, Germany was the first foreign country to publish and translate my work. They started with *Catherine Carmier* under the title *It Was the Nightingale*, which was taken from Shakespeare's *Romeo and Juliet*, one of those romantic stories. I started writing it when I was in Stanford, and it took me a long time to do it because I didn't know how to write novels. Anyway, Germany published that story in the seventies, and they also published *The Autobiography of Miss Jane Pittman* and, of course, *A Lesson Before Dying*. They might have published *A Gathering of Old Men*, too, but I am not sure.

Interviewer: Did you get the impression that critics in Europe react differently towards your novels than in the States?

Gaines: Not all critics. I have a good friend in Paris who taught at the Sorbonne, and I think he is as perceptive about my work as many American critics are. But he knows a lot about Afro-American writing. He is the executive of Richard Wright's papers, Michel Fabre. Michel has given me some good criticism, and my French translator has done an excellent job. Unfortunately, I haven't met critics who can explain the German translation to me, but I have met people in Paris who have explained the French translation. I don't read French. I have met the French translator, and, as a matter of fact, we had two or three readings together in Paris. I would read in English, of course, and she translated it into French. And we were sitting right there reading to an audience. Others who had read the novels and short stories both in French and in English have agreed that she is very good. So, there are those who understand the work and state it very clearly.

Interviewer: What I think is very important in your works is that you are depicting the same area in all of them, and you are very specific; it is really so authentic that it almost becomes universal in a way so that many people can relate to it even if they have never been there.

Gaines: I got that technique from Faulkner, from his Yoknapatawpha County—and I can only say Yoknapatawpha County before I drink. And there is, of course, Joyce and Dublin. And Faulkner might have gotten the idea from Joyce.

I think that in each one of the books, there is some other little detail I might bring out about the area. The area is one which I know pretty well. I lived there the first fifteen and a half years of my life. Since I am teaching in Louisiana, I travel those roads and the rivers and the towns.

Interviewer: In the project I'm working on, I am trying to work out your "philosophy of progress" as it may be implicitly reflected in your works. I start out by concentrating on those people who more or less openly rebel against the status quo, figures like Jackson Bradley, Marcus Payne, and Grant Wiggins. What I found very intriguing is that you seem to have much sympathy for all of your characters. Jackson Bradley, for example, is mainly a nihilist, but you make him very understandable so that we can really relate to him and to his inner feelings.

Gaines: I suppose I got a lot of these ideas from reading European novelists, especially looking at Bazarov in Ivan Turgenev's *Fathers and Sons*, but also from other characters in Dostoevsky's works, and, of course, Stephen

Daedalus in James Joyce's *Portrait of the Artist as a Young Man*. At the time I was writing about Jackson and Catherine Carmier; these were the influences. These young men who were at odds with their community, with their family, with religion, in other words, who were questioning these different things in their lives. And, yes, I agree with you. I suppose the only way they could free themselves was by questioning things.

Interviewer: But, on the other hand, they don't have any vision; they don't have any values that can replace or complement the older ones.
Gaines: Well, that is the search; that is the quest; that is what they have to find out. They don't have it at that moment. But they are very educated, except Marcus, who is just a rebel anytime and anywhere. But, in order to go someplace else and in order to make progress, you must leave something. And most of those young men are in the process of leaving the old order and moving to another order, which they do not yet recognize themselves.

Interviewer: Could we read *A Lesson Before Dying* as a sequel to *Catherine Carmier*?
Gaines: You mean Grant and Vivian?

Interviewer: Well, all of the characters really. Grant in a way parallels Jackson, and Vivian recalls Catherine. And also Tante Lou is reminiscent of Aunt Charlotte. The difference seems to be that the characters in *A Lesson Before Dying* seem to be one step ahead of those in *Catherine Carmier*.
Gaines: Well I hope I have progressed a little bit over the last few years. I think that's a very good reading. I think you have read very well.

Interviewer: A character like Marcus Payne in *Of Love and Dust* is very fascinating to me. On the one hand, he is very egocentric and individualistic. But, on the other hand, he cannot be broken or defeated. He has created his own way of resistance, which makes him really likable.
Gaines: [*laughs*] You know, a lot of people both in France and in Germany have said the same thing. A lot of people here really love Marcus and consider him a really great character, but I know of others in the States who didn't. But I feel the same way about Marcus. I feel that he is a rebel, a troublemaker, but I love him. I created him. And Jim, he learns at the very end to appreciate Marcus and to see what kind of character, what kind of person he really is. No, I think he is a great character. Marcus and Miss Jane, I think those were the two characters I had most fun writing and creating.

Interviewer: And a similar character in a way is Copper in "Bloodline." But he is a bit too militant.

Gaines: Well, you know, he is a bit mad. That's why he has that vision of armies and tearing up things. But I was thinking of Procter in "Three Men." After I wrote "Three Men," it was then that I wrote *Of Love and Dust* and invented Marcus. I said, OK, suppose I get a person like Procter out of jail. Let's say Procter does not do what he does at the very end, when he goes to the penitentiary in order to become a man and when he has to save this kid. But suppose I had gotten him out of prison and put him out on a plantation, then he would have become Marcus. So those two are very similar. And Copper is as well; they're all that same kind of rebel. I hope that I am not repeating myself. I hope they are not copies of each other.

Interviewer: No, surely not, but I found it a little dangerous to conclude "Bloodline" the way you did.

Gaines: [*laughs*] How was that; why dangerous?

Interviewer: It's because you close the story with Copper saying, "I'll come back with my army and bathe this whole plantation in blood, if I don't get my rights." But then, of course, "Bloodline" is followed by "Just Like a Tree," and that modifies the picture of violence and militancy.

Gaines: Well, as I said, Copper is mad. Copper has no army to come back. He has nothing; he is mad. That's all I can say. He has nothing to come back; he will never come back. He might turn out to be in an insane asylum because he's nuts. He is a pathetic character really. I mean he is a lovable character but a pathetic character really.

Interviewer: That's why I think it's good to have "Just Like a Tree" as the closing story in *Bloodline*.

Gaines: Some have compared the stories to an episodic novel because it began with a child, and then in each story the character is a little bit older. For example in "A Long Day in November," the child is six years old. In "The Sky Is Gray," the child is eight. In "Three Men," Procter is seventeen or eighteen, and I think Copper in "Bloodline" is a little bit older. And then you reach the old lady, Aunt Fe, in "Just Like a Tree." Then, of course, you have the young Emmanuel, the civil rights worker, who is something like Jimmy in *The Autobiography of Miss Jane Pittman*.

Interviewer: Did you use the name *Emmanuel* because of its meaning, "God be with us"?
Gaines: Yes, that's right.

Interviewer: What I find very fascinating in your works is that you never pass judgment on anybody, not explicitly. This is true, among other works, for *The Autobiography of Miss Jane Pittman.* I'm thinking about the scene with Albert Cluveau and also about the massacre scene. And I think the way you are depicting these events is very successful in drawing the reader in and really arousing his feelings.
Gaines: Yes, that's absolutely true. And that's what I've said to many of my students. Especially African American students ask me, "How could you write such a scene as the massacre scene without being angry at those who do the killings?" And I said, "Well what I wanted to do with that scene is to write it so well and make you to see and hear and feel that you will try to never let something like that ever happen again. That you will stand up and speak." It's not that I try to arouse certain violent feelings but a feeling of sympathy, a feeling of compassion, a feeling of empathizing with the characters. And that's what I'm trying to do with this particular scene and with Albert Cluveau. Cluveau is controlled by the society in which he lives. He was Miss Jane's best friend, and he was very close to her and would do anything for her.

That character actually existed. Of all the characters in the book, he is the one person or character who actually existed. He and the professor, the young black professor who, in 1903, or at the turn of the century, was teaching young black children how to read and write, how to swim, how to do gardening. The whites in that area felt that he was doing too much, and they got this man, this assassin, to get him. This assassin had killed other men, though. This professor was not the only person he had killed, and later, he would also be killed himself. I did not know all the details about it, and most of what I have there is created. I created all these situations. I did not know exactly how he killed the professor. It was not the way it is in the book. I did not know how it happened. I only knew he had killed this guy, and I created everything around it. So I didn't know how this man looked. But after the film was made, which became very popular in the US, there was a very old lady, a French lady—real French and not Cajun—who was in her nineties, and she came up to me and told me that she could remember the day when the teacher was killed. She was a little girl at that time. But she said, "Oh, but your Mr. Cluveau in the movie didn't look like the real one. The real Cluveau had a long beard." She said he had a very long beard. So she had remembered that, too, and I, of course, had no idea what he had looked like. I just created him.

Yes, and I tried to give him humanity.

Interviewer: You do that also in *A Gathering of Old Men*, which I find so fascinating because one doesn't see that as much with other writers.
Gaines: Oh, you've read well. Someone told me, "You gave life to the Ku Klux Klan. You made the Ku Klux Klan look good." But that's something I would not have done. I just give them humanity.

Interviewer: You bring in your criticism other ways. As for example by the description of clothes, when you contrast figures like Luke Will and Deputy Russell. Luke Will is depicted as wearing his shirt out of his pants and having dirty hands. On the other hand, Russell, the deputy, is described as neatly dressed, thus paying tribute to the mourning in the Boutan house.
Gaines: Yes, that shows the character Luke really is. You have really read well.

Interviewer: What's your assessment of the Schlondorff movie?
Gaines: Well I liked some of it [*laughs*]. I think Volker worked well with what he had. The script was not exactly the way it should be. He could have had a better script, but, as I've said, I think he worked well with what he had. But he didn't have time. If you're making a film for television in the US, you have about five weeks for a two-hour film. And when it is raining, you cannot shoot outside. And it rained all the time. There are some good points in the film; there are other points where I think they could have been stronger. For example, the scenes in the yard where the old men are standing around and waiting. I thought there was not enough intensity there. You know, someone was throwing a ball around. You don't do that. When you are waiting for a mob scene, a lynching scene, and someone is playing baseball, or someone rode a bicycle! Little things like that should not be there. But I am sure they had told him to loosen it up a bit. And the ending, of course, is not the ending I have in the novel.

Interviewer: I wanted to ask you about that. Because some critics have said that the movie places too much emphasis on the mere gathering, disregarding that a struggle for changing things often entails the use of violence. I've always felt that your emphasis is on the internal victory of the men.

Gaines: Well, it's really on both. It's the internal victory of Charlie, and the old men gathering and standing. When I saw the movie, I could understand why it ended that way. But at the time I was writing the story, I thought it should end with Charlie, and with Luke Will, dying. But the gathering is really the important thing, and the second most important thing is that Charlie is coming back. Remember, these old men had never done anything like that before, and one day they had found the courage to do that. That spirit is very important.

Interviewer: The way you describe the shooting at the end is full of humor. It shows the absurdity of old men having to fight. That's why I thought that it is probably too hard to translate the humor onto the screen, and that's why Schlondorff may have left it out.

Gaines: Well, people have different opinions about this ending, depending on the group. There are many black students who are against that ending. Many white students felt that Charlie's coming back and that standing were the big victory. I have been criticized for the very last chapter of the book by those who think it's too much of a farce. But at that particular time, I was not thinking about that. And now . . . I don't reread my books; I don't do that.

Interviewer: So why exactly did Charlie have to die? Couldn't he just have gone to prison and take his stand like Jefferson does in *A Lesson Before Dying*?

Gaines: Well, you know, that's the Chekhovian theme. If the gun is there, if the gun is over the mantle, the gun must come down at the end. Since all the old men gather with their guns, the guns have to be used. And that's why Luke Will and Charlie had to shoot it out.

Also, when I wrote that story, it was a different time in my life. Not that I was any more angry at that time than I was when I wrote *A Lesson Before Dying*, but at that time I felt that this was the way to write the ending. Maybe I was not as mature as I was ten years later when I wrote *A Lesson Before Dying*. Maybe if I had written *A Gathering of Old Men* after *A Lesson Before Dying*, I would have had a different ending. But at that particular time that was the ending that I could see.

Well, I had other endings. At one time, I had old man Marshall and Mathu shooting at each other. I had all kinds of things. Originally, the book had been written entirely from Lou Dimes's point of view, just from a single point of view. But I realized that Lou Dimes couldn't get inside the minds of all these old men, and they wouldn't have told him all the things they have said among themselves through multiple narration.

Interviewer: I had problems with the figure of Lou Dimes. He was the only one I could not really relate to. Well, I guess he is a journalist and he has to be somewhat detached, which makes him able to recognize things that other people can't; for example, the true relationship between Mathu and Candy. But I am not sure whether he has learned enough at the end, whether he has really understood what was going on at the end and what significance this day had.

Gaines: Well, I was sort of hoping that he had learned something at the end. But Lou Dimes is sort of an outsider, really. He is not part of Candy's crowd, the plantation owner's crowd. Lou Dimes is from a poor family; he would have played basketball with blacks, but he did not grow up or live with them. And, of course, he would not know the older people who lived on the plantation, who Candy knows or Mapes would know. Sheriffs always know these people. You know, in the state of Louisiana, I think we've had about four different sheriffs within the last hundred years, who when they die, their wives take over [*laughs*]. It's really a family thing. So these guys get to know everybody. And Lou Dimes hasn't been around long enough to know the people. So Candy and Mapes know the people, and Miss Merle because she goes from one house to the other, gossiping all the time.

Interviewer: Many people I have shown the movie to were overwhelmed by the way the atmosphere was captured. That's also why I think it is an important movie in order to fully understand your work, particularly for those who have never been to Louisiana.

Gaines: Yes, the atmosphere is perfect. Especially with the opening scenes they have done fantastic things. The first different shots of the row of houses and the cane burning scenes. The atmosphere is captured very, very well. When they were shooting the film, I was invited to the set, and I spent quite a bit of time with Volker. We dined together and had coffee together quite a few times, and we were talking. I was not officially involved in the film, of course. When he asked questions, I, of course, tried to answer, but I did not volunteer any information. I was just there.

Interviewer: Another thing I'm interested in is the importance of cross-generational relationships that have always been prominent in your works. In this sense, I regard *A Gathering of Old Men* as a kind of synthesis of your previous works. When the old men take their stand, this is witnessed by the young boys like Toddy and especially Snookum. And when Charlie is coming back, he is also assuming a symbolic father role for these boys, which is also manifested when they are touching his dead body.

Gaines: That scene, and also the importance of Salt and Pepper, the two football players. Maybe I became too obvious about what Americans are supposed to be like: blocking, tackling, and running, you know. When I think of the story, maybe even Charlie is too obvious. I had to have him come back. And there are a lot of people who don't feel that Charlie could do this, who think that Mathu is the actual killer. I really had to convince people very hard that Charlie is the killer and has that courage.

But to run away is something that none of my little people have been able to [do]. Miss Jane tried to get to Ohio; Grant went to California, but he came back; Charlie tried to go but could not go; Catherine would like to leave, but she cannot leave. They are rooted there, and they just cannot escape it. And Aunt Fe is just like a tree; she dies before she can leave.

Interviewer: So by witnessing what happened on that day, Snookum might become a more mature grown-up and get rooted there and tell the story to his descendants.

Gaines: Oh yes, definitely so, that's what happens in *A Lesson Before Dying.* Grant must go back to that school and that's when he turns around to his kids, and he is crying in the very last sentence. He's gonna put everything now into being a better teacher and try to save these kids. And they will probably grow up and become rooted there. Otherwise, some of them might have run away and done the things this dying professor had told Grant he should do. But now the kids will stay and do all the work that is necessary. And those are the ones that have made all the difference in the South, staying, working there, living there, fighting, and dying. They are the ones.

Interviewer: I have discovered that you share several viewpoints with Martin Luther King Jr., as far as communal progress is concerned. First of all, the integrationist impulse, which in this case means that if you imprison one, you imprison all. Progress can only be achieved for the whole society or for no one.

Gaines: Yes, I do admire him very much. You know, we were born on the same day, though he is four years older than I am, but we are both born on January 15. There were three of us in San Francisco who were born on January 15. And after he was assassinated, we would always have a birthday party where we put a large picture of him in the back. And we'd have a birthday cake which would have Martin, Ernie, CB, and Mary written on it. Yes, I am a great admirer of his, but I never met him personally.

Interviewer: Also, King had this concept of creative suffering, by which is meant that if you stand up for what you believe, you may have to suffer for it, but this will have a redeeming effect and will restore your dignity.

Gaines: Yes, I have that as a sort of constant theme from one book of mine to the other. There is a line. Most of my characters are willing to go over that line, whether that means harm or death or whatever, when they cross that line. Jimmy Aaron, Marcus, and Jackson, who loses Catherine. You do suffer; you have to suffer in order to make any changes, especially when you have something so ingrained as racism, and over so many years, in order to have any change at all. And it has to begin with one person, and others will follow. It's usually one person that must be willing to pay a big price to make this change.

Interviewer: Does that on the other hand mean that if you are holding back, you are in a way guilty of your own oppression, that "silence is betrayal," as Dr. King said.

Gaines: Yes, ah, I don't know how to say this. Most of my characters don't look at themselves as revolutionaries. They just feel that "I have to do this" and don't think about whether others will follow. On the other hand, in *A Lesson Before Dying*, Jefferson has been convinced by Grant to make this move to change things for others.

Interviewer: I found it remarkable that the more I read Dr. King's speeches, the more similarities I discover.

Gaines: You know it's not that I have read his speeches that much. But I think it was that at that time we had the same sort of feeling about how things ought to be changed. I remember that Alex Haley wrote *Roots* at the same time I was writing *The Autobiography of Miss Jane Pittman*, and neither of us knew the other. But we were writing about the same sort of thing; he was writing about Africa at a certain point in time, and I was writing about slavery at a certain point in time.

I think that's what happens among people. It just had to happen at that time.

Interviewer: So you were not consciously trying to adopt King's philosophy?

Gaines: No, but it was there. I have been asked if I was influenced by Malcolm X when I created Procter in "Three Men." No, I was not. He had to go to prison and suffer there in order to change things. No, I did not have that in mind. But there was something going on; there was something in the air, in the spirit at that particular time.

I have been a great admirer of Hemingway. A man who loses out physically but some way comes up morally stronger, and the spirit rises. But when I am writing, I don't have Hemingway or Malcolm X or King in mind. It's that my characters take over. I think I do it subconsciously. These things gather deep down in me, and they come out when I am creating a character. But I am not influenced directly by it when I'm sitting at the desk and writing.

Interviewer: But you have always admired people who have stood up for their beliefs, like Dr. King or James Meredith. You have once said that you would like to translate into your works what Meredith stood up for.

Gaines: Meredith was the reason why I went [back] to Louisiana. I was supposed to run away with some friends to Mexico in 1962. I was supposed to leave America because we thought it was too commercialized. It did nothing to help the writer to be creative. Everything was already there, everything was dying. Friends of mine, both white and black, were leaving America, going to Africa, to Europe, to Mexico. I was supposed to join two friends in the summer of '62. But I didn't have any money in my pocket, and I had to work. And then James Meredith went into Ole Miss in September of that year, and it completely changed my life around. If I had gone to Mexico, I would have been running away. Running away from my writing. I would have been running away from myself, really. I would have been running away from life. But because he went to Ole Miss, it made me face up to life. It made me see that in order to accomplish something, you have to stay and not run. At that time I thought he had to be the bravest man in the world. The bravest man in the world. And, of course, I felt the same way about King. And because of Jim Meredith, I went to Louisiana in January of '63 and I spent six months there. I am sure those six months saved my writing career because I had been trying to write *Catherine Carmier* for four years, and I could not do it. But after spending six months there and working on the book, I came back to San Francisco and finished the novel. I don't know that I would have ever finished that novel, had I not gone back to Louisiana. And I don't know that I would have gone to Louisiana had James Meredith not gone to Ole Miss. He is really a hero of mine.

Interviewer: That leads to the question about contemporary heroes. Where do the heroes come from today?

Gaines: I don't know where they are. Our writing is not taken as seriously as I would like to see in the States. I think there are some very good writers there, but we are not in the forefront as the civil rights demonstrators were or our religious leaders or our athletes or our entertainers. I think that if we read more in the States, and if more attention was paid to writers, I think we could find the heroes there because we have some very good African American writers in the States today, like Toni Morrison or Alice Walker. There are quite a few.

But I don't know where the heroes will come from next. I have no idea who will be the next heroes.

Interviewer: You also have a lot of athletes as heroes in your works, but again, if you look at the contemporary scene, the whole sports scene may be just too commercialized now to produce outstanding models.

Gaines: Yes, when you look back at the Joe Louises and Jackie Robinsons, they were real heroes because we had nothing else. We had absolutely nothing else.

I've gotten this idea of bringing in athletes from Hemingway and also from Joyce's "Ivy Day in the Committee Room" and how they talk about past heroes.

Interviewer: In your recent interview with John Lowe, you mentioned that you were planning on writing two novellas. How much progress have you made with them?

Gaines: Actually, I have three novellas in mind, but they are really very sketchy. I haven't been able to concentrate any time on it. I need a block of two or three months where there is nothing else to do but to concentrate on that, and I haven't had that kind of time since I've been in Europe. As I said, it is sketchy and I will continue to work at it, but these novellas are not even half developed.

Interviewer: As a Gaines aficionado, I am, of course, looking forward to reading anything new from you.

Gaines: When I go back to the States in January, I will spend a lot of time working on these new stories. And I will be teaching creative writing at the University of Southwestern Louisiana next fall.

An Interview with Ernest J. Gaines

Allen Gee / 1998

From *Gulf Coast: A Journal of Literature and Fine Arts* 10.2 (Summer 1998): 25–35. Reprinted with permission.

Editor's note: The following conversation took place at the Wyndham Warwick in Houston, Texas, on April 10, 1998.

Gee: I read a short piece you wrote titled "A Very Big Order: Reconstructing Identity" that appeared in the *Southern Review*. You write about your beginnings, about going to the library, trying to find something there about your people when you were young, and not finding anything, exactly, reading Twain, Faulkner, Welty, and later, Steinbeck, Cather, Turgenev, and Chekhov. Who are you reading now to try and find something?

Gaines: Well, usually, I'm reading manuscripts now. More manuscripts than anything else. There's always someone sending me galleys to read. Recently, I read James McPherson's *Crabcakes*. I've just received a book by Ernest Hill, who teaches at Southern University in Baton Rouge. His first novel was *Satisfied with Nothing*, and he's just written out another novel, *A Life for a Life*. I just started that; it's a galley form now because they would like me to make a little blurb about that. And I'm reading a collection of essays by Sean O'Faolain, the Irish writer, on the vanishing heroes in contemporary fiction, so I only read novels now that somebody will send for me to read, for a blurb, or manuscripts that former students of mine would like me to read. I'll make some comments if the manuscript is a solid piece. That's what I'm doing now, and I'm doing a lot of travelling because we're pushing the book (*A Lesson Before Dying*) since the Oprah thing. Since my interview there with Oprah, a lot of people have gotten excited about the book again. The book was out four years before Oprah had me on her program, and suddenly there's more excitement. And we've sold more copies in the last six months than we did in the past four years. So my wife and I have been travelling all over the country, and Vintage Press, which publishes the paperback version of the novel, is sending us about. So I'm not doing too much reading since I'm doing more travelling now than anything else.

Gee: You mentioned reading about heroes, and I've seen that often in your work with *Miss Jane*, and reading through *A Lesson Before Dying.* Are you going to return to motifs again with heroes in your work?

Gaines: Oh, I really don't know. In most of my work there's a common theme, a common motif. And that is, what is manliness? What really is manliness? Is it a guy who can knock a guy out with his fists or a guy who can—you know, the John Wayne type who can shoot a guy with a black bullet and the guy dies—you know things like this. Or is it someone who really stands up at a moment because no matter who you are in the world, you can be the richest guy, you can be Bill Gates, or you can be yourself or me—there comes a moment in life when we have to say "yes" or "no," and what do we say at that moment? And I think this is where what I consider manliness comes in. Not only what you say at that moment, but what do you do at that moment. What do you do? If you saw someone out there bleeding to death right now, falling off one of those scaffolds out there and bleeding, what do you do? Do you go there? Do you try to help this guy? Or do you say, "Well, that guy's a different race than I am"? I ought to forget it. The hell with it. So what do you do? This is the kind of thing, the kind of theme that I suppose I will always write about because I've been writing about that since my very first novel back in the sixties. And I've been writing about rural Louisiana, rural stuff when everybody else—when you were supposed to write about urban, northern urban cities. I was writing about rural plantation life, field life, men working with their hands, and that sort of thing in the South, and I like to write about that sort of thing.

Gee: Are you going to go back there again?

Gaines: Oh, yes. I've tried to write about other things. I've tried to write about Bohemian life in San Francisco, and I've tried to write about interracial love affairs in San Francisco. I've tried to write about my army experience on Guam. I've tried to write about all sorts of things. But none of it has really come out. None of it has been good enough to be published. We have it in a suitcase at the library in Louisiana where I'm writer-in-residence. We have them in the archives there. So I don't think I'll look at it now, but after I'm dead I want students to go in there and search through it to see exactly how bad the thing was. It's really bad stuff, and I'd like for students to see that because they think that writers write what they—what gets published. But a writer goes step by step, makes all kinds of mistakes, puts manuscripts aside, and takes on something else, and puts that aside, to get the work done. So we're saving those manuscripts where I know I failed. They'll be there for scholars, or whoever would like to read through them. Not now, but when I'm dead.

Gee: Do you think your finished novels, that you consider to be more successful now, does their strength come from the impressions of your childhood, from those emotions?

Gaines: Yes, I think writers are really impressed by their early childhoods. I left Louisiana to go to California when I was fifteen years old, and I think I learned a lot about the place and the people and the way of living there, from those fifteen years. I worked, went into the fields when I was a very small child, when I was eight years old. I went into the swamps to pull the end of a saw to cut down wood because that's how we cooked our food and warmed the house, with wood. We didn't have gas or electrical things, so when I was about eleven years old I had to go into the swamps to do this kind of work with my uncles. I knew about the swamps; I knew about hunting. I knew about fishing. I used to fish in the bayous, in the river. I picked cotton, cut sugarcane. I knew all of these things before I went to California. I learned a lot. But I think if I'd have stayed in Louisiana for another five years until I was twenty or twenty-one years old, I think I could have been destroyed as so many of my contemporaries were. They no longer went further into education. They became quite bitter about their situations. Many of them ran away, went into the military, did other things, but I was fortunate my folks took me away from there. At fifteen years old, they took me to California to be educated. I went to school in a completely integrated area. I lived in government projects, and a lot of the poorer people lived in those projects at that time, just after the war. My classmates and my playmates around the recreation center and on the playing fields were of different nationalities. Asians, Hispanics, whites, the blacks. I got a chance to get around and be with people, much—so different than the experience I had in the South, where everything was white and black. There were no other groups. Whites here, blacks there. You didn't see anybody else. You didn't see Hispanics or Asians or any other group. It was just white and black. So this kind of experience that I came from, I was fortunate that I went to the North when I went to the North to see that people were different and that they were the same in so many ways, but they were different in so many ways.

Gee: Do you think you'll ever write about that experience in a memoir or essays?

Gaines: I think I've done this many times in interviews. I don't think I've ever tried to write an essay about it. In interviews, I'm sure I've said something about the different stages in my life, from being a fifteen year old in California to being sixty-five.

Gee: Who were the most important writers you had as mentors early on?

Gaines: My mentor was Wallace Stegner at Stanford, and there were a couple of writers at San Francisco State. The person who was the most influential at San Francisco State was not a creative writing teacher, but a teacher who taught composition writing. The only reason why he was so influential in my work was because I was flunking his class, and he gave me the opportunity to write fiction instead of writing those essays which I just couldn't get. I was getting Ds in writing essays.

Gee: Did you know that you wanted to write fiction, that that's what you wanted to do?

Gaines: Oh, I knew I wanted to be a writer even before I went to high school or college. I wanted to be a writer when I was about sixteen years old. I knew I wanted to be a writer. It's all I wanted to do with my life. I had discovered that when I went to California at fifteen and went into a library when I was about sixteen years old. It was the first time I had done that because I was not allowed to go into the library in Louisiana, in my town. The library was for whites only. I couldn't go to the library there. But when I went to California I found myself in the library just reading and reading and reading everybody, and I didn't understand what I was doing. But I loved what I was doing.

Gee: Do you think it's the love for fiction that keeps you writing novels, and not writing in other forms.

Gaines: Well, I think so. I love reading great works. I love reading great plays, poetry, and of course novels. That's the only thing I can do. I used to write little skits—I had to take a drama class, and I used to write little skits for that. But I never took it seriously, you know, that I would try to be a playwright or anything like that. I prefer the novel. I was much more free with the novel. I could do things. I didn't know anything about acting or setting up stage, although I use a lot of dialogue in my work. But I never thought about putting this in play form.

Gee: Can you tell me about how your style evolved because it's very distinct?
Gaines: Well, I don't know what style is, but style is the man. I can't do any-thing else. I suppose my style comes from the way I walk or the way I talk or the way I make gestures or something like that. I don't know anything else. I don't know any other way to write. I remember when I was in college I was imitating everybody. I imitated Hemingway a while. I imitated Faulkner a while. And I remember one professor told me at Stanford—this is Malcolm Cowley—he said, "Ernie, one Faulkner a century is enough, so stop imitat-ing this guy." Then I started imitating Hemingway, and I tried to write like Joyce. And then, finally, I just began to rewrite and rewrite and rewrite, and began to find myself.

Gee: The style is deceptively simple.
Gaines: Yeah. Yeah, right. I may have gotten some of that from Hemingway, but I think by listening to the way people would talk and what they're say-ing and what they're not saying, especially among my own people, my own black people. Many times they're not telling you everything that they want to tell you, and you have to sort of figure out what exactly they are telling me. Especially when they're talking to very well-educated people or when they're talking to other races, you know, they don't say everything. But, I mean, that's common among man. A man's gonna hold back—say maybe he doesn't trust a guy for a while, you know, he's just gonna hold back. But you have to be the guy who should learn to read between the lines, and as Hemingway once said, also, a writer must have a great shit detector. I mean, what if a guy is bullshitting you . . .

Gee: A built-in one.
Gaines: Yeah, built-in shit detector. Right. You better know what you're talking about because this guy could pull things on you that you have to understand. You have to separate the husk from the grain and be able to figure out exactly what's going on here. This is what I try to do in my work.

Gee: Can I ask you about your writing process, for stories or novels, in terms of how you handle plot? Do you do entire plot sketches, or do you start from one moment?
Gaines: I never plot out anything. I sort of plot it out in my mind. Well, I never really plot it out completely. I'll use an analogy of going from San Francisco to New York by train, and I get on the train in San Francisco and I know I want to get to New York. I know I want to get there, but I don't know

all the things that are going to happen during those four or five days between the trip. I know some things. I know some of the states I'll go through, but I don't know—for example, until today I didn't know that you'd be wearing a white shirt. I didn't know what you'd look like. I wanted to meet you, but I didn't know that you would have glasses. I didn't know that—whatever—all these little things. But these are the things that come about during that trip from San Francisco to New York. The weather changes. It gets cloudy in some places. You go down into valleys, over the hills, and the train is moving around curves. All these sorts of things come in while you're going. Now you have a destination. You know some of the things that you're going to try to bring in, that you'd like to bring in, but you don't know all the things.

Gee: Do you know the end point?
Gaines: Well, sometimes I know the end point. Sometimes I don't. Sometimes it changes during that route. For example, I did not know when I started *A Lesson Before Dying*, I did not know that Jefferson would die. I did not know that. But as things accumulated during the travel, there was no other end but that he should die and that he should die that particular time of day.

Gee: Can I ask you about Paul, the deputy in *A Lesson Before Dying*? He really reaches out.
Gaines: Yeah. I've written about Pauls before, and sometimes I've named a guy Paul in other stories and not realized it, forgetting what I've named people. But Paul is . . . if there were not any Pauls in the South during the whole civil rights movement, then we'd still be fighting out there today. There would still be a lot of bloodshed. But there were those kind of guys out there, who, caught up in the system, had to go along with the system but would like to change the system, would like to do something else, and that's how Paul is here. That's what he is supposed to be here.

Gee: I'd like to ask you about American fiction. Where do you think it's going?
Gaines: I don't know where it's going, but I think that the writer has in the past, and always will, write about what the hell he wants to write about it. And I think this is what you should do. Just write about it. Write your kind of work, the way you want to do it. If you want to write history, write history. If you want to write a contemporary event, write it. If you want to write about racial clashes, if you want to write about difference in classes, if you want to write love stories, crime stories, whatever kind of thing you

want to write about, you write about that. And I think America is so vast, so broad, with all its multiple races that you will find different races writing about different things. So I don't know what someone should or should not do, whether you should write about family or not. You make that decision. You should make that decision. We have all—among African Americans, you can see that my work and Jim McPherson's work are two different kinds of work. Jim is predominantly a short story writer. He writes more about urban life. I'm predominantly a novelist. I write more about rural life. There are commonalities there, but Jim and I are different kinds of writers. We look at things differently. And Ishmael Reed or Al Young or Toni Morrison, Alice Walker, we don't write about the same thing, and I'm just talking about one race. Get that Asian race. Chinese or Japanese or Filipinos or Koreans or Vietnamese. They have the right, and they will, they will interpret life as they see it. That's what you're supposed to do. That is what you're supposed to do. There's no such thing as a blueprint as to what a writer should write about. See, the world will let a writer starve to death, and then as soon as he makes anything, then they'll start telling him what he should do. Well, hell, they weren't telling him what he should do when he was starving out there, man. When you starve, you starve on your own. But after he starts becoming somebody, then everybody wants to tell you, well, you should write about this. You should write about this protest over here. You should write about this political thing. You should not do this. I don't agree. I don't agree.

Gee: Is there an elusive novel that you want to write, something you've thought of, a story?

Gaines: I have a couple of stories I'd like to write about, but as Hemingway once said, "It doesn't do to talk about it until you write it." There are a couple of things I'd like to write about. The most elusive novel that I've completed that I always wanted to write about was *In My Father's House*, and I think in ways—I just reread it about a month or so ago—and I think it's much better now than I thought it was before. But that novel, I feel that it could be one of my weakest, maybe my weakest novel.

Gee: No.

Gaines: Good. Occasionally, you run into a person who says, "I like that novel very much," and then you find a whole group of people who say, "Well, that's your darkest novel because it doesn't have the humor that, say, a *Miss Jane Pittman* has, or, *Of Love and Dust*, or even of *A Gathering of Old Men*." It doesn't have that kind of humor that comes out, you know.

And there's a little humor in *In My Father's House.* But that was the novel I knew that I just had to write. I just knew that. The others I wrote, but this one I had to write about a father. And the father and son theme is another theme that runs throughout my books. Fathers looking for sons, and sons looking for fathers.

Gee: And spirituality, always.
Gaines: Yes. True. Absolutely true.

Gee: On the subject of fathers and sons, can I ask you about what you think of the portrayals of African American males today?
Gaines: By whom?

Gee: Oh, you don't have to name names.
Gaines: Do you mean by female writers? By African American female writers? As I said, you can interpret anything any way you wish. Now, if they want to look at, if African American female writers want to look at the African American male as brutal or uncaring or inconsiderate or whatever, I think it's their right to look at or interpret life that way. But, as I said, I don't think there should be a blueprint as to how it should be interpreted. I don't think Toni should tell Alice or Alice should tell Terry McMillan or Terry McMillan should—I mean, one writer or another shouldn't spread a blueprint—as to say, "This is how those black SOBs are." No, I don't agree there. But the individual writer I feel can do anything he or she wishes. Now, you can be shot, you know. I mean, that's your problem. If you write certain things, that's your problem.

Gee: You write women well, and you have strong women in your books.
Gaines: Well, I believe, that's because I love women. I love the lady who raised me. I love my aunt who raised me. I love my mother. I love my sisters. I love my wife. So, you know, I try to see the whole person. The same when I'm writing about whites. I can make them decent people or not, depending on how it balances the work.

Gee: Whether it's the chief deputy or the younger deputy.
Gaines: I've done the same thing in all my books. So it depends on the kind of character I'm trying to portray in a certain position in the book, whether it's a good character or a bastard. For example, both of those characters—if Paul was like the other deputy, the chief deputy, I think something would

have been lost there, in the entire story. It would have been lost. It would have been too much of a race thing, then, too much of white versus black. I didn't want that. I wanted what Jefferson could give to Grant, and what Grant could give to Jefferson, under those conditions. This is what I wanted to do, and since people like Paul did exist at that time, alongside of people like the chief deputy, then they should be in that book.

Gee: Can you tell me about the differences in how you approach your writing now that you're an experienced writer? There's the baseball metaphor, of the younger pitcher, throwing fast balls, and the more experienced pitcher being able to throw the change-ups and curves . . .

Gaines: When I was younger I thought I'd win the Nobel Prize by the time I was forty. I remember one guy telling me once, "Gaines, your ego is so big you ought to carry it around in a trunk." I said, "Listen,"—you know I was in my early twenties—I said, "What the hell, I can compete with all those other people out here. I'll compete with Hemingway and Faulkner." He said, "You have to remember, now those guys are white." I said, "I don't give a damn what they are. I'm as good as those guys. I can compete with those guys." He said, "Gaines,"—you know this was a black guy telling me this, a very intelligent man, a critic,—he said, "Your ego is so big you ought to carry it around in a trunk." When I was much younger, I could write eight, ten hours a day. You know, I'd get up and I'd write. I'd write. I didn't give a damn about anything in the world except my writing. I would not get married. There were women in my life, but if she didn't want to hang around, okay, leave, because she wasn't going to take the place of the writing. I was too poor to buy gifts for my family at Christmas or anything. I didn't have anything. I was ready to eat pork and beans, crackers, just to be able to write. I worked just enough, held part-time jobs. I worked at the post office, at a print shop, at a bank, did some mail work, just enough to make just enough money to pay the rent in my little apartment in San Francisco. Just enough. And I'd write eight to ten hours a day because I only worked part-time. Now, of course, it's different. I work, but I'm in a marriage and do things for the family. And I've slowed down a hell of a lot. And of course, now today I write maybe five hours a day and concentrate much more now. There I could just take pen—I still write longhand—I'd take pen and pad, and I'd go anywhere and just write and write and write. But today it's slower. I think more about it. I think a lot about my work long before I write it. Then I go to work, sit at the desk. So this kind of thing changes between that time and now. I'm much more conscientious about things around me now. At that time I cared only about the writing. Nothing else mattered in the world. Nothing mattered. Only my writing. Now, of course, I'm aware of other things.

Gee: Part of manliness?
Gaines: Yeah, you grow. At least you're supposed to grow.

Gee: John A. Williams came through here, and he said he wasn't going to write fiction anymore because he was discouraged by publishers and editors. How do you feel about that?
Gaines: I have a good relationship with my publishers, Knopf and Vintage. I would never ever tell some young writer not to write because of publishing. It's always been difficult for most minorities to get their works published and accepted because the first thing the publishing house is interested in is making money. And they feel that, okay, who's going to be your readership? Who's going to read this? Can I sell enough books? And until you get a reputation, you don't sell those books if you're a minority. Some publishing houses, like Knopf, will publish my work, as well as publish Anne Rice's work. Now, they know they're going to sell Anne Rice's work, but they may not sell a "literary" piece of work over here. They say, "Well, we're not going to make any money here, but it seems like a good thing to have. We should have some of these books here, too."

Gee: Until Oprah holds it up.
Gaines: Well, when Oprah speaks, people listen. It's like that old commercial. When she speaks, people listen, and here's what happened.

Gee: They couldn't win the lawsuit against her down here in Texas.
Gaines: No, no, no, no. She's very popular. She's so popular. She brought the whole show down to Amarillo. She brought the whole show down here, and she brought in the biggest names. When she put Garth Brooks on, the Texans down here, you cowboys with that beef stuff might as well give it up because the world loves Garth Brooks. The kind of people you are representing, who you are supposed to be representing, worship Garth Brooks, and here he is on the Oprah show. So you'll have a hard time trying to convince those people that Oprah is wrong, since this is the kind of person she can have on her show.

Gee: I see race relations in so much of your work. You can read *A Lesson Before Dying* set in the forties, and of course see so much then, looking at it as a historical novel, that's pertinent to now. Do you think so much hasn't changed?

Gaines: Yes, it's true. So much has not changed. That was the way of life at that time. We wish, that after the whole civil rights movement of the sixties, that that way of life would have changed. Of course, there are still problems. I mean they're not as stringent as they were at that time, but you find the same things. When I left the South in '48—it was the same year *A Lesson Before Dying* would have taken place—I could not go to the local library there. That was why I was brought to California. Today, of course, my books are in all the libraries. I'm writer-in-residence at the University of Southwestern Louisiana. Those kinds of things have changed. However, only four or five years ago, David Duke almost became a senator in Louisiana. Sixty-five percent of the white people there voted for him. And if we were not able to vote, if blacks were not able to vote in the state of Louisiana, this guy could have become senator in the nineties. So the old French saying, "The more things change, the more they remain the same"—so you have some of the same problems today that you had in the forties, yes. But I don't write entirely about race. Race comes after. I think what I try to do is ask, How can I, or my character, live as a man? How can he make it as a man, in this oppressive society? And I think I'm much more interested in that than I am in the race thing, blacks, whites, cutting at each other's throats all the time. Because in the story of *A Lesson Before Dying*, the relationship is between two black men most of the time, not between, not the clashes between Grant and the sheriff or the sheriff beating up Jefferson. That's not even there. It could happen, but it's not there. That's not the story. Someone, in reviewing the book, has said that "Gaines is not interested in whether Jefferson goes to the electric chair or not. His interest is how Jefferson and Grant communicate?" And that is the point of the story. How do they communicate? How can Jefferson help Grant? How can Grant help Jefferson?

Gee: I have one last question. In "A Very Big Order: Reconstructing Identity," you reveal that as a younger man your audience—who you were writing for—was the black youth of the South, and the white youth of the South. . . .

Gaines: Well, Wallace Stegner asked me, "Who would you write for? Who do you write for?" Well, I said, "Mr. Stegner, I don't write for any particular group because when I look at that wall, when I look at that paper, I don't see faces down there. I don't see any face. I just try to write as well as I can because I've been influenced mainly by Western writers, white writers. The European writers: Joyce, Turgenev, Tolstoy, Chekhov. American white writers: Hemingway, Faulkner, Twain. So I never pick groups to write for." And he said, "Well, what if a gun was put to your head?" So I said, "Well, then I'll come up with an answer." And I said, "Write for the black youth of the South so that he could—I hope to have him find his humanity." And he said, "Suppose the gun was still at your head?" I said, "Maybe the white youth of the South. Because I hope, I would like to inform him, that unless he knows his neighbor of the last three hundred years, he knows only half of his own history. Unless he knows the black over here, who's been next door to him, and in the South, more than in any other part of the country, your next-door neighbor is—we grew up like that, where I grew up. The white guy was next door but still segregated—I said unless he knows that neighbor, he knows only half of me. He's on the other side of the street. He doesn't know very much."

Gee: If Wallace Stegner were to ask you the same question today, how would you answer it?

Gaines: I don't know how I would answer that. When Stegner asked me that, I hadn't published anything. Today, my books are translated all over the world. Germany, Russia, Japan, China, Israel, Portugal, all over the world. So I would just try to write for a man, I guess. Let him know a little bit about this little—this little space, in this time, where I am. And I hope that in that way, I can—and in letting him know about this, I would show him that we're all here together. The world is so much smaller. I think I said something on the Oprah show, about how what I try to do is write character in my character so that the reader can better his own character; that is, create character with character, so that the reader can develop his own character. That's what I like to do with anyone who picks up one of my books.

An Interview with Ernest J. Gaines

Jennifer Levasseur and Kevin Rabalais / 1998

From *Missouri Review* 22:1 (1999): 95–111. Reprinted with permission from Jennifer Levasseur and Kevin Rabalais.

Ernest J. Gaines is the author of six novels, including *Of Love and Dust, The Autobiography of Miss Jane Pittman*, and *A Gathering of Old Men*, and one collection of stories, *Bloodline*. His most recent novel, *A Lesson Before Dying*, won the National Book Critics Circle Award in 1993. He has received a literary award from the American Academy of Arts and Letters, a Guggenheim Fellowship, and a MacArthur Foundation Fellowship. Gaines was born on a plantation near New Roads, Louisiana. He now divides his time between Lafayette, Louisiana, and San Francisco. This interview was conducted by Jennifer Levasseur and Kevin Rabalais on the University of Southwestern Louisiana campus in Lafayette on August 26, 1998.

Interviewer: You've been writer-in-residence at the University of Southwestern Louisiana since 1984. What do you feel are your responsibilities as a teacher of creative writing?

Gaines: I approach the teaching of creative writing—if you can possibly teach creative writing—from the Socratic method. The students have their material ready on Tuesdays, and they will have read and written critiques of the material by the next time we meet. I write a critique as well. Each Tuesday night, we discuss two students' work. The students who have stories being discussed that night read aloud for five or ten minutes so we can feel the rhythm. After the student reads, I open it up for discussion. I don't lecture. I sit back and direct the discussion; if it slows down, I speed it up, or if no one has anything to say, I raise a question. This is my approach to "teaching" writing. I set requirements. I believe the students should all write critiques of each other's work, and they must also discuss the stories in class. I feel students usually learn as much about writing from discussion among their peers as they do from me. I don't assign books for them to read because they should read everything. I always recommend books—the Bible, Strunk and White's *The Elements of Style.* My six words of advice to writers are: "Read, read, read, write, write, write." Writing is a lonely job; you have to read, and then you must sit down at the desk and write. There's no one there to tell you when to write, what to write, or how to write. I tell students if they are going to be writers, they must sit down at a desk and write every day.

Interviewer: The students read from their own work for the first few minutes of class so readers can get the sound of the rhythm. You've also said you write your stories to be read aloud.

Gaines: When people hear stories, they identify more closely with the characters. When I read aloud, people always come up to me and say, "I understand it much better now that I've heard you read it. I can hear the characters' voices much clearer." Many of the students use dialects or words and phrases we are not familiar with, but once we hear it, we tend to understand it much better.

Interviewer: Dialogue is something you've said you are proud of in your work.

Gaines: In dialogue, I'm dealing with the sounds I've heard. One of the reasons I often write from first person or multiple points of view is to hear the voices of different characters. Omniscient narration becomes a problem because, for me, the omniscient is my own voice narrating the story and then bringing in characters for dialogue.

Interviewer: There is a strength in the many voices in your work, a weight you give to each character's voice no matter how small a role he or she plays. One very minor character, a drunk in *In My Father's House,* gives Reverend Martin directions. When he speaks, his voice is as strong as any in the novel.

Gaines: My ear is pretty good. As a small child, I listened to radio a lot. During that time—this was back in the late '40s—there were always great dramas and actors on radio. I liked listening to them because I had to follow the story through dialogue. I like reading plays, and I like listening to the ways people speak.

Interviewer: Does this oral approach help when you are editing your work?

Gaines: What I usually do is record my work on a tape recorder. If it sounds good, then it is. I never read my work to anyone else and say, "Okay, what do you think?" Editors recommend certain things, but usually, at this point in the game, I can stick to my guns and say, "This is how it's written, and this is how it sounds." I write about south Louisiana, and I feel my ear is pretty good for the dialects of that region, at least better than the people in New York who have never been here.

Interviewer: In *The Autobiography of Miss Jane Pittman*, it is Miss Jane the reader sees and hears. How did you find Miss Jane's voice?

Gaines: I did a lot of research to get the historical facts right and read quite a few slave narratives to see how the slaves expressed themselves and how they used their vocabularies. I grew up on a plantation on False River, Louisiana, and I was around older people—my aunt, who raised me, and the older people who visited her because she was crippled and couldn't walk. Those were the voices I had in mind while creating Miss Jane Pittman. She was not based on any one person or any two people but on the kind of experience someone who lived during that time might have gone through. Her voice came fairly easily. I had read enough and could recall the dialects and the limited vocabularies of the older people on the plantation where I lived to create an authentic voice for Miss Jane. The first draft was told from multiple points of view, with people talking about her after she had died. I did that for more than a year and then realized it was not exactly right. I needed to get her to tell the story, so I concentrated on one voice rather than several.

Interviewer: Have there been some characters' voices that were easier to get into than others?

Gaines: Jim's in *Of Love and Dust* because I was thirty-three years old when I started writing that book, and I created him to be the same age. He's uneducated, but he's thirty-three years old. He uses the language I grew up around living in Louisiana. Also, it wasn't too difficult to find Jefferson's diary voice in *A Lesson Before Dying* because I wrote the diary after working on the novel for five years. I knew his character and what he would say, how he would express himself. Sometimes I have to rewrite and rewrite to get the exact phrases I want. I stick with south Louisiana, not places with unfamiliar accents.

Interviewer: How do you approach a novel like *A Gathering of Old Men*, with its distinct multiple points of view?

Gaines: I try to concentrate on voices of different people I knew as a child. I left Louisiana at fifteen but always came back. While writing *A Gathering* *of Old Men*, I could recall that different people spoke differently, and they would never describe the same thing the same way; they never used the same expressions. So when I went from one of the characters in that novel to another, I had to concentrate entirely on that character and how he would express himself. Then when I went to another character, I would concentrate on another person's voice and give it to that particular character.

Interviewer: You've said before that you were influenced by Japanese films, including *Rashomon*, the story of a murder told from several points of view.
Gaines: I saw *Rashomon* many years ago, and it has had some effect on me, as have Faulkner, Joyce, and whoever else's work I've read. They say if you steal from one person you are plagiarizing, but if you steal from a hundred people you are a genius. You don't pick entirely from Faulkner, entirely from *Rashomon*, or entirely from Hemingway. You learn from all of them, just as all writers have done. You learn from people you read.

Interviewer: What are some other important influences on your work?
Gaines: I've been influenced by the great French filmmakers of the fifties—Truffaut, for example, particularly *The 400 Blows* and *Shoot the Piano Player*. When I was writing *A Lesson Before Dying*, I saw a film on television with Danny Glover, and it had a tremendous effect on me. Danny Glover plays a social worker who visits prisons. There is one prisoner who will do anything to annoy him. The little things he would do to irritate Danny Glover made me think, "Hey, that's good!" I've never been to visit anybody in prison repeatedly. A couple of weeks ago, I was talking with some kids in a jail in Orlando, Florida. These were murderers, dope peddlers. They were sixteen and seventeen years old. But I've never gone back and forth like Grant does in *A Lesson Before Dying*. Watching this film with Danny Glover, I thought, "This is what happens when you keep going back to a prison to visit one guy. He will always do something to irritate you." That's how I decided to have Jefferson not speak, or say something to annoy Grant. What I'm saying is that you learn from all these things. You learn from music, from watching great athletes at work—how disciplined they are, how they move. You learn these things by watching a shortstop at work, how he concentrates on one thing at a time. You learn from classical music, from the blues and jazz, from bluegrass. From all this, you learn how to sustain a great line without bringing in unnecessary words. I advise my students to keep their antennae out so they can pick things up from all these sources, everything life has to offer,

but books especially, which is the main tool they have to work with. They should not close their ears or eyes to anything that surrounds them.

Interviewer: One book you've recommended is *Max Perkins: Editor of Genius* by A. Scott Berg. How do you feel about the hands-on style of editing, exemplified by Perkins, that doesn't seem to be as present in the publishing world today?

Gaines: I really like Maxwell Perkins because of all the great writers who were around him. A. Scott Berg did a wonderful job with that book. He did a lot of research and brought out the different characters of F. Scott Fitzgerald, Ernest Hemingway, and Thomas Wolfe. I knew some good critics and editors. Malcolm Cowley, who had the sense to rediscover Faulkner, was a teacher of mine at Stanford. Wallace Stegner was my mentor at Stanford. He was the person who brought me there. Ed (E. L.) Doctorow, who later became famous as a writer himself, was my editor at Dial Press. He was a very good editor. I have a good editor at Knopf now, Ash Green. These people are wonderful. They are not as famous as Max Perkins, and not all writers are fortunate enough to get great editors, but I've been lucky. You need a good editor because every writer thinks he can write a *War and Peace*, but by the time he gets it on paper, it's not *War and Peace* anymore; it's comic-book stuff. If you have an honest editor who knows what literature and writing are about, he can give you good advice. You don't necessarily have to follow it all. It's good to get the material away from you after you've finished something, to send it out and let another person comment on it. I had a wonderful agent, Dorothea Oppenheimer, and she saw everything of mine for thirty-one years. We had our fights. When she criticized me, I would say, "Well, you don't know what you're talking about. I'm the writer." But I apologized later. I think those editors and agents are necessary. I didn't get along with all my editors, though.

Interviewer: You began work on what later became your first novel, *Catherine Carmier*, when you were sixteen years old. It went through many rewrites and titles. What type of learning process was this?

Gaines: I tried to write a novel around 1949, which later became *Catherine Carmier*. Of course, I sent it to New York to a publisher, and they sent it back. We had an incinerator in the back yard, and I burned it. I was falling back in my class work, so I started concentrating on school. When I was twenty, I went into the army. I wrote a little bit. I came out when I was twenty-two, and I went to San Francisco State to study literature and theater writing. Then I went to Stanford. I was writing short stories during that time. Someone gave a lecture, and he told us that young writers without a name would have a hard time publishing a collection of stories. So that day, I put the short stories aside and said, "No more short stories. I've got to write something I can publish." I didn't have anything else for a novel but that one story I'd tried to write about ten years earlier. I started rewriting it, and I wrote about fifty pages and won the Joseph Henry Jackson Award, which was a local award given to residents of California. That helped me get through 1959. I got jobs at the post office, a print shop, a bank. I would write in the morning and get these little part-time jobs in the afternoon. From '59 to '64, I wrote that novel over and over. I must have written it more than ten times. Each time I rewrote it, I came up with a different title. I was always changing things: somebody would die in one draft, and another person would die in the next. Malcolm Cowley and several other editors saw it, but no one was ready to publish it. It is a simple story about a guy coming back to the old place and visiting the old people, and he has changed so much that he doesn't fit in anymore. The model I used was Turgenev's *Fathers and Sons*. I was reading something from it every day. It's about a young doctor who has just finished university and comes back to the old place and falls in love with a beautiful woman. He loses her and dies. My character does the same thing, but he doesn't die. He has to go away again. I was using Turgenev's novel as a model for how to write a novel.

Interviewer: In that novel, you explore a situation—a young man who leaves Louisiana to receive an education, then returns—that you examine again in your most recent novel, *A Lesson Before Dying*.
Gaines: My characters seem like they can't get away. Miss Jane tries to walk to Ohio, but she never gets out of Louisiana. Charlie, in *A Gathering of Old Men*, tries to run away, but he has to come back. All my characters are like that; they go so far, and then they return. They must face up to their responsibilities.

Interviewer: They know they must accept responsibility and go on because it is the graceful thing to do.
Gaines: Yes. They have to make the effort to go on, and sometimes it brings death. But they must make that effort before the moment of death. In *A Lesson Before Dying*, Jefferson must stand before he will be executed. Marcus, in *Of Love and Dust*, can't escape, but he rises before he dies and becomes a better human being. In *A Gathering of Old Men*, Charlie must come back, and he dies when he does. There are certain lines they have to

cross to prove their humanity. I could not write about a character who did not have these qualities—a person who struggles and falls but gets up, who will go to a certain point, even though he knows he might get killed. That's a common theme in all my work: those who cannot escape by running away, and those who go to a certain point, even if it means death. For example, in *A Lesson Before Dying,* Grant will not try to run away anymore. Vivian is going to keep him in Louisiana.

Interviewer: In *A Gathering of Old Men,* you give the reader both points of view—black and white—to show what each side is going through and how they are living.

Gaines: That's what writing should be about: presenting as many facets as you possibly can. I'm not interested in seeing one side of anything. One of the reasons I make both Grant and Jefferson tragic figures in *A Lesson Before Dying* is because I wanted this to be a story about more than just a young black man sitting on death row. I needed someone to go to the prison and teach Jefferson, but also someone who would learn while teaching because he is also in a prison; Grant is in a prison of being unable to live the way he would like to live. I had to discover how he could break out of that. Jefferson, of course, finds release in death, and Grant must take on the responsibility of becoming a better person, a better teacher. I did not want a simple story about someone being executed; we have had lots of them, too many. I wanted something else, another added component to that novel.

Interviewer: In your body of work there are examples of almost every point of view.

Gaines: I change point of view when one does not work for me. *A Gathering of Old Men* was originally told from one point of view, that of the newspaperman, Lou Dimes. Then I realized he could not tell the story. He could not see Snookum running and striking his butt the way you would if you were trying to make a horse run faster. He could not see Janie going to that house, and so many other small things that could make the story better. He never would have known the thoughts of these people. So much of the story is internal. There is very little action. You don't see Beau being shot. What you see is Beau lying there and all these other people talking and thinking. I knew I had to write it from multiple points of view rather than omniscient. *The Autobiography of Miss Jane Pittman,* as I have said, began as a multiple-point-of-view narrative, but it did not work. I rewrote it as a first-person narrative. I recommend taking the easiest route in writing, not making things harder than they really are. If you can tell a story better from the omniscient point of view, then tell it that way. If you can tell it better from first person, tell it that way. I never say, "Well, I'm going to tell some first-person stories and some omniscient ones." I think, "What's the easiest way to tell my story without cheating?" I cannot cheat myself in writing.

Interviewer: Earlier, you mentioned that you were warned off trying to publish short-story collections when you began writing. The same warning is given to young writers today.

Gaines: Thirty-five hundred copies of *Catherine Carmier* were printed. Only about 2,500 were sold. The rest were remaindered. I had written the short stories that later appeared in *Bloodline* by the time I wrote *Catherine Carmier*. There are only five, so I may have been writing the fourth. I then wrote another one, the title story, which is the last in that collection. I sent it to Bill Decker at Dial Press, and I said, "Those stories are good; they will make my name." Bill said, "Yes, we know the stories are good, but you need to be a name in order for us to publish them." It's a catch-22. They might make your name, but you need a name before you can publish them. Who's going to pay attention to an unknown young writer? It was then that I wrote *Of Love and Dust*. I wrote the first draft in three months and sent it to Bill Decker. He said, "I like the first part of your novel, and I like the second part, but they don't have anything in common. You need to make it either a farce or a tragedy." I rewrote it in three months and sent it back to him. He said, "You've improved it ninety percent. Now I want you to run it through the typewriter one more time and do anything you want to do because I think you know where you want to go with the novel." I did that and sent it back to him within two months. He told me, "I'll publish it, then I will publish your stories." The novel was published in '67, and the stories were published in the spring of '68. That's how I got my stories published.

Interviewer: You have not published a story collection since *Bloodline*. Have you written stories since then?

Gaines: I've thought about it, but I never came up with any that were in the same class as those. Also, whenever I finished one novel, I was always ready to start another one. I don't have one in mind now, but in the past I've always had a novel in mind while working on another one.

Interviewer: The first story in *Bloodline*, "A Long Day in November," was later revised and published as a children's book with the same title.

Gaines: Yes, we cut out some sexual terms and then added illustrations to make it a children's book. But it's not a children's book. My wife tells me it's still an adult book told by a six-year-old child.

Interviewer: Whose idea was it to turn that story into a children's book?

Gaines: The people at Dial Press recognized that I had two stories in *Bloodline* narrated by children, so they said, "Can you write a children's story?" I said, "I can write a story from a child's point of view, but I don't know anything about writing children's books." Someone at Dial said, "Well, maybe we can take one of these stories." I wish they had taken "The Sky Is Gray." It would have made a much better children's book than "A Long Day in November."

Interviewer: Was writing something you always thought you would do?

Gaines: I did not know I wanted to be a writer as a child in Louisiana. It wasn't until I went to California and ended up in the library and began read-ing a lot that I knew I wanted to be a writer. I read many great novels and stories and did not see myself or my people in any of them. It was then that I tried to write. There were very few people on the plantation who had any education at all, especially the old people my aunt's age and my grandmoth-er's age. They had never gone to school, and they didn't have any books. I used to write letters for them. I had to listen very carefully to what they had to say and how they said it. I put their stories down on paper, and they would give me teacakes. If I wanted to play ball or shoot marbles, I had to finish writing fast. So I began to create. I wrote about their gardens, the weather, cooking, preserving, anything. I've been asked many times when I started writing. I used to say it was in the small Andrew Carnegie Library in Vallejo, California, but I realize now that it was on the plantation.

Interviewer: What impact have your many years of teaching had on your writing and reading?

Gaines: My students keep me aware of things around me, but I don't know that my "style"—and I hate using words like that—has changed in any way or that my views on life have changed in any way from teaching. I do learn things from certain students. Most of my students are middle-class white females. I learn about their ways of thinking and describing things, their backgrounds and social values. So when I come to write something of my own, that knowledge is there to use, if necessary. For example, when I was writing *A Gathering of Old Men*, I had someone in mind just like Candy. In fact, she's still on that plantation, and she knows I was writing about her in some ways. I am always getting information from the things and people around me, the sounds, the sights, the weather. I do learn from my students, but I don't know how they have changed my view of writing.

Interviewer: In the past, you've said if you had a student come to you who had the potential and desire to create a great work, you would put the student's work in front of your own. Do you feel being a mentor would be as fulfilling as working on your own writing?

Gaines: I can't say that, but I would say the objective of teaching is passing on what you know. I am slowing down now as a writer. Most American writers slow down in their fifties, though some people say I wrote my best book, *A Lesson Before Dying*, at sixty. But I'm not as aggressive now. I'm not writing for five or six hours a day anymore. It's possible to devote more time to a student, to a young writer, and not feel cheated at all. I think I was given a talent to be a writer, and I should use that talent. I don't know that the student's work would be more important than mine—that I would be able to quit writing and devote all my time to him or her—but I would give a heck of a lot of time to that work.

Interviewer: Were there goals you set at the beginning of your career?

Gaines: Well, I thought I would win the Nobel Prize. I thought I would make a lot of money and be able to send it back to my aunt who raised me, but she died many years before any of my work had been published. I told myself I would write for five, six hours a day every day and try to have enough money to support myself to write. I wanted to have enough money to write as much as I wanted to write, but I never set any goals to be rich or travel the world.

Interviewer: Your novels are all close in length, but *The Autobiography of Miss Jane Pittman* spans more than one hundred years, while *A Gathering of Old Men* follows characters through one day.

Gaines: I am proud to have accomplished this, to have concentrated on one day with flashbacks and also to have written something as broad as *The Autobiography of Miss Jane Pittman*. The novels are all about the same number of pages, and the time span in most of them is the same. In *A Lesson Before Dying*, I had to stretch the time to what would be equivalent to the semester of school blacks were getting in the rural South; at that time, we were getting less than six months. I knew exactly the kind of time I had to put into that novel as far as story line, when it would begin and when it would end. But the other novels are all about the same size. I never decided beforehand how long a book would be. It just so happens I learned more from Turgenev than I thought I did in the beginning. His novels were very short compared to Dostoyevsky's or Tolstoy's. I feel after writing so many pages, maybe at most four hundred, there is nothing else to say, so it is time to close it down. I knew *The Autobiography of Miss Jane Pittman* would cover a hundred years and that it would be a longer novel than my earlier ones. I have been influenced by so many different forms of writing. I studied Greek tragedy at San Francisco State, and I've always thought the idea of having things in a single setting and limited to twenty-four hours was the ideal way of telling stories. For example, "A Long Day in November" takes place within less than twenty-four hours, as do "Bloodline" and "The Sky Is Gray." "Just Like a Tree" takes place in three hours. It's all concentrated. *The Autobiography of Miss Jane* was a different thing altogether.

Interviewer: Jefferson's notebook is one of the most moving parts of *A Lesson Before Dying.* You get inside his head, but as readers, we know Grant doesn't get the notebook until the end. It is powerful not only because of its content, but also because the reader sees the diary before Grant receives it. How did you decide on the placement of the diary?

Gaines: I did it so it would work chronologically with the rest of the novel. That book has been translated into German, and they moved the notebook chapter to the end. I thought it should be before the end, so you would still see Jefferson after he dies, after Grant is given the notebook. I've sold the rights to HBO. They are supposed to start shooting it in October of '98. I have no idea what they are going to do with it or where they are going to film it. It has also been adapted as a play for the Alabama Shakespeare Company.

Interviewer: The novel is cinematic in the same way Tolstoy's "The Death of Ivan Ilyich" is. The reader sees every movement of the characters as if they are on a stage.

Gaines: One of the things I learned from Turgenev's *Fathers and Sons* is that something is always happening in one setting, then you move on to something else. If you look at the chapters in that novel, I don't think any one is longer or shorter than the others. I wrote a rough draft every week and then went over it. They would always end up the same number of pages. I had to write that book over a period of seven years, writing only half the year because I was teaching at USL. I would go back to San Francisco at the end of December and start in late January, writing until the end of July, when I was ready to come back to Lafayette and teach. *A Lesson Before Dying* is the only novel I've ever written that way, and it really scared me because I didn't know how I would go back to it the first time I put it aside for six months. I was afraid the reader would see those breaks, so I worked on smoothing them out. It may have been good because if the novel had been written in three years, I might not have had as many different elements coming into the story. I don't know if I would have had the notebook in the story. But because I was thinking about it over a period of seven years, those things just came into it.

Interviewer: You received a lot of publicity when Oprah Winfrey chose *A Lesson Before Dying* for her book club. How did you feel when you learned this?
Gaines: She called me personally, and I didn't believe it was her. I had met her when the book first came out. She said, "We've chosen *A Lesson Before Dying* for the Oprah Book Club. This is all hush-hush until I announce it on my show." I said, "It's okay with me, just as long as I can tell my wife." She came to Louisiana to the plantation at False River. We spent two days together.

Interviewer: The novel had already drawn attention when it won the National Book Critics Circle Award in 1993. Did you feel a rush of new readership because of Oprah's influence?
Gaines: Oh, yes. Before, the book was selling well, but it was selling to high schools and libraries. With Oprah, it sold to the general public. There were between eight hundred thousand and a million copies printed as soon as she announced it. Everybody knew *The Autobiography of Miss Jane Pittman*, but they never knew who wrote it. Now they know Ernest Gaines wrote *A Lesson Before Dying* because they saw me on the show. I receive many letters from people all over the country and different parts of the world, and most of them are coming from white, probably middle-aged males. It's the first time I've received letters from this particular group. Bill Gates said *A Lesson Before Dying* was one of his favorite books, along with *The Catcher in the Rye*. That's good to hear, but he never sent me any computer stuff. I've always received many letters from students, but it seems *A Lesson Before Dying* has touched a lot of people.

Interviewer: How do you feel about all the attention?
Gaines: I'm happy people are reading the book, but other than that, I just do the same thing. I teach. My wife and I still go to the same restaurants. We still visit our friends, things like that.

Talking with Ernest J. Gaines: Religion, Spirituality, and Belief

Marcia Gaudet / 1999

From *Louisiana Literature* 16:1 (1999): 54–66. Reprinted with permission.

This conversation/interview took place on March 2, 1999, on the sun porch of Ernest and Dianne Gaines's home in Lafayette, Louisiana. When Darrell Bourque asked me to interview Ernest Gaines for this special issue of *Louisiana Literature*, I asked that he sit in on the interview as well. The memory of conversations the three of us have had together through the years as friends and as colleagues at the University of Southwestern Louisiana suggested this to me. The result, I believe, is a very special and intimate talk with Ernest Gaines among friends.

Marcia Gaudet: Although south Louisiana is part of the predominantly Protestant South, it has a large Catholic population. You were, of course, raised Baptist, and your portrayals of religious figures are basically Protestant. But you went to a Catholic school for three years. Do you think that having gone to a Catholic school, having grown up in a culture that was unlike the rest of the South—one that really was mixed and had the large Catholic population—influenced in any way how you portray religion and religious people in your work?

Ernest J. Gaines: Quite possibly. Of course, I grew up Baptist and most of my people were Baptist, although my stepfather who raised me was Catholic. His side of the family was Catholic, and the aunt who married into my family was Catholic. But the people on the plantation where I grew up, and most of the people on the plantations, were Baptist people. I don't know if going to Catholic school changed my views—I went to Catholic school [in New Roads] when I was twelve years old, between twelve and fifteen years old—other than that I realized I was beginning to get a little confused about things because the Catholic kids would tease me about being Baptist or Protestant because that was sort of country. That was sort of, I suppose, backward as far as they were concerned. So, at a very young age, I reached the point that one or the other did not matter anymore—being Baptist or Catholic. Because if you can be Catholic and serve the Christian beliefs, you can do the same thing as Baptist and believe in the Christian God too. The reason Catholicism has not been an influence—I don't mention Catholics—is that I didn't have nuns [as teachers]. We had lay teachers who taught in the Catholic school. Of course, there was a priest there. But other than studying the catechism and Bible history and stuff like that, and rules to go by, I had no close contact with Catholicism. I never thought about becoming a Catholic or anything like that—like my stepfather was—because my close family was Baptist. My aunt who raised me was definitely a Baptist. The old people, my godmother and godfather, most of the people on the plantation were Baptists. So it never entered my mind to become Catholic. Of course, Dianne [Gaines's wife] is Catholic—goes to Mass all the time, every day almost.

MG: South Louisiana is colored by cultural Catholicism—things like festivals, rituals, lifestyle, beer drinking—things separate from theology that seem to influence the culture in general. The other thing that interests me is the influence of Catholicism in other places in the South, where Catholicism is seen as strange or different. Does your portrayal of Catholics (mainly the Creoles) reflect your community's attitude toward Catholics when you were growing up?

EJG: I don't think we had conflict there where I came from. We were mainly Baptist, and the Catholics came into our lives on the plantation. In my writing, usually the Catholics are the more fair-skinned people in the black community, although my stepfather was my color. And they came with certain attitudes. They had certain attitudes toward others as well, Protestants as well as lower whites. They sort of set themselves apart and away from them. In this part of Louisiana, they felt above others around them.

MG: You have those very important black ministers, but quite often they are not able to help their people, at least not until *A Lesson Before Dying.*

EJG: For that period of time. If you look at "The Sky Is Gray" or *A Gathering of Old Men,* many of these ministers were illiterate. They had a blind faith in what they believed in. My ministers—not all ministers, but the ones I had on the plantation—had a blind faith in what they believed in, and God solved all problems, no matter what it was. God solved all those problems. Usually they came up against someone who resisted this blind faith in anything. In "The Sky Is Gray," this guy says, "I'll accept nothing." So the minister, of course, represents the white church, the white religion, everything completely unacceptable as far as this young guy is concerned.

MG: Do you think the Baptist minister represents the *white* church?

EJG: He represents God—he represents Christ. And as far as the young student is concerned, that's white. In *A Gathering of Old Men*, you had people here who had never, ever, ever stood. And, here's a minister who comes and says, "Hey, calm it down, keep it calm." And this is what we'd been taught all our lives. You don't get in trouble if you keep calm, if you stay cool, if you stay good. You don't get in trouble. And this is what the old man, the minister here wanted the people to do, saying you're going to get in a lot of trouble. You're going to bathe this place in blood if you do this kind of stuff. And these old men, who had never, ever stood, were ready to be bathed in blood by standing. In *In My Father's House*, I was dealing with something different in that I was speaking for someone whose religion had made him very strong. Believing in God had made him strong, but this person ended up by—. Religion had broken down racial barriers, but had religion closed the gap between generations? Among us, among blacks in this country—and I suppose the world—there are those who believe in accepting the Christian religion and those who will not accept it. That's always been there, and it will always be there as long as we have people who associate Christ with people like Jerry Falwell. There's no way in the world that I can believe in anything like this. No way in the world can I believe in this. I cannot believe in anybody whom this guy here can call on and say, "That's our savior." You know, Dianne and I talk a lot about conservatism among the black middle class, and we feel that among the black middle class there's as much conservatism as you'll find anywhere else in this country. But we refuse to accept conservatism as a political ideology because it is associated with those kinds of racist attitudes. So we will not accept that. You believe in God, but you will say, "Okay, if this guy believes in him, if that's his God, I will not have anything to do with it." So you try to find some other way of serving God. You find all those young men changing their names and finding some other religion. And, of course, there are those who can't believe in anything—who can't accept another culture or religion that they don't know anything about. So these are the kind of people whom you find in much of my work.

MG: You said something a while ago—that there was a complete acceptance of God or religion. That they accepted that God would provide for them. In *A Lesson Before Dying*, you have these two old women who don't seem to ever question God. Yet, when they want to save Jefferson, their idea of being saved includes something more than God.

EJG: They felt that "walking," that being a man, was very important. They were afraid that Jefferson would accept how the man [his defense attorney] described him. And when he first goes to prison, he does. And his god-mother knows that God can take him to heaven, but she does not know that God can change him—this person—in that way. You see, her faith is blind faith. Her idea of God is that God, after death, will be there. Her faith is not that God will make you a whole man. I don't know that that perception, that state of intelligence—. He can change him from a sinner, from someone who does not believe, to believing in him. The idea is to get you into heaven. But something else is needed here. For example, he wants to go to school. He wants to go to school; he wants to be certain things; he wants to be better educated; he wants to do certain things. He wants to achieve a certain discipline. That is necessary here without thinking that God is going to do those kinds of things for us. We have to do those kinds of things on our own.

Darrell Bourque: So there's a separation between God's work and man's work.

EJG: Well, it is something that you have to do—for everybody. We don't think that God is going to destroy this guy King [John William King, the white supremacist convicted of first-degree murder and sentenced to death for the 1998 dragging death of James Byrd in Jasper, Texas], put this guy King in the gas chamber or the electric chair, or whatever. Man has to do that. Man has to do certain things. God has other things. We can pray for this guy's soul to go to heaven, but we know darn well we have to punish him down here. We have to do certain things. And what they were saying about Jefferson is that Jefferson has to learn not to believe in what this guy is saying about him. And Jefferson could not do this on his own. Jefferson could not do this on his own. And we don't know that God could have done that for Jefferson, but they hope Grant can do it. But not God. We don't expect

God to stop Hitler; we don't expect God to stop Stalin; we don't expect God to stop these people. We have to go there and do certain things ourselves, and then God can do—but we have to do some of these things ourselves. And this is what she is depending on. She's not denying that God can help, but God helps those who help themselves. Even if you become a religious person, you have to make that attempt to become that religious person.

God gave you a choice. You want to become religious—give up all your evil ways. You become religious and follow me. But, you don't have to do it. Nor can you become religious without doing it. The only way that Jefferson could have ever changed—in my book—was that Grant became a part of it. And the only way that Grant could become a real, whole person, too, was for Jefferson to help him as well.

MG: And I think that's one of the things that's so beautifully done—and one of the many reasons people see so much in the book. The old ladies want Jefferson to be saved, but they go to the teacher, not only the minister. So it's not just the body or the soul.

EJG: Well, they want both of them.

DB: They provide for both.

MG: The minister can take care of the soul—

EJG: Right, but the body and the *mind*—the *mind*, the *mind*. The physical being here had to be taught, had to be trained. It's the same thing, you know. I'm repeating myself in my books because that's the whole thing about "The Sky Is Gray." It's the brain and the heart. But then you have the teacher here who has to condition you about how to live.

MG: The idea of the whole person.

EJG: Yes, right.

MG: At first, it seems that Grant is totally rejecting religion, and in some ways he is. But, over and over again, Grant tells Jefferson that he believes in God but that he doesn't believe in heaven. He doesn't believe in an afterlife. How did that develop in the character of Grant—that he makes such a distinction?

EJG: Oh, I don't know. He probably read some book on philosophy. [*laughs*] He read that stuff somewhere. I think he would accept it just through his education that there is something greater than me, that there is something greater than that white man out there who chose everything here around me. To me, there's something greater. He tells Jefferson, "I see children laugh, I see flowers grow, I see things happen. So there must be something else other than just this sort of thing." And he keeps telling them—tells his students—well he may not tell them directly, but when he's sitting at that road waiting to hear about Jefferson's death, he says to himself, "I do not believe, but you must believe. You must believe in something, because to not believe, you're a slave." He says, "I'm a slave; I don't believe." He says that. But I think he believes. He has this disbelief until Paul brings that letter—Jefferson's notebook. And when Paul tells him what kind of person Jefferson was at the last moment—and then Grant goes back into his place, I think he begins to change here. Maybe not believe in God at that moment, but he has accepted his role, I think, and commitment, and eventually he can grow into belief—believing in God—because he has both Catholicism with Vivian on one side and those old ladies on the other side. But eventually, I think he can accept it.

DB: I think one of the real powers of the book is that quiet transformation that takes place with Grant. The book has been trying to articulate another story, but that's a changed man.

EJG: Oh, yes. I think you'll notice that even more when you see the film, and you'll notice how he's affected by Jefferson. Both of them become transformed. Jefferson dies for more than one reason, but one of the reasons why I felt his death was important was that no one has ever died for the black woman in the United States. We have fought wars since the first war in this country. Black men have fought wars, for independence and so on. And yet, we've died for capitalism, we've died for independence, we've died for America, but not just for that black woman—the mother, the sister, the wife. When we went to war, we were not going to war to fight for them. We were going to war to keep America safe, for American ideology, to do our part for democracy, or whatever, to destroy this evil, this Hitler or Stalin or the Japanese nationalism. But it was not for that person. They were not fighting for Miss Emma. In many cases, we could not even stand up for Miss Emma in our own state, our own community. It was the first time that anyone had ever stood up for her. And this is what I think she wanted as much as anything else. This is what *she* wanted. At the same time, of course, she wanted him to believe in God, but she wanted him to be able to stand. And this is why Grant is brought in—because no one had ever stood for her. No one has ever done anything like this. This is probably the last time that any black male will ever—in her lifetime—stand up for her. And for Miss Emma, Jefferson is the only person there. And so she needs that. And she tells that to Pichot, she tells that to Grant, to everybody. Someone must do something for me one day. Someone must stand for me one day. And this is one of the reasons—by standing, he stands for her. He also stands for the children around. He stands for the future. And he stands, of course, also so that Grant would stand—that Grant would stay and commit himself. So it's both the religious stuff and the secular reasons. He must grow. And *my* emphasis in the story was really much more on his standing as a man, rather than on the religious thing.

MG: He becomes a full person. We can think of what goes on in "The Sky Is Gray," where the mother insists on one thing—survival—at the expense of other things for her son. Grant is completed as a man.

EJG: I feel that I have continuous themes running through those books. I don't realize it until after I've written the book. Just like Catherine and Jackson [in *Catherine Carmier*] and Grant, you know. The guy comes back, falls in love with the beautiful girl. In *Catherine Carmier*, Jackson leaves. And here, Grant must stay.

MG: And the theme of belief is there all along too. You hint at this before, but it's brought full circle in *A Lesson Before Dying*. When Jefferson asks Grant if he believes in God—as you were saying earlier—he says, "Yes," but he explains that he doesn't believe in an afterworld. He believes in it in terms of what he sees now in this world. He redefines what he means by his belief or what he means by God. He talks about the children's need to believe.

EJG: Well, Grant would not accept the fact that what he sees around him is absolutely all there is to the world. This is the trap I'm in—I'm caught in—but this is not all there is.

MG: Earlier, Darrell and I were talking about how your work affects people. Darrell, would you tell Ernie what you were telling me as we walked here?

DB: Sometimes it strikes me as interesting and strange the way literature really does get into the individual minds and private lives of people. We hope that that's part of what happens when we make art. But I was talking to a guy in the gym this morning, and he was asking me about the reading series (*Significant Voices*) that's in progress right now. And I was telling him about the schedule, and I said Ernie Gaines would be reading on March 14. This is a guy who works in the medical profession, and he said, "Ernie Gaines." He said, "I've read everything that Mr. Gaines has written. And I'll tell you what my favorite line is in all his work." And I don't know if he got it exactly right, but it was the way he was remembering it. He said, "'Lord, what I done done?' in *A Lesson Before Dying*, that moment when the woman says, 'Lord, what I done done?'"

EJG: Yeah, right.

DB: And he said, "From time to time that book has given me that prayer." You know, because we find ourselves in the midst of all kinds of hell.

EJG: Yes. "What I done done to deserve this?"

DB: That's right. And it's a variation of Christ's words on the cross. It's a great moment of trial, but a moment of trial that brings us real close to truth, to a spiritual truth and a religious truth. And I thought that it was really wonderful that her words live in a real human being, who needs those words, and who's moved and affected by those words.

EJG: Yes. I got a letter from a fellow in Georgia, and he said one of his favorite lines was when Grant tells Jefferson, "I want you to chip away at this block, just chip away at this thing where people think they are better than anyone else in the world. And until you stand, it's going to continue to be like that. But if you stand, you can chip away at that myth—because it's a myth. But if you don't stand, it continues to grow."

DB: One of the things—and I've told you this before—that has resonated for me over the years, and I got it into the little brochure that we did for the readers' series, is that mention that Miss Jane Pittman makes about when she's asked about the old people and about the Indians who lived there and about praying to rivers and trees. And she said, "Of course, you don't pray to a chinaball tree." [*laughs*] "And you have to know the differ-ence between a ditch and a bayou." I love that.

MG: You have to use your sense, too.

EJG: Right.

DB: Yes. What I love about that is the sense of humor that emerges there. It's a funny story at the same time that it's a really moving story. But it's that kind of pantheistic belief that religion is about believing in the things of nature.

EJG: Yeah, right. I got that from some book I had read about Indians and their worshipping of water and their worshipping of fish. To protect the bal-ance—return the bones to the water—to become a fish again. But that's okay with a river. You don't do that with a crawfish [*laughs*]—and put it back in the ditch. Not ditches and bayous and china ball trees. But with an oak tree, it's different; it's okay. I just love oak trees.

MG: Yes. As Miss Jane says about oak trees, "It's just the nobility you respect." Another question—recently David Madden (writer-in-residence at Louisiana State University) said at a conference at Loyola that the book that had influenced him most was the Bible, not the Bible as read but the Bible as spoken by the preachers, listening to the preachers tell the stories of the Bible. Do you feel you were influenced in this way by preachers or ministers?

EJG: Maybe the rhythm of the preaching, but I can't see how the ministers affected me. I could hear preaching all the time whether I was in church or not. I guess the rhythm, the repetition. I must have gotten that. I never try using the metaphors they used in their preaching.

MG: When you were growing up, were you aware or was there a real distinc-tion in the Baptist church between what was God's music and the devil's music.

EJG: Oh yes, right. We were definitely aware of that. We could not—that was one of the things we had to stop when we became little Christians. We couldn't do that anymore. We couldn't sing those little blues songs anymore—at twelve I had to stop. And we had to sing the Christian songs. That was one of the things we had to give up. They didn't want you to shoot marbles anymore. You couldn't play cards; you couldn't do anything for a while. I could go just so far, but you weren't supposed to do those things anymore. You weren't supposed to dance. The Catholic kids could, you know. I went to a Catholic school, and all the little Catholic kids danced. That's the reason I can't dance today. Darrell can. [*laughs*] That's why I can't dance today because when I was a child, at that age, I was not supposed to. And I suppose then I went to California, and I was so shy that I was afraid. I was fifteen, sixteen years old, and I was afraid to dance. The other kids could dance, but they weren't Christians. But I suppose it was when I went out to California that I started changing. I don't think I did too much changing in Louisiana because I was too close to my aunt [Augusteen Jefferson, the sister of Gaines's maternal grandfather] to make any kind of definite change from the Christian upbringing, the Baptist upbringing, to become skeptical or whatever.

MG: The dichotomy of the church music being God's music and representing good, and the blues and jazz as the devil's music could be seen as a simplistic thing. But it was also associated with a general concept of good and evil. Our new folklorist, John Laudun, teaches a class on concepts of good and evil. The class explores how our own concepts of good and evil in our world structure our thinking, and then also how it influences the things we create—whether it's the films or the novels or the poems or the jokes we tell. How we conceive of what is good and what is evil is going to affect how our creative ability is going to channel or direct us. Do you think, first of all, that religious concepts of good and evil have been important to you?

EJG: There's always two forces in just about everything I've written. There is that religious force, and then there is that other one—maybe not evil, but that other force that does not follow the religious pattern. In *Catherine Carmier*, Aunt Charlotte is very, very religious. She's just as religious as Miss Emma is here or Tante Lou is here. I don't think of Jackson [in *Catherine Carmier*] as being evil, but he was not following a pattern of religion. In *Of Love and Dust*, you have the very religious lady there, Aunt Margaret, who looks after little Tite all the time and is doing the right thing. And you find that throughout, in *In My Father's House*, in the short stories, in the minister in *A Lesson Before Dying*—because I don't know how my folks would have survived without it. They could not have made it without it. And those religious people were the ones who could help the nonreligious survive because many of them had the poorest kind of job and no respect for whatever they did. So those who had that strong faith could always keep them going, even if they went to work for nothing. Something about the ones at home reaching God—their faith, their strength was strength enough to carry the other ones along. Without Tante Lou and Aunt Emma, I don't know that Grant ever would have stood. You find the same thing in just about all my work. The young may be rebelling against it because he believes in education or resistance for this, but if he survives, it's through religion that he survives, through the strength of the older ones. So it's a tremendous force in all the books I've written. In *Of Love and Dust*, the older people are very religious. Of course, Marcus is a rebel, but the older people are religious.

MG: Coming back to the question of good and evil—

EJG: You see, I don't know what good and evil is. I don't know the definition of good and evil.

MG: Well, when we see something that is extreme, like the racist murder in Jasper, Texas, we all agree, "This is an evil act."

EJG: Yes, sure. But I look at life as balancing. Nature is balancing. Everything is there. There's good and evil out there. Somebody does something awful— somebody is going to do something good. I think—. Our little moment here on earth is so minute, so small that whoever's on top today, it doesn't mean anything. It means something for that moment, yes, but that is something that can be reversed. There's good and bad, good and evil—. We throw terms on these different phenomena, but I think it's much more gray than one extreme or another. There are evil things, but when someone goes out and just murders people, I think first that they're very sick.

MG: Are there any portrayals of ministers by other writers that influenced your portrayal of them?

EJG: Not that I'm aware of.

DB: Many of us grew up in parable-speaking cultures where it's not what the minister says, but what your aunt says. Your aunt talks to you in terms of parables, and I think it gets somewhere in the imagination. And when we begin to tell a story, a parable is a good way to do it. And sometimes that's a more influential thing than things that we can actually touch on.

EJG: My aunt was a big hero to me, and the obstacles she had and how she overcame them. That she crawled over the floor all her life. And this is the thing that I feel has given me strength in order to write as I write—as I feel about the world around me. And I know she was extremely religious, she was extremely religious, and it was this, I'm sure, that enabled her to continue going on, to feed us, to wash our clothes, to do all these kinds of things. She could not go to the church, as you know, so they would bring the sacrament to her. But it was through her strength, I think, much more than any religious person, or even the Bible. I read the Bible; I had to read the Bible as a small child, but I don't know that the Bible really influenced me morally. I don't know that. Later, in college, I read the Bible as literature. I loved the beautiful writing and the beautiful story and poetry and music and everything. And maybe it did in some ways. I believe in treating someone else as I would have someone treat me, but I don't know whether I got that from Christ or Confucius. You know, just as Darrell was saying, those things can come through some other way. Maybe I am influenced, believing in that teaching much more than I realize. I was taught responsibility, and I was taught to respect people.

MG: Montaigne says that often an astute reader will see things in a work that an author didn't know he had put there. You know that several people who have written about *A Lesson Before Dying* as well as the publisher's study guide for teachers have interpreted Jefferson as a Christ figure. For example, Jefferson dies on a Friday—

EJG: Well, the reason he dies on Friday is that Bertrand DeBlanc [former district attorney in Lafayette] told me that the executions would take place on Friday between noon and 3:00 p.m. I did not know that before. You know in so many of my works, when someone dies, it is that someone else goes on—or the people go on. They die, but someone else goes on. When I visited an academy in Washington, DC, a kid told me, "Mr. Gaines, my teacher told me that Jefferson is a Christ figure." And I said, "Oh, really." He said, "Yes." And this is what he goes on to say, "The two guys who were killed— Brother and Bear—they were the two guys who were on the side of Christ on the cross." I said, "Wow, I never thought of anything like that." [*Laughs*] So when I go to these places and the kids ask me questions—"Mr. Gaines, what is that symbol?"—the first thing I ask is "What did your teacher say?" [*Laughs*] 'Cause I don't want to disagree. Jefferson in a way does have this kind of meaning.

MG: He has a redemptive function. He does bring about a redemption.

EJG: Yes, yes. But I think others do the same thing. They've said the same thing about Hemingway's *Old Man and the Sea*. The mast he carries is like Christ's cross on his shoulders. In Faulkner's *Light in August*—

DB: Joe Christmas.

MG: JC.

EJG: Yeah, Jesus Christ. Maybe Faulkner had that in mind in the beginning. So those things can come in. And I'm sure in the artist's subconscious it's there. But he's not completely aware of it. We put in things like a carpenter building a house. You have to put in so many bricks in there to support it and so many nails to get this thing up. But if you say, "What's that particular nail for?"—I'd have to say, "Well, I had to put a nail in there." Or this particular size brick—"Well, it worked there." Or this color—"Well, it worked." And quite often this is what happens. But, we know we're building a house. And we know that a house cannot protect people from the weather and all those things, unless you do all the little small things. I think much of it is in there without our being aware of all the little details. I think it would be very artificial to think, "Well, I'll put this here—." I think once you put it all together, we can see that there are certain meanings—what might seem like a close reading.

MG: But you don't object to—

EJG: Oh, I don't object to anything. [*laughs*] Some things maybe I was not aware of. You know, there are all kinds of interpretations of what Hamlet is all about, some by very brilliant people, and I'm sure if Shakespeare were around he would disagree with fifty percent of it. But, whatever critics say, I just let them say it.

DB: I think one of the things that you do so beautifully and you do so well is to work these themes of religion and to work the ideas of God—how we're wrestling with the idea of God and what God might mean to us and so forth—into the literature that you make because it is important to the way we go on. But one of the things that I love and one of the things I think you're a genius at is humor. So the religion and the God that is at issue in

Catherine Carmier and *A Lesson Before Dying, Jane Pittman,* and all of the stories is also there in a story like "My Grandpa and the Haint." That's such a different take on religion and spirituality, and on what it's like—. It's going to come and shape you and affect your life.

EJG: Oh yes, I believe in humor. You've got to have humor in this stuff. I don't know how much religious faith there was in "My Grandpa and the Haint." I think Mom went to someone who was not quite—well, she went to someone who was religious but not Christian religion. Same thing as in "A Long Day in November," he goes back to this old hoodoo woman who says, "Give it up. Burn your car."

I do believe in religion. I believe there are so many different kinds and that you can believe in any one you wish to believe in to help you survive.

DB: In your humorous stories, I hear echoes of the rich tradition of Jewish literature. There are funny stories about God, funny stories about spirituality.

EJG: Yes, [Isaac Bashevis] Singer is one of my favorite storytellers, and maybe I read those Singer stories when I was much younger. Dorothea Oppenheimer [Gaines's literary agent, friend, and mentor, until her death in 1987] introduced me to Singer's work.

MG: The portrayal of God in Zora Neale Hurston's *Mules and Men* is often compared to that of a trickster figure, somebody you had to negotiate with or outwit. The whole tradition of humor as part of belief or humor as part of dealing with God is there, too, in African American folklore.

DB: Yes, and that Jewish notion that you can argue with God. He's there to argue with. And I find that real appealing too.

MG: He's not infallible, either. He makes mistakes sometimes.

EJG: I remember Singer's story, "The Spinoza of Market Street." I wrote the story that I read here at Deep South Writers' Conference one time, and I'd still like to write it better, "Christ Walked Down Market Street." [Note: Gaines later said he remembered Singer's story—set in Warsaw, Poland—and also remembered seeing a man who often had his hand out for donations walking down Market Street in San Francisco. Gaines said that inspired him to write a story about a person who was looking for God but in all the wrong places.]

MG: You never published that, did you?

EJG: I never have because I've never been satisfied with it. I think it's the best thing I've ever done, but I've never been satisfied with it.

MG: I love that story.

EJG: I do too. Christ in his trench coat. I like thinking about him like that—a guy hanging around, talking to you, listening to you, instead of all of these evangelist programs. I never see him there. I don't see him in the churches I go to. But I think he can end up at a bar, standing listening to you, saying, "Okay, tell me your problems." Without you knowing who he is, in a trench coat. Or maybe when you first meet him, he doesn't have a trench coat. He has these old clothes, and he's dragging along on Market Street, has his hand out, begging for a dime. Next time you see him, he's a different person. My idea of Christ is that he was this wonderful guy. I don't know if I would have had the nerve to follow him at the time [he lived]. Since they were doing these things to Christians—throwing them in lions' dens and all that. But, I think he was a wonderful guy. I wish I had the guts to follow him, like one of his disciples. But I think I look at Christ as one of those great heroes—his teachings, his beliefs. I don't know what good it's done, throughout the years, but he made a good try. He had many good disciples. Martin Luther King is one. Gandhi and all the others. Seems like that's the only way you're going to get things done in this world. I wish we could have religion—and use it to help man and not to take advantage of man, not to hurt man. But religion, it seems, separates us as much as it brings us together. It seems the most segregated hour in the United States is the eleventh hour on Sunday morning. Yes.

My church is the oak tree. My church is the river. My church is walking right down the cane field road, on the headlands between rows of sugarcane. That's my church. I can talk to God there as well as I can talk to him in Notre Dame. I think he's in one of those cane rows as much as he is in Notre Dame. At least to us. And that's where I meet God. That's where we communicate.

But really, I think for the mass, we needed something else—this gathering, that community, coming together because not too many people have time to walk and be alone and communicate with God.

MG: Not all people have the capacity to communicate in solitude.

EJG: Yes, we need coming together as a group to communicate too. If we come together as a group to communicate—. But that's the problem—we come together to communicate with our own group, our own surroundings. When Wallace Stegner asked me many years ago, "Whom do you write for?" I said I don't write for anyone in particular. And he said, "What if a gun were put to your head?" In that case, I said, I write for the black youth in the South and let them know that this life is worth something—and I'm writing about him." And he said, "What if the gun is still at your head?" And I said I'd write for the white youth of the South to let them know that unless he knows his neighbor for the last three hundred years, he only knows half his own history. He only knows a little about himself. I feel that way. Until we can really communicate with each other, we'll always have those problems—no matter what else we do, no matter how much education we have. Unless we can communicate, unless we can all gather together. You know, we see that there are different races on campus, but they're not pulled together on campus. They're there, but they're not together. This is the kind of thing that religion can do.

DB: Or literature. [*laughs*]

EJG: You know, for *A Lesson Before Dying,* I've received more mail from white males than any other group, and most of it is from attorneys. I also get many letters from teachers.

DB: In a lot of ways, the book is about how to be a man, and it transcends race. It's about how to stand up for some concept of personhood. So I can see how it speaks to a particular group of people.

MG: And also why it has such a wide appeal. It transcends gender as well—how to be a person.

The Last Regionalist?: An Interview with Ernest J. Gaines

Rose Anne Brister / 2001

Callaloo 26:3 (2003): 549–64. © 2003 The Johns Hopkins University. Reprinted with permission of Johns Hopkins University Press.

Although Ernest Gaines laughingly referred to himself as an "old relic" in this interview, he still possesses confidence in his writing and a demeanor indicative of a long and prosperous literary career. Gaines enjoys a personal and professional poise accrued over the last four decades that I observed as I interviewed him on two occasions: in person on November 27, 2001, at the University of Louisiana at Lafayette and via the telephone on December 11, 2001. We visited familiar themes in his fiction and discussed his current projects, literary and otherwise. Also, he exhibited a willingness to explore the present state of southern literature and to contemplate its future state. Gaines's textual concerns, such as a sense of place and community, are an endangered species in contemporary literature. Just as these "pet themes" recur in his texts, similar themes recur throughout interviews he has given and in criticism about those texts. If Gaines himself does not adopt contemporary literary concerns, likewise many interviewers have deferred discussion regarding his position in the contemporary literary environment and his recapitulation of, by his admission, ideals not valued in today's culture. To this end, I presented several excerpts from previous interviews for his analysis in order to encourage him to evaluate his career retrospectively. I found that, while he does not consider criticism about his texts nor does he read much contemporary fiction, Gaines continually exorcises the "Louisiana thing" that drives his fiction. But, even in light of this possible obstacle and his warning that he "said some stupid things in the past," I observed an introspective and retrospective Gaines, willing to review his distinguished career, to analyze his position in the current literary world, and to anticipate his future work.

BRISTER: I have researched the southern pastoral and a sense of place in your writing. I focused on your use of imagery, location, and the extent to which the pastoral is manifested in *Catherine Carmier* and *Of Love and Dust*. I want to ask you some questions regarding a sense of place, and also I want to talk about your craft and teaching.
GAINES: What do you mean by pastoral?

BRISTER: Well, valuing the rural space over the urban, the simple over the complex. In my research, I read many of your interviews and much criticism on the two novels. I want to ask you about a few statements you have made in the past and see if you still feel the same way now. A lot of these are older quotes and . . .
GAINES: [laughs] Well, I said some stupid things in the past.

BRISTER: [*laughs*] You did? To begin, I am interested in your relationship to the land, given that you went into the fields at age eight. In 1976, when you were living in San Francisco, you said, "I come back to the land to absorb things." Since home is now only one hour away, how often do you go back?
GAINES: I was there just yesterday because my wife and I recently bought a piece of that property. A few acres on the plantation where I grew up, where my mother grew up, where my grandparents grew up, where my folks probably had been slaves. We also have a camp down on the river in the area that I write about. It's Pointe Coupee, which I call St. Raphael Parish. New Roads is Bayonne. The river is the St. Charles River because I named it after my brother, and Raphael is my stepfather who raised me. I sort of name things after them. Yes, I am very closely related to the land because, until I left from here, that's about all I knew. That's where my family had been for many, many, many generations. You could probably go back to slavery, and they were there. So the land is very important to me and to my work and to all the things I write about. It is one of the main characters in my work.

BRISTER: In 1990, you told Marcia Gaudet and Carl Wooton, "There is no future for blacks on this place at all . . ." You were referencing the area in and around River Lake plantation. What is the future now for River Lake?
GAINES: I'm the only one who has bought a piece of that property. I don't think they'll sell it to anyone else. I guess because of my name, I suppose,

and teaching here [University of Louisiana at Lafayette] and because we've had a relationship with the owners of the property. We don't call it a plantation anymore, just formerly River Lake plantation. They know who we are. So many people own parts of this place, sixteen or more. The people who sold it were not spending any amount of time there anymore. They just put it up for sale. We saw the sign, and, without knowing who they were, we called. It just so happened that we knew the people. We got together and bought the piece of land.

BRISTER: What are your plans for this land?

GAINES: We are planning to put a house there. I live a block from here (ULL); it's a university house. It's called the "Gaines House." They might as well put a plaque up there now. [*laughs*] My wife feels that it's better to have something out there on the land where my ancestors were, to have a "Gaines House" out there. So we intend to put a house there within the next year or so.

BRISTER: Is it true that you are involved with the local community to save the buildings at Cherie Quarters?

GAINES: I am not involved specifically with those buildings. I've been involved in saving the cemetery, which we have done. My wife, another friend, and I have established a nonprofit cemetery corporation which now owns the graveyard. We pay for the cleaning and the upkeep of the cemetery. We want people who have relatives buried there to come in and contribute. Once a year, All Saints Day, we organize a day to clean up the tombs, paint the tombs, cut the grass, get the weeds out of the tombs, plant flowers. Every month we send someone out there to cut the grass. We do that on our own. There are only about two old shacks remaining in the quarters, and I have no input there at all. Only the cemetery. There's a church there, the same church where I attended school. We're also interested in moving that particular building onto our property as well and restoring it.

BRISTER: Do you think that's feasible? Are you in talks with the owners of that land?

GAINES: We've already discussed it, and it's okay.

BRISTER: Perhaps due to my upbringing, it's my impression that, even in the late twentieth and twenty-first century, a native Louisianian usually doesn't leave home or, if he or she leaves home, will come back quite often. Does Louisiana cast a spell over its children?

GAINES: Well, not all of its children. I'm the oldest of my siblings, and there are twelve. Seven of us were born here; five in California. Besides myself, there's only one other brother who would like to come back and stay here. He's talking about coming back within the next few years or so. The others have forgotten about it altogether. They have good jobs and nice homes, so they have no plans to come back to Louisiana. My ties are here because of my writing. I was taken away when I was fifteen years old. I had to be taken away because I could not go to high school here. I couldn't go to the library, and my folks wanted me to be educated. Because of segregation, there was no high school or library for blacks. I didn't want to leave, leave my aunt who raised me. Something of me just stayed here. I was always coming back to Louisiana.

Then, finally, when USL made me a professor in 1981, I stayed here but not permanently because I was only here during the semester when I was teaching. The rest of the time I was in San Francisco. But, since 1997, I have lived here and in Miami. I was always coming back here. I have done all of my writing in San Francisco. But the only place I could write about was Louisiana.

BRISTER: Do you feel that you can only physically do the writing when in San Francisco?
GAINES: I really don't know. I've done some work here on what I hope turns out to be a novel, but I think it's about the fourth or fifth thing I've tried to do since *A Lesson Before Dying.* And I just hope that this does turn out to be a novel. Of course, I'm writing it here because I'm no longer living in San Francisco. I visit San Francisco. As a matter of fact, my wife and I are going to San Francisco for New Year's. My mother's out there. My brothers and sisters are there. So, we go back and forth.

BRISTER: You have anticipated my next question. You told Marcia Gaudet in 1985 that if you had gained access to Wright's *Native Son*, you would not have been influenced by it because it deals with the urban space. In your childhood, you remained in and around Pointe Coupee Parish, in the rural space. Did your confinement to the rural encourage a strong sense of place in your writing?
GAINES: Oh, right. Definitely so. If I had lived in a city—New Orleans, for example—I could not have written about this part of the state. Yes, I was confined to the area; it was part of my everyday life. I suppose that's why it is so involved in my work because I didn't know anything else as a child. A lot of the things that I recall in my work are from my childhood. Faulkner

did all of this with his Yoknapatawpha County around Oxford, Mississippi. He concentrates all of his work in and around the town of Oxford. I thought if Faulkner can do this with Mississippi, then I can do that with Louisiana. So I concentrate all of my work in one area. I don't know if that has been limiting or not. I've spent most of my life in San Francisco, and I have often thought about writing other novels about San Francisco, about my army experience. But nothing really came off. I think the body was in those places but the soul was not. Whenever I try to write these things, they just don't come out very well. So I discard the work and go back to my Louisiana. I suppose had I written about those areas I could have written four or five more novels, maybe short stories. I would save all my energy just to go back to the Louisiana thing.

BRISTER: You wrote three California novels early in your career and called them "bad." What exactly makes them "bad"?

GAINES: They're bad because there's no soul in them. I think the three manuscripts are in the Dupré Library, drafts of these things. I call them "things" because they surely were not very good. [*laughs*] I have one about my bohemian experience in San Francisco, one about my army experience, and one about something else.

BRISTER: How has living in San Francisco influenced your writing? Has it facilitated your writing?

GAINES: When I lived in San Francisco from the 1950s through the 1980s, I communicated with writers. I attended creative writing classes at San Francisco State and at Stanford. I never could have had that kind of exposure in Louisiana at that time. Maybe now I could do those things, but back in the 1950s, 1960s, and 1970s, I never would have been able to get that exposure. Young writers should communicate with other writers, better writers, more mature writers. I really think San Francisco was a great place for any young artist in the 1950s and 1960s, especially the 1950s and 1960s with the Beat Generation. I was not caught up in it, but I was part of it. I stood outside of things. When I wanted to talk to people, I was at the university. There were always writers autographing their novels. So I thought it was quite healthy for a young writer at the time. For me, it was.

BRISTER: A good situation to observe but not necessarily participate in?

GAINES: Well, I participated in some of it. For example, I was at Stanford with Ken Kesey. He was sort of the guru of the drug scene and that sort of thing. We were in class together, so we would get together. But I would never participate in the drug scene. I'd be around and watch these things. But I'd never get involved in it because I could see that it could mess with your mind.

BRISTER: Do you know of any modern-day equivalent of that creative atmosphere? Or has that atmosphere declined with the increase of technology?

GAINES: I really don't know too much about it because I don't follow it too closely. You have a lot of writers writing for conferences. Places all over the country that teach writing. Usually, I've been going to Sewanee [Writers' Conference] in the summer. I didn't go last summer, but, previous to that, I'd gone about six consecutive summers. It's where you get a group of people together for about two weeks. I don't know that there is a community where you have the sort of thing that you had in San Francisco back in the 1950s or Greenwich Village in the 1920s and 1930s. I don't know if we have those kinds of communities anymore.

BRISTER: You've said you won't explore San Francisco in your work now because your soul isn't in it. Do you foresee yourself ever writing about it?

GAINES: I don't know. I know I have not succeeded in the past. There may come a time when all of the Louisiana stuff is all dried up. I haven't written anything since *A Lesson Before Dying* in 1993. This is 2001. That's eight years. Maybe if I had written a San Francisco story, I would have had a book out by now. I just haven't had that drive.

BRISTER: You said in 1976 that you won't write about California until you "get over" this "Louisiana thing." After many years and an extraordinary body of work, have you gotten over that "thing"?

GAINES: I don't know that it's quite out yet. I am working on a project now that I hope will turn out to be a novel. It's starting out really good, but I don't know what's going to happen with it. I'm sticking with my Louisiana stuff.

BRISTER: Do you think the reading public expects all of your fiction to be Louisiana fiction, to have that "Louisiana thing"?

GAINES: Well, I don't know what they expect of me. I think they like to identify people with certain themes, certain subjects, and certain areas. I think it would be a surprise to quite a few people if I changed. But I never think about anything like that. How can I write a decent novel or story about the subject I'm interested in? I never think about what readers would think of me or how they would accept me.

BRISTER: Are all of the early manuscripts in the Dupré Library at ULL? Are those open to the public?

GAINES: No, they are not. Only the published material is open to the public. The other stuff I just don't want anyone to read until I'm dead. [*laughs*] Then I won't be able to answer for it. Then I won't have to answer for that stuff because it's so bad.

BRISTER: I'd like to talk more about your craft and teaching. Is it true that you received Ds in composition class?

GAINES: Right, when I first came out of the army. I took Expository Writing 110 at San Francisco State. I'll never forget that number because of the teacher who was there in 1955—I just saw him again a year or so ago. My wife and I, whenever we go back to San Francisco, will call him and have dinner together. I always remind him about it. He says, "Well, Ernie, I bet you could teach me a little bit about writing today."

BRISTER: Well, I bet he'd give you an A now.

GAINES: [*laughs*] Yes, I think so. Anyway, I was getting Ds from him, and I approached him once and said, "Mr. Andersen, let me try to write a story." He said, "This is not a creative writing class, but if you think you can prove yourself better than what you're doing now, go ahead and write the story." So I wrote the story, and he liked it very much and passed it around to the other creative writing teachers there. It turned out to be the first short story ever published in our literary magazine [*Transfer*]. We were just organizing a magazine at that time, 1956. And my story, "The Turtles," was the first short story published in that magazine. I keep reminding him that it was he who gave me that break.

BRISTER: I recently read "The Turtles." And it's a hard one to come by. It seems very "Gainesean," if I may say so.

GAINES: [*laughs*] Yes, it was very early, when I was a young kid of twenty-three. I guess it has that rural and pastoral thing you were talking about.

BRISTER: Yes, it does. It also deals with fathers and sons, which is what you have called your "pet theme." It's also a good coming-of-age story as well. And when you mentioned Faulkner earlier, it reminded me of the introductory literature class I'm currently teaching. I knew I wanted to have a section on southern literature. I taught "Barn Burning" and "The Sky Is Gray" together, and we compared the two, along with Ellison's "Battle Royal" and Walker's "The Flowers." We looked at all of the stories as ones of initiation. The students enjoyed these stories because of the young protagonists, which are more readily identifiable to them.

GAINES: Did you see the National Endowment for the Humanities film version of "The Sky Is Gray"?

BRISTER: Yes, several years ago. I think the interpretation of the end is interesting. What do you think about Octavia smiling at James at the end? I don't think there's any indication in the text to suggest that she would smile.

GAINES: Well, I always say, "They didn't tell me how to write my stories. I won't tell them how to make their movies."

BRISTER: You recently attended a stage version of *A Lesson Before Dying* at the Southern Repertory Theater. How did you like it?

GAINES: Yes, they did a very good job. I think they're going to try to bring it across the state. I know at one time they were thinking about doing that. Nicholls State wanted it and a couple other places.

BRISTER: How do you feel your fiction translates to other genres: film, stage? Is there a certain flexibility in your fiction that lends itself to this translation?

GAINES: Well, I've been told that I write a lot of dialogue and have a lot of small settings. Maybe that's why it's adaptable. I know that the director there told me that whenever she found that she got caught up—that the play itself was not explaining everything that she wanted—she would always go back to the book and see exactly what I was doing. And, if she had a question about the dialogue, she would go back and read the original dialogue. Ann Peacock, who wrote the script for the movie, also said the same thing, that she relied on my dialogue as closely as she could.

BRISTER: You've taught at the University of Southwestern Louisiana—now the University of Louisiana at Lafayette—since 1981, permanently since 1983. You also taught at Denison University and other schools. Is it true what you said in 1986, that you accepted the Southwestern position because you were "broke as [you] could possibly be"?

GAINES: Yes, I was broke. I had just written *In My Father's House*, and it hadn't done anything. I said, "Well, I'll teach; I need the money."

BRISTER: Given that you do "double duty" in the academy as a writer *and* teacher, do you find the classroom arena rewarding?

GAINES: Well, I write one semester and teach one semester; I never write and teach in the same semester. As far as the classroom, yes, I think I can benefit from being in the classroom if I don't have to teach the entire year. I took off an entire year to write *A Lesson Before Dying*; I had never done that before. I don't think it hurt me but rather helped me. Over the period of that year I think I began to grow. I began looking at things in a much broader way. These kinds of things came into the writing. The students would come in during the discussion. I was able to use material and ideas there. When I was doing the work for *A Lesson*, the students were professional people from whom I got help. I had several attorneys in my class. They introduced me to different books. I had one attorney who had someone on death row in Angola during the time I was writing the book. And then I had another student of mine who introduced me to an attorney who had witnessed the execution of a young man about forty years ago here in south Louisiana. It was he who described the electric chair and the generator and the noise and sounds. I was always asking them questions. If I had tried to write that book all in one year or two years, I probably would not have met those different people. Every one of them gave me something that I could use, through our conversations, our interviews. The book took me a period of seven-and-a-half years. But I do get things from my students as well as from other people. As far as my students now, I don't know that I receive any kind of help from them. But this kind of thing soaks in. You might not need what they're giving you at the moment, but eventually you can recall things. I know the students in my class are mostly white, and most are females. They can describe things and write about things that I cannot experience. Most of them are middle-class and educated women who come from a different kind of society than I have experienced. So they bring things like that into the classroom. I get something from all of them.

BRISTER: Which contemporary authors do you study? Which books are on your nightstand now?

GAINES: I don't have any contemporary writers on my nightstand now. I usually read the old writers that I read many years ago. Now I'm reading parts of Turgenev's *Fathers and Sons* and Salinger's *Catcher in the Rye*. I'll read a chapter out of someone else's book.

BRISTER: You revisit the classics by which you were influenced. Do you find new and different ideas when you reread these books, things applicable to your writing now?

GAINES: I don't know. I like certain scenes and the way the writer addresses those scenes . . . what I learned from those scenes . . . dialogue. I'm still learning how to write. So I like going back to them. I read more manuscripts by contemporary writers than novels. I have former students always sending me manuscripts and people around me sending me manuscripts. I can't read them, of course, because I have my students' manuscripts to read. I let my wife read more of the contemporary novels. She tells me what they're about, and, if they sound interesting, then I try to read some.

BRISTER: What do you mean by "I'm still learning how to write"?

GAINES: Well, you should see some of the first drafts of my writing. [*laughs*] It's really awful. I go back and read a great passage from Tolstoy's *Anna Karenina*. Tolstoy can work with such little details. He makes such things come to life. I think to myself, "Why am I not doing that sort of thing?" It seems so natural to what he's doing. These are things I know that I can do if I concentrated more. I remember a little scene not too long ago in *Anna Karenina* where she's punishing one of her children for doing something bad, eating somebody's cake. Then she sees him playing with the little girl whose cake he had eaten, and she [the little girl] is sharing with him. The way Tolstoy describes that scene is fascinating. Why don't we do the same sort of thing, those little things? We always describe the great big things: explosions, violence. But that's what I mean about still learning how to write. When you read the great masters, they show you much.

BRISTER: Are there any "up and coming" writers in your creative writing program?

GAINES: There are people with talent. But to write you must have more than talent. You must have discipline and time. You must have time to write. When I graduated from college in 1957, I gave myself ten years to make it. It took just about ten years for anyone to recognize my name, but students today want an agent after they write their first short story.

You ask if I find talent; yes, I find talent there. But not too many are willing to stick to the writing. They feel they must eat and have a television or home. They should marry a rich wife or husband. You just go out and do the work and give up all those luxuries.

BRISTER: In 1996, you gave an interview at the University of Bonn. When referencing sports heroes in *A Gathering of Old Men*, you said, "I don't know where the heroes are." Do you still feel this way? Are there any heroes in sports or otherwise?

GAINES: Well, I think as far as sports figures, there are no heroes as fifty years ago in the black community. We had Joe Louis or Jackie Robinson. They were definitely heroes to African Americans all over the country. There were no Martin Luther Kings at that time or political heroes out there. I think when I was saying that I don't know where the heroes are I was thinking about the athletes. I don't know if there are any heroes among athletes today . . . maybe Tiger Woods or Michael Jordan. I don't know. You know, when you start getting older and older, you don't recognize the younger people. I've always felt that the heroes were those people who went to work every day, did menial work, and were able to keep their sanity with little pay and look after their families. Those are my heroes because those are the people I come from. I did not know the greater writers or baseball players or actors. I come from a farm. So I always saw those stronger men there. Those are my heroes.

BRISTER: What is the future of southern literature? Do you have an idea in which direction it's headed?

GAINES: I don't know that anyone's going to continue writing what I've written about because the land is not there for the individual anymore. The land is there for the big machinery and the companies. So you won't find that kind of a place for the individual. I have no idea where southern literature is going. I think eventually we're all going to write alike. We will have our individual subjects to write about, but I can't see a big distinction between a southerner in Atlanta and a southerner in New Orleans or a southerner in Jackson or a southerner in New Jersey. I think regionalism is going to be disappearing faster and is disappearing faster and faster. I think we're going to write about general things that everyone else is writing about. I won't be doing it because I have a novel in mind. And I should hope I have another one in mind before I kick off. So I won't have to deal with that sort of thing. But, it seems to me that in my classes now—my advanced creative writing classes—that so few of my students are writing about "the South" as we knew, as I knew it. They're not writing about the problems. They're writing more about themselves or their relationships with their families or other relationships but not about the race thing or injustice or things like that.

BRISTER: You don't feel they're socially conscious?

GAINES: Right, yes. I see less and less of that happening. That's what I mean by they're all going to be alike. I don't think so many of the southern writers feel that that [socially conscious fiction] is the only thing to write about. And a lot of them don't want to be "southern writers," just a writer who lives in Louisiana or Mississippi or Georgia but not classified as a "southern writer."

BRISTER: So, there's a sort of stigma attached to regionalism?

GAINES: Right, well, that's what some people think. I know that William Styron said that and Walker Percy said the same thing: "I'm a writer, not a southern writer." So as far as where "southern" literature is going, I have no idea. There are those who will always write about the past, the Civil War. But I think you'll find as many people writing about McDonald's and Popeye's chicken as anything else now. And you can write about Popeye's and McDonald's from anywhere in the country. It seems like this is what we're up against.

BRISTER: Similar to that idea is a sense of community and family, which is just as prevalent in your fiction as a sense of place. It seems to me that community is an antiquated ideal in this hypertechnological age. Do you think so?

GAINES: Yeah, that's what I'm talking about. I think it's going to be a sad thing to happen, but it seems to me that's where we're headed. They're [contemporary writers] not taking on these issues as Faulkner did or Eudora Welty or Carson McCullers or Flannery O'Connor. I don't see them taking on those issues anymore. Maybe I'm one of these old relics that's hanging on there because I'm from the old school. [*laughs*] Those writers I just mentioned are the ones that I learned from, whose work I studied when I was in college. I suppose it still has influence over me. But I'm much older than the students that I'm teaching. I'm a generation or two older than they are. So it's one of those things.

BRISTER: Well, I didn't mean to imply that you are a relic. [*laughs*]

GAINES: [*laughs*] Oh, no, no. Sometimes I feel that I am. I question myself: "Why are you still writing about these things?" But it's the only thing I can write about. I cannot write about anything else. I've tried to write about San Francisco and my army experience, but it didn't come off as well.

BRISTER: Given your distinguished body of fiction/essays, do you see *your* influence on your students' writing?

GAINES: I try to discourage it. I don't want to see it. But, yes, they tell me that I've influenced them in structure, and I tell them to keep things simple for me. I was looking over a story last night, and the guy had several different references to other things, similes and metaphors, in the first opening sentence. And I said, "No, for the first opening sentence just make it simple, make the opening paragraph simple. Then later in the work you can go through all of the other things if you wish. I don't want to see them at all. But, if you want to do it, do it later." I've been told I have some influence. But I don't want to see anyone write exactly the way I write. I know how much students do imitate for a while. I imitated Faulkner as well as Hemingway until Malcolm Cowley told me, "Ernie, one Faulkner at a time; one Faulkner per century is enough." [*laughs*]

BRISTER: Well, it's a new century and . . .

GAINES: [*laughs*] Well, someone else can write like Faulkner or Hemingway.

BRISTER: Even though you don't keep up much with contemporary authors, do you see your influence on any contemporary authors besides your writing class?

GAINES: Oh, I don't know. I know once Alice Walker had read everything that I had written, and she said she liked what I had done and short stories influenced her work, that simple way of writing "A Long Day in November" and "The Sky Is Gray." But I never think about that when I read their work. I think we draw from everybody. When you draw from one person, that's plagiarism; when you draw from a hundred, that's genius. I draw from everybody. I've read the Russians, Shakespeare, Greek tragedy, American novels. I think I've learned something from all of them. After a while you find your way. So I'm sure at certain stages I picked up lines of Hemingway or tried to write long, convoluted sentences like Faulkner. I try not to.

I was at the academy today in Grand Coteau, and a woman compared my fiction to Faulkner's Yoknapatawpha County. And I said, "Yes, I was influenced by Faulkner. He showed me that I could take my little postage stamp of land and write forever about it." But, other than that, I'm sure some of his [Gautreaux's] thinking and philosophy I agree with. I'm not sure that anything is influenced by much more than *the idea* [Gaines's emphasis] of setting my work in one place, which I learned from Faulkner.

BRISTER: It seems you set up a relationship between your fiction, Faulkner's fiction, and contemporary fiction—Gautreaux's in this case. What is the parallel there?

GAINES: Well, I think most southerners have been influenced by Faulkner . . . southern writers my age and younger than I. I know definitely I have. I've been influenced by others as well, Hemingway and others. Well, Faulkner's greatest influence on me is writing about place, and he shows us how to write about a place. I've said that I don't know whether that's good or bad because I write so much about place that I just don't go out any further. Faulkner just went from the Civil War up to the contemporary, so he had so many things to write about. I don't know that I have those kinds of subjects to write about. But, yes, he has been a tremendous influence on me, especially writing about place, use of multiple points of view, and characters.

BRISTER: We can't get around Faulkner, can we? Is it inevitable that any southern writer . . . ?

GAINES: [*laughs*] Well, that's entirely up to those writers. Maybe they can get around Faulkner. I know that some of them feel that they don't want to be influenced by Faulkner. But I don't know that they can avoid him.

BRISTER: I am told that you have an interesting story about your first conversation with Oprah Winfrey.

GAINES: Well, she called one day. I usually don't answer the phone, but I was sitting by the phone and answered. She said, "I would like to speak with Ernest Gaines." I said, "Speaking." And she said, "This is Oprah Winfrey." I thought to myself, "Oh, yeah?" She said again, "This is Oprah Winfrey." And I said, "Oh, how are you Oprah?" Just like that. [*laughs*] I didn't believe her at first. She said, "We've chosen your book [*A Lesson Before Dying*] as the Book of the Month. This is to remain hush-hush." I said, "Well, I have to tell my wife." And she said, "Yes, but not the papers. The publisher will have to know about it because, once I announce it, everyone will go out and buy the book." The publishers had to have books in bookstores by the time she announced the choice. Well, she came down here because she wanted to come to Louisiana for the food and just to be here. She's originally from Mississippi. We spent two days together, eleven hours on a Friday and a Saturday. She's a wonderful person to be around, just as she is on television. We walked through the plantation where I'd grown up. We walked the row and went to one of the old cabins there. We went to the church-school where I attended my first six years of school. As a matter of fact, she got down on her knees as I showed her how we used to write our assignments either on our laps or got down on our knees with paper and wrote on the seat of the bench. She did the same thing. We went to the cemetery. There I pointed out graves to her where my folks have been buried for the last four generations. I broke a piece of sugarcane for her. [*laughs*] I had a pretty hard time breaking it across my knee. I had my knife and peeled it. I asked her if she knew how to chew sugarcane. And she said, "Of course, I know how to chew sugarcane. I'm from Mississippi." So we had a wonderful time.

BRISTER: What is your feeling on her book club and television as an outlet for noncanonical or lesser-known authors to reach a large audience?

GAINES: Well, I think it's the greatest thing to happen since paperback books. She has reached so many people. Before we had paperback books in the late 1940s and early 1950s, you had to go to the library to read books. But with paperbacks, if you had a quarter or fifty cents, you could buy the classics. I think what she has done is a tremendous thing for people who have never read a book. I know it benefited me with *A Lesson Before Dying*. It was on the *New York Times* Best Seller list. I can't see anything wrong with it, although some people lately have put it down.

BRISTER: I think a recent National Book Critics Circle award winner criticized the book club as literature for the masses, less intellectual.

GAINES: Yes, he thinks the people who read her [Oprah's] books might not understand what he's writing. But I think she's chosen some serious books out there. I should hope mine is sort of serious. [*laughs*] I think he's wrong for saying something like that.

BRISTER: And I think her audience is exactly the audience a writer would want to reach, a group that might not otherwise know about these kinds of books.

GAINES: Yes, sure. Well, that book of mine would not have sold nearly what it sold. And because it was well known, many of the schools knew about it, the university level, high school level, and added it to their curricula. I think she did as much for it as anything else.

BRISTER: That's another benefit of the book club: to get the book to the students who should read these books. You said in 1986, "I don't think I'm taken seriously as a writer yet . . . [no] books have been written about me." Since then several books have been written about you, and you have received many honors and citations. Do you feel like you're taken seriously in literary circles?

GAINES: Well, since 1986, I've written two books, *A Gathering of Old Men* and *A Lesson Before Dying*. Maybe that's all my critics wanted out there. I think in each one of these books . . . well, I hope that I've grown. Maybe now I am taken seriously. But I really don't know. I might say things like that, but I really don't think that much about what critics say about me.

BRISTER: Much literary criticism has been written about your fiction. Do you keep up with the criticism?

GAINES: Well, not really. I've had several people to write their dissertations or master's theses. A book just came out by Mary Ellen Doyle, *Voices from the Quarters*. There're about as many books written about me now as I've written. Most of these have been published since 1986.

BRISTER: Well, Cliff's Notes published a booklet on *A Lesson Before Dying*! I guess you've made it now.

GAINES: [*laughs*] I guess so.

BRISTER: Regarding Doyle's new book, she recommends a compilation of your "college" stories and your nonfiction works. However, you said earlier that you will concentrate on novel writing for now. Will you consider the collection she suggests, or will you revisit the short story in the future?

GAINES: I really don't know. If I came up with a good idea for a short story, I might do that if I have time. But I don't know.

BRISTER: Earlier in our conversation, we discussed the direction of southern literature and the decline of the individual and regionalism. This reminded me of what you said in 1995, "I'm doing what the others are doing, just more quietly." You referred to writers like James Baldwin and Richard Wright, who used their texts to effect political and social change. In light of this quotation and the shift in southern literature, do you see yourself as an activist or a historian now more than ever? Is there a greater need for that kind of writing now, given the literary changes?

GAINES: I really don't aim at history or historical writing. I suppose it comes into my work. Other than *The Autobiography of Miss Jane Pittman*,

I don't try to write history. I make references to history. My writing is different from their writing in that I write about where they came from and because I still live where they came from. Baldwin was born in New York, but Richard Wright was definitely from Mississippi. Baldwin's folks were from the South. All I'm doing is writing about the place they came from, and they write about the places where they are. I never did go to a large northern ghetto. I went to a small town in California, a naval town. At the time, I went to a completely integrated community. So my views were quite different from theirs. I never did forget where I had come from, the old people here. My aunt who raised me. These are the ones I wanted to write about. I don't know that Baldwin and Wright saw that in their writing. I don't know that they thought about this sort of thing. I know that they've been hurt . . . hurt a lot. They've taken it with them to New York, to Chicago. So have my folks, and so have I. I saw racism and prejudice when I was here in Louisiana before I left. But, at the same time, I still had these old people there who I cared very much about, brothers and sisters here who I cared very much about. So just because we're all African American doesn't mean that we all have to write the same way. I think, unfortunately, too many of our writers emulated Richard Wright's *Native Son* and *Black Boy*.

BRISTER: In that they are too political?

GAINES: Well, not only political. Someone said that every novel is a protest novel. But it's that they felt that this was the *only* thing to write about. Even those who were not in the ghetto wrote about lousy housing and drugs and alcohol and whatever you find in large cities. They were very naturalistic about things but not looking at the whole picture. As Ellison preached and preached it in *Going to the Territory*, our lives are not as narrow as some of these people make the world seem. Our experience is much broader than what they were saying. This is what I try to do. It's not that I'm not writing about conditions. It's that I've used a different approach to coming to my conclusions.

You mentioned the pastoral. That comes up in my writing where it does not come up in their writing. I can talk about the trees, the grass, the people working, the roads, the quarters and how it affects the lives of the people around them. Those are the things that really interested me, not just the hard concrete of a large, city ghetto. No, I didn't experience this as they did. But I think we're all writing about the human condition and especially the African American condition in the United States. I think we're all doing the same thing . . . just doing it differently.

BRISTER: In 1990 you said that, if you could rewrite *Catherine Carmier* or *Miss Jane*, you would include "people sitting around and eating gumbo and talking and shelling peas and making quilts and moss mattresses." Is this an idea that you will explore, more of "the folk stuff" as you call it?

GAINES: Well, if it comes up. In the project I'm working on now, I put it in there. The book I'm working on now is told by several different people, from multiple points of view. So, all of these little things come in there, which distinguish the characters from one another. Maybe somebody will talk more about gumbo and have some more gumbo. Someone already told me that I have enough food in *A Lesson Before Dying*. [*laughs*] As a matter of fact, one of my former students wrote a paper on just the food in the story. I think she had it published. Well, there are things I could add to *Catherine Carmier*. But once the child is there, you cannot reborn him again. He's out there and on his way now. You just try to improve on the next book. Yes, there are things I would have included in *Catherine* and *Miss Jane*, if I had thought about it at the time. There are things I would have taken out of *Miss Jane* now. But I'm not going to explain what those things are. I would have taken some things out there and maybe even in *Catherine Carmier*. But the child is out there and running around.

BRISTER: That is a good metaphor for writing, given the amount of time and labor that goes into producing a piece of fiction. Do you feel that your books are your children?

GAINES: Yes, you fight with them for nine months—well, seven years with the last one. Then, after you've finished, you've lost something. You're glad it's over, but you feel very empty about it being over. It's happened like that with every book. I would think a woman feels that way about carrying her little load for nine months.

BRISTER: You mentioned that your new project will contain multiple points of view. It seems a difficult feat to balance the characters' voices to produce a cohesive story. You accomplished this in "Just Like a Tree," for example. I'm also thinking of Faulkner's *The Sound and the Fury*. Do you find this device liberating or rather challenging?

GAINES: Once I find the voice of each character, then it's easy for me to do. For example, in *A Lesson Before Dying*, it's very easy to distinguish between Jefferson's voice and Grant's voice. I suppose if I had to tell the story from Miss Emma's point of view, I think I could get her voice down to be distinct from the others. Or from Paul's point of view or Guidry's or the sheriff's. I think I could do it. I think they are their own characters. They'll throw in words and phrases and nuances that others will not do. I think I can get six or eight voices out of it.

BRISTER: Well, it can be very rewarding for the reader—to get a "complete" picture. And I look forward to reading your new novel.
GAINES: Well, I don't know when that will be. I just have to take some time.

Works Cited

Doyle, Mary Ellen. *Voices from the Quarters.* Baton Rouge: Louisiana State University Press, 2002.

Gaines, Ernest J. *The Autobiography of Miss Jane Pittman.* 1971. New York: Bantam Books, 1986.

Gaines, Ernest J. *Bloodline.* 1968. New York: Random House, 1999.

Gaines, Ernest J. *Catherine Carmier.* 1964. Chatham: Chatham Booksellers, 1972.

Gaines, Ernest J. *A Gathering of Old Men.* New York: Knopf, 1983.

Gaines, Ernest J. *A Lesson Before Dying.* New York: Knopf, 1993.

Gaines, Ernest J. "The Turtles." *Transfer.* San Francisco: San Francisco State Press, 1956.

Gaudet, Marcia, and Carl Wooton. *Porch Talk with Ernest Gaines: Conversations on the Writer's Craft.* Baton Rouge: Louisiana State University Press, 1990.

Lepschy, Wolfgang. "A MELUS Interview: Ernest J. Gaines." *MELUS* (Spring 1999).

Lowe, John, ed. *Conversations with Ernest J. Gaines.* Jackson: University Press of Mississippi, 1995.

A Lesson for Living

Dale Brown / 2001

From Dale Brown, *Conversations with American Writers: The Doubt, the Faith, the In-Between* (2008): 94–111. © 2008. Wm. B Eerdmans Publishing Company, Grand Rapids, MI. Reprinted with permission of the publisher; all rights reserved.

Dale Brown and Ernest Gaines spoke in October of 2001 in an airport lounge in Columbus, Ohio, where Gaines had traveled for a speech at Ohio Dominican College.

DB: So how do you handle this celebrity business?
EJG: My wife usually travels with me. She keeps things in check. We handle it pretty well. Someone asked Wallace Stegner, after he had won the Pulitzer Prize, how he felt about it. He said, "Well, I'll go out and get a bourbon."

DB: So you try not to be too caught up in it?
EJG: I do, but they usually catch me up in it. If the interviewer has read the books, that's one thing. But if a newspaper reporter or a radio show host just wants to chat—I don't believe in that kind of junk.

DB: What about the "Oprah" appearance?
EJG: Of course it elevated *A Lesson Before Dying* to the top of the bestseller lists. We were six weeks at number one of the *New York Times* list. Everyone sees *Oprah*. I don't know if everyone saw *Oprah* on that particular day, but I've met a thousand people who said, "I saw you on *Oprah*." All different ages, races, ethnic backgrounds. I don't know how some of those people have free time to watch *Oprah*. She was a wonderful person to work with. We were together for about eleven hours there on the plantation where I grew up. She came to Louisiana. Usually she would have the writer come to her studio in Chicago, but she wanted to get down to Louisiana to try some of the food down there. Although she is from Mississippi, I don't think she'd

been in that part of the country. I took her to a restaurant, and she liked the food, liked the piece of sugarcane we shared. We had dinner in the big house, the same house where the plantation owners lived and where my maternal grandmother worked for many years. I had worked in that yard myself, more than fifty years ago.

DB: How has your world changed since September 11?
EJG: I've just gone on with my work. I had to speak in Washington, DC, that following week. That was a long limousine ride from New Orleans.

DB: Will this historical moment change what writers write about?
EJG: I don't think it's going to change what I write about. It is still about love and hate, the young and the old, race, and the rest. And for me it all still goes back to Louisiana.

DB: Will a good book make any difference?
EJG: Well, I'm working on something I call "a thing." I don't know where it's going. My latest novel, *A Lesson Before Dying*, was published eight years ago, and I've been trying to figure something to write about ever since. Just in the past few months a subject has started to come together. After *A Lesson Before Dying* became popular, my agent wanted me to get something out right away because my name was hot. But I'm not controlled by the market. I have to keep my own pace, my own subjects.

DB: What is your new book shaping up to be?
EJG: I read a part of it at MLA in December. A chapter of it was published in *Callaloo* magazine. They printed chapter three—"The Man Who Whipped Children." I will probably change it many, many, many times. I have no idea how many times it's going to change. Chapter three is probably one of the toughest chapters to write. Maybe that's the reason I wanted it published. No, I think chapter four is going to be the toughest chapter in this particular book. By the time I get to chapter twenty, maybe I will have changed chapter three and chapter four and chapter everything else. I hope I don't have to change the first chapter.

DB: It sounds like whatever chapter you're writing now is the toughest one.
EJG: Yeah. Well, chapter four is a transitional chapter. I have a murder, and the police come on the scene to ask a few questions. Then you really have to get down to work. What happened, and why did it happen? You can always

write that first chapter and maybe you can write the second one, but when you start getting around to the third and fourth chapters, you really have to start thinking. It's just like Beethoven's Fifth Symphony. "Buh, buh, buh, bum," is okay. Then he has to start working.

DB: And you try to keep the chapters to a certain length and pace?
EJG: I usually do. In *A Lesson Before Dying* I was able to hold to around ten or eleven pages.

DB: Does Dianne, your wife, read your work?
EJG: No. She'll hear the stories when I read them in public, but I never ask her for an opinion. I wouldn't do that, though I think she'd be pleased. She may be too critical. You can fight your agent or your editor a couple of thousand miles away, but you don't want to be sleeping with someone and fighting with her. I avoid that.

DB: And this all started for you on the plantation in the 1930s and 1940s where you wrote letters for neighbors?
EJG: Yes, I wrote letters for the old people.

DB: And your first performances were in church?
EJG: I tried to put on a little play. I had to be producer, director, and actor. I even had to pull the curtain. I think I was thirteen or fourteen.

DB: Your church background comes up in each of your stories. There's "Determination Sunday," for example.
EJG: That was the day that the people would get up and sing, and the meeting would be about three hours. Third Sunday of every month. They would sing and talk of their plans for heaven. Each person had his own particular song. You could identify people by their songs. If you were not in the church, even from a distance, you could tell who was testifying.

DB: It was a way of saying, "I'm still carrying the cross."
EJG: Oh, yes.

DB: And this was a Baptist church?
EJG: Yes, I was baptized as a Baptist, baptized in the same river that I write about, the same river where we'd fish and wash our clothes. We washed our souls in that same river. My wife and I just bought a piece of property

on that same plantation recently. We have a pier on the river about maybe three hundred yards from where I was actually baptized, when I was twelve years old. White folks were baptized there too. We were all baptized there because we all lived on that same plantation. But my stepfather was Catholic, and I went to a little Catholic school during my last three years in Louisiana.

DB: Do you feel indebtedness to this religious background? Is it gratitude, ambivalence, or connection that you feel?

EJG: Certainly there is ambivalence, but I would not be the person I am today if I had not had that background. The old people had such strong beliefs, and they tried to guide me. The civil rights movement began in those churches, but I was gone by then. Of course I read about it in San Francisco and saw it on the news. That little church was my school as well. The building is still there, though it is about to fall over. My wife and I are arranging to move it to our property this spring. We want to restore it. No one looks after it. So we want to move it to our six acres, repair it, and keep it up.

DB: Do you frequently get invited to speak at churches or church-related institutions?

EJG: Yes, but I usually talk only about my writing. I don't ever get into any kind of religious discussion. I avoid it. Religion and politics I avoid. Religion, politics, and family problems, I stay out of those areas.

DB: But it seems to be the case that people pick up on spiritual matters as they read your books.

EJG: Yes. I may not be a particularly religious person, but my characters usually are. One character may have a strongly religious position while another pushes the other way. These arguments make a book.

DB: You have many endearing characters, usually the older women who live in the stream of faith. The ministers and the professionals, however, are often treated with considerable satire.

EJG: I was educated in the 1950s in San Francisco, and I was reading books like *Fathers and Sons* by Turgenev and Dostoevsky's *Crime and Punishment* and Joyce's *Portrait of the Artist as a Young Man*. And those books began to make me aware of myself and what was really going on. I began to ask myself about these folks who claim to be Christians. I'm not talking about the old people on the plantation; their faith was real enough. But those folks on television and those who fought against antilynching laws made me question the whole business. Many of the younger people at the time developed the same attitude.

DB: So you give us Reverend Jamison, say, in *A Gathering of Old Men*, who seems, as part of the religious hierarchy, to recommend accepting injustice. He's the only one who didn't have a gun, the only one who won't stand up to the sheriff.

EJG He knew what the result would be. He was trying to save the people from the suffering. But it was time for these old men to stand up. They had to do something big in their lives. They were pushed beyond where they have ever been pushed; they were pushed to the extreme. He just couldn't get there with them.

DB: What about Phillip Martin, the minister from *In My Father's House*?

EJG: Phillip has felt that everything has been solved for him when he became a Christian. When his son comes back, he finds that he's still weak. He had this great strength to lead the people to vote, to be a spokesman for Christianity, but when that son shows up, the program collapses.

DB: So the past does matter. Despite his conversion to Christianity, he still has to stand up to his guilt?

EJG: People ask me about Grant Wiggins at the end of *A Lesson Before Dying*. "What's going to happen to him?" They want to know. I'm not sure what comes next, but Grant will be okay. So will the Reverend Martin.

DB: They've both had to carry the load of representing the community, being "the one"?

EJG: People in those little communities years ago did not vote, so they chose somebody to look up to, someone to lead them. When I was a child, I was always the one to write letters for the old people.

DB: And you felt the pressure of representing the community?

EJG: Yes, I wanted to play baseball and cowboys like the others, but I felt I had to do these things for these people, and my Aunt Augusteen, who raised me, insisted that I do those things. I would have done anything in the world to keep from hurting her.

DB: Was it a burden?

EJG: It's like a big rock on my shoulder. My agent told me I ought to be happy to have this weight because so many writers don't have anything. I told her I'd be glad to share it with them. It's too big for me to carry alone. I've been chipping and chipping away at that huge load for forty-five years now. Each little book, each story, is another little chip gone.

DB: Your books also speak powerfully to the issue of displacement. Each of your books, in one way or another, notes the difficulty of leaving and the terror of staying. So many characters, like Grant in *A Lesson Before Dying*, get caught between two worlds.

EJG: I was finally able to come back when I was fifty, about eighteen years ago. I'd written *The Autobiography of Miss Jane Pittman* and *In My Father's House*. I'd just finished *A Gathering of Old Men*. If I'd tried to come back when I was thirty-five or forty, I'd have been just like Grant Wiggins. All kinds of things kept pulling me back, all my stories went back there to the plantation, but I couldn't have accepted conditions in the South. I had a connection. I had a real close connection to the South and to the memory of my aunt. When I left, I left because I had to, because there was no high school nearby for me to go to and there was definitely no library for me to go to. I didn't have any relatives in the cities with whom I could live while I studied. I had to leave, but I left something I loved. I left my aunt and my brothers, sisters, and friends. Those times were mean in many ways. I left some good things, and I missed them. But I was able to come back. So many southern writers, like Richard Wright, say, "That's it. Forget it. I will never go back there again." They took everything with them. I have brothers who I don't think will ever come back here to live.

DB: How would your life have been different if you hadn't gone to San Francisco?

EJG: I probably wouldn't have lived. I think I went to San Francisco precisely at the right time. I was fifteen years old, and I'd learned a lot in those fifteen years about the South, small towns, plantation life, and work in the fields. I went to the swamps when I was eleven or twelve. I was in the fields at that age. I worked with a handsaw. I knew about hard work. I'd washed dishes. I knew those small towns. I knew what segregation was. I'd felt racism. I knew how to throw trees; I cut them down with my uncle. I traveled with one of my aunts across the parishes. She sold cosmetics. I began to know the people there in the little towns. I rode in the back of the bus many times. Had I left Louisiana at age ten, I never would have experienced all these things. I could never have written about the things I've been able to write about. If I stayed in Louisiana another five or six years, I probably would have been destroyed. So many of my playmates died in their twenties or thirties. Very few of them got to be fifty. I would not have been able to do the kind of thing that was inside of me. Something inside of me made me want to do something else. But Louisiana at that time was a place of great limitations. There was no high school in the parish where I lived. And no library. I had this brain, and I wanted to do things. I'd put on that little play, remember. I wanted to learn more about those kinds of things. There was no place for me. I would have been destroyed or gone mad. I had to go away to understand, to interpret.

DB: In San Francisco you discovered?
EJG: Good teachers and advisors and agents.

DB: And the library?
EJG: Yes. Of course I could not enter a library here in Louisiana. When I went to California in 1948, I used to hang around with my friends on the street corner after the school day. My stepfather ordered me off the streets, so I ended up in the library. I saw books for the first time. I never saw so many books. I just started reading. I found myself trying to find something about rural life because I grew up on a plantation. But I came up empty. I found lots of books but none by or about blacks. So there was nothing about me in those books. Then I found the Russians and read anything that had peasantry in it, anything that dealt with the people, the people who worked the earth. I was about sixteen years old. I thought I knew what I was doing. I was looking for *me* in those books, and it was when I did not find me there (or find my brothers and my aunts and my uncles and the people I knew) that I tried to write about my own place.

DB: Your Aunt Augusteen was somehow at the center of that too?
EJG: Oh yeah, Auntie has always been in the middle, always will be, I guess. It was she who raised me and my other brothers and other siblings.

DB: You say that you sometimes tried to write about San Francisco subjects, and those stories had "no soul."

EJG: There was no root there. I was writing about things I didn't know enough about. But when I came to the peculiar subject of the South, what my people had lived, the flavor of things here, the particular parish of my youth, I felt so close to the earth and my ancestry. I could dig deeper inside of me and hear not only my voice but their voices. This is what I mean by the sounds of the singing and the sounds of the church and the praying and all those things that would come through when I wrote about my own area in the South, but that didn't happen when I tried to write about San Francisco or my military experience.

DB: Do you think it's true for many writers that it's the childhood that nourishes?

EJG: Well, someone has said that at fifteen years old you've just about experienced everything that you're going to write about anyway. I still write about things that impressed me at that age, but I've learned to look at it from a perspective of an adult. I tried to write a novel when I was sixteen years old, and I didn't know anything about it. Now, I think I do know.

DB: And the sounds and the smells and the "earthy" part of it goes all the way back to your childhood?

EJG: Yes, but remember I was always coming back to Louisiana from San Francisco. I would come back every two years. I had to go back to the well every so often to smell the earth again and listen to the songs again and visit the boys and listen to the church songs and be around the people who were devout and be around those who were not. I was constantly coming back. I continued to grow in my understanding of those first fifteen years in the South.

DB: You've clearly worked hard at the craft, first in San Francisco with Wallace Stegner and since. And the time you take on each book suggests considerable revision. How many edits, for example, did you go through on *A Lesson Before Dying*?

EJG: Not so many, actually. I must have written it three times at most. I worked on *In My Father's House* daily for seven years. I worked on *A Lesson Before Dying* for seven years, too, but I was working on it half the year. When I teach, I don't write. When I write, I don't teach. But the slow pace was a good thing in this case because a lot of things happened to me in those years that changed the novel. I don't know if Jefferson's notebook would have occurred to me if I'd written that book in two years. I don't know if the radio would have been there. I don't know what would have happened. At first I thought the story would be set in the 1980s. It would have been a different thing altogether. It was a blessing in disguise that I was delayed during my work in *A Lesson Before Dying*.

DB: So a book evolves slowly for you?

EJG: I know where I want to go, and I know what I want to do. It's like a train trip from San Francisco to New York. You have the general plan, but you don't know all that will happen. You may even wind up in Philadelphia. I would write for a time and then put the book down for six months. The first time I put the book down, I was at the chapter where Grant had to go to the jail for his first visit with Jefferson. I'd gone that far, and I had no idea in the world what Grant was going to talk about or what he was going to do once he went into Jefferson's cell. For the whole semester I was teaching, I was wondering, What's he going to do when he gets there? I'd never gone inside a jail cell and talked to anybody. I just reread everything I had written and got back into that character, and when he got into the jail cell he said, "Jefferson, Aunt Emma couldn't make it this time," or something like that. And then it went on from there. But I knew from the start that Jefferson was going to be sentenced to death. I did not know that he would actually be executed. While I was still on the book, I met a retired professor who told me about "Gruesome Gerty," the portable electric chair that was in use in those Louisiana parishes in the 1930s and 1940s. I knew that had to come into the novel. I kept a picture of "Gruesome Gerty" on my desk during the last months on the book.

DB: You dedicate *The Autobiography of Miss Jane Pittman* to your Aunt Augusteen: "To the memory of my beloved aunt, Miss Augusteen Jefferson, who did not walk a day in her life but who taught me the importance of standing." Does "standing" mean taking responsibilities?

EJG: Right. You've got a responsibility to yourself and to the less fortunate others. I felt responsible for my siblings and for the community. Aunt Augusteen died in 1953, but I'm sure if I had been in the South in the 1950s and 1960s I would have been expected to be the one going to the demonstrations and marches.

DB: Even a character like Marcus in *Of Love and Dust*, through Jim Kelly, his mentor, is learning that he's going to have to recognize what he's done. He's going to have to stand up.

EJG: It's a common theme throughout all of my work. You find it in the *Bloodline* stories: "Three Men" and "The Sky Is Gray."

DB: You seem wary of many of the labels with which critics try to corner you. To say "Ernest Gaines writes about race" or to call you a "southern writer" isn't quite adequate?
EJG: Someone asked me recently if I was limited by writing about the South. Faulkner wrote about the South and won a Nobel Prize. Joyce wrote about Dublin. I think Louisiana is a little bit bigger than Dublin. Balzac wrote about Paris, so why can't I write about Louisiana? Wally Stegner asked me once who I write for, and I said, "Everybody." I learned from Russian writers of the nineteenth century and French writers and Hemingway and those guys. Then he said, "If I were to put a gun at your head?" I said, "Then I'll come up with something."

DB: That's when you said you were "writing for the young black men of the South."
EJG: Yes, and the young white youth. If they do not know their neighbor- hood, they know only half of what's going on.

DB: Gordon Thompson says, "Gaines writes about the small-minded and misguided only if he can love them." You are startlingly even-handed in your books. In *A Gathering of Old Men*, for example, the reader is ready to despise the vile character, Fix. And then we meet him as he sits with his granddaughter in his lap. Or there's the kind white woman in "The Sky Is Gray." And there's Candy in *A Gathering of Old Men*, a character we like, but you show her maternalistic streak. You complicate characters like the white jailer, Paul, in *A Lesson Before Dying*. We're all set to see a stereotype, and you jar us with a good white person.
EJG: Yes, they virtually deleted the Paul character for the movie, but they've given him a prominent role in the play. I saw the production in New Orleans a few weeks ago, and Paul has a significant place. But I don't know where that comes from. When I first went to California, we were living in govern- ment project housing, and there were different races there—white, black, Hispanic, Asian, Native American—all there together. I met some bastards, but I met some white guys who would just do anything to help; some of them would bend over backwards to help you. So I knew the Pauls; I knew them in San Francisco. I've known Pauls who have come back to Louisiana to teach. Paul has always been popping up in my life. He's always been there.

There were times when he could not afford to show his humanity, but he's always been around. That's something.

DB: You don't really have heroes and villains. One theme of *In My Father's House* is the difficulty of knowing someone's character. Even the good people have flaws, and the bad folks have their moments of grace.

EJG: Sure. Someone criticized the ending of *A Gathering of Old Men* because of my treatment of Luke Will. They said I was helping the KKK because of Luke Will's speech asking someone to look after his wife and kids. "Why'd you make him so human at the end?" someone asked. Well, he is human. He just cannot accept certain things. He cannot accept this black man, but he loves his own little child. He's a human being.

DB: Do you know Will Campbell?

EJG: I met him just recently. We both received the National Humanities medal from the president at a ceremony in Washington, DC.

DB: Campbell talks about these same kinds of things, about loving the KKK, about how they, too, are trapped in a system.

EJG: I'm not sure about "loving." Luke Will is still a son of a bitch, but I made him a human being.

DB: I wonder how *A Lesson Before Dying*—both the book and the film—is affecting your critical standing. John Lowe says you have been "shockingly underrated." How do you respond to the critical judgments?

EJG: I don't worry about them. Somebody asked me what I think of the film versions of my books. I tell them I don't like everything I see in the movies, but I've seen what they've done to the Bible. I've seen what they've done to Shakespeare, to Faulkner, and to Hemingway. And since they didn't tell me how to write my book, I will not tell them how to make their film. That's how I look at critics.

DB: You don't read too much contemporary literature?

EJG: I read my friends, but I go back to the masters: Tolstoy, Turgenev, Faulkner, and Hemingway. I don't keep up, really. And I think it's a shame in a way because so many of my contemporaries do. They always ask me what books have I read lately and what I thought of it and who said what about the book. I always have to say, "Well, I don't know." They must think I'm the most illiterate person in the world. I keep going back to my old books. The other day I picked up Turgenev's *Fathers and Sons*, which I've read maybe twenty times completely through. Now I only read a chapter or two, and then I put it aside and read a chapter or two of something else, like *War and Peace*.

DB: Is this a good time to be a writer?

EJG: Well, this has been the only thing in the world I wanted to do since I was a child, so I don't know. Being a writer was not a choice. I still think there're wonderful things to be said.

DB: If *In My Father's House* was the most difficult to write, which was the easiest?

EJG: *Of Love and Dust.* I wrote it in about eight months. My editor read the first draft and said he liked the first part of the book and second part, but they didn't have anything in common. So he sent me back to the typewriter with instructions to make it a tragedy or a comedy. He thought the Marcus character needed to be more consistently pictured as having to face his actions; he shouldn't have too much fun. After that edit, he said I'd improved it 99 percent. "Now go over it one more time," he said. When I sent it back, it had been about eight months.

DB: What about *Catherine Carmier*?

EJG: That was the book I learned to write on. That's the book that had Turgenev's influence. I had no idea what a young man might do when he comes back to his old place. How does he react? And then I discovered Turgenev's *Fathers and Sons*. Turgenev is writing about much the same thing.

DB: So with the world exploding, Bull Connor in the South and S. I. Hayakawa in San Francisco, you were writing novels?

EJG: Yes, especially at San Francisco State, my friends, black and white, said I should be out there on the line with them. They wanted me to carry their protest signs. I told them that I was writing a book about a little lady born in slavery who lived to be 110. And they said, "Listen, Gaines, nobody wants to hear about a little old lady in slavery; we're talking about changing times." I said, "But I thought she would be important." So I just stuck to that.

DB: And all the way back to *Catherine Carmier*, the issue seems to be more than race. Jackson Bradley, in that first novel, longs for a place beyond race. His restlessness strikes me as fundamentally spiritual.

EJG: He wants something to believe in, yes. Like many of my characters, he's looking for something, and I think it's God as much as anything else. He is like Grant Wiggins in *A Lesson Before Dying* or the young man in "The Sky Is Gray." He's after something to believe in. They all feel this, but they can no longer accept much of their pasts. Their education means a certain lostness. Grant Wiggins, remember, unlike Reverend Ambrose, hasn't the strength to go to Jefferson's execution. Ambrose can go. Grant cannot. When I was writing the book, a friend of mine, a lawyer, had a client on death row. He asked me if I would like to go to visit the prisoner. I couldn't do it. I just don't want to look in a guy's face who knows he's going to die in an hour. Maybe that's why Grant doesn't do it in the end.

DB: *A Lesson Before Dying* can be seen as a debate between Ambrose and Wiggins over Jefferson—a battle for Jefferson's soul. And you leave it an open question at the end. Ambrose goes to the execution. But the camera goes back to Wiggins. You often do that. You mute the dramatic possibilities.

EJG: Yeah, I think everything should be that way. The big battles are off stage. In *Of Love and Dust*, Marcus has already done the killing. In *The Autobiography of Miss Jane Pittman*, the war has already been fought. In *In My Father's House*, the deed has already been done. The big thing is the revealing of character. What's going on inside this character? What happens after the tragedy? That's where you get at human nature. And the characters drive the story. I still wake up sometimes at night and wonder what Grant is up to now.

DB: *The Autobiography of Miss Jane Pittman* was the first big hit for you. Was that because of the film?

EJG: Oh yes, I think so. The book came out in 1971 and the film in 1974. The book sold more copies during the three months after the film than it had up until that time.

DB: Now with the explosion of sales for *A Lesson Before Dying* and *Oprah* and all, maybe they won't put something about Miss Jane on your tombstone. But lots of people thought she was a real person?

EJG: Oh man, I lived with that for a long time. I'm still living with that. I was at a university recently where this old man got up with a Bible that had red rubber bands around it. It was an old leather-bound Bible. He said it was a Bible Miss Jane had left for the folks. My completely fictional character had suddenly left a Bible!

DB: Is Hemingway a big influence on the plain style of that novel?

EJG: Maybe it's Hemingway, but I find that in jazz, in spirituals, in the Baptist churches, and in the language of my people. But I have been influenced by Hemingway, definitely so, just as he was influenced by Gertrude Stein and others.

DB: You have the marvelous sounds of the South in phrases like "root hog or die." And great stories of the folkways. I'd never heard of smoking children, for example. Have you seen that done?

EJG: Sure. Our neighbor would tie his children up in croaker sacks and tie the sacks to the tree limbs. We kept moss in the yards, and we'd put leaves over the moss and set fire to them to keep the mosquitoes away. (We sat on the porches; he had no screens or anything.) So the smoke was a way to punish those children.

DB: There's considerable humor in your books. I remember when Mary tells Miss Jane Pittman that the Lord will take care of her at the demonstrations, and Jane jokes that the Lord may be taking care of somebody else. Does that emerge just from remembering the voices, paying attention to the past?

EJG: I think so. I have a brother who is very funny. He can talk about the most serious things and make you laugh. It is part of my inheritance. I saw the Ken Burns show on PBS the other night, the Mark Twain biography. That reminded me of a fellow I knew who was a writer for the *Sacramento Bee*. You know Mark Twain once was a newspaperman in Sacramento. And the guy said that whenever they needed some money at the *Bee* they would always get an old desk and sell it as "Mark Twain's desk." He said they did that about three or four times. Lots of Mark Twain desks drifting around. I thought of that. Great story. But I don't know who could be funnier than African Americans or Jews. Their humor is linked to their sorrow.

DB: Why was *In My Father's House* so difficult to write?

EJG: I didn't know what point of view to use. I tried to tell it via Chippo Simon, but he didn't know enough about Robert X in San Francisco. And Chippo didn't understand the anger and frustration the young teachers felt. I tried to tell it from multiple points of view. That didn't work. And I couldn't figure out exactly what Robert X, the abandoned son, would actually try to do to his father, Phillip Martin. I had trouble with point of view and theme. So I just went over and over and over and over trying to get it together.

DB: One of the remarkable things about that book is the suggestion that one of the legacies of slavery, particularly for the black man, is paralysis.

EJG: Yes, being unable to act at the time when one must act. Phillip Martin could not move when his young family left him. He cannot act to save his family. And twenty years later, when Robert X shows up, Phillip literally falls to the floor. He's paralyzed.

DB: In a letter to Walker Percy, Shelby Foote said, "I seriously think that no good practicing Christian can be a great artist." Can a believer write a good book?

EJG: I don't know if he can. I think he has to have doubts. I think the writer must feel that nothing is absolute, nothing is perfect. And he questions, questions, questions. Two and two is four, I suppose, but we don't live by figures like that. I feel that you can't really believe in any one thing to the point that you can look at all aspects of the world through one keyhole. I don't care what that one thing is. You cannot see the entire world if you believe in one thing that strongly. You have to have some doubts. Mark Twain says that novels should neither preach nor teach, but in the end do both, and I think that's what I try to do in my writing. I do not believe in standing on a soapbox. I don't know if I could tell anybody how to live. I don't know how to live. I just try to get something going, something comic, something tragic. And then I try to write it well enough so that anybody could pick it up and say, "Oh yes, this could be me."

DB: *A Lesson Before Dying* is consistent with all of your books in showing a certain doubt about institutional religion. Jefferson is executed two weeks after Easter. You note that the people will have forgotten by then. But Ambrose, the representative of the church, is there at the end. Do you mean to approve of him?

EJG: I do. I do approve of him being there. I think he has tremendous strength. He shows something, faith, and that was impossible for Grant Wiggins. Grant is still asking questions. Ambrose must be there for the people.

DB: Despite the burden, you still take considerable joy in this writing business, don't you?

EJG: Yes, yes. It's the only thing. It's my life.

The Influence of Multi-Art Forms
on the Fiction of Ernest J. Gaines

Marcia Gaudet and Darrell Bourque / 2002

From *Interdisciplinary Humanities* 20:1 (2003): 76–92. Reprinted with permission.

This interview was conducted on December 17, 2002, at the home of Ernest Gaines, near the University of Louisiana at Lafayette campus. At the time, Gaines, Gaudet, and Bourque had been friends and colleagues in the UL Lafayette English Department for over twenty years.

DARRELL BOURQUE: That whole idea of influence or use or whatever you want to call it is really broad. I mean, to a large extent any of us who are writers or musicians or visual artists are all influenced by the larger culture that we encounter. But what we could do in this particular set of interviews is to ask some more specific questions about how artistic expression impacts a particular imagination. As we've talked to you over the years informally and in other essays or interviews that you've given, you know, there are instances where you talk about the way in which you listened to Joyce, read Joyce, read Turgenev, loved the work of Vincent van Gogh, and so forth. And so in a lot of ways, I think that's one of the reasons why your name immediately came up for me is because I know that as you've talked through the years, you've touched on some of those ideas. But I was wondering, Ernie, who would you say is a nonliterary artist who has maybe had an impact on you as a writer or as an artist yourself? Are there any people who come to mind?

ERNEST J. GAINES: A nonliterary artist?

DB: Right, either a musician or—

EJG: Well, I've listened to music all my life, all my adult life I should say, and especially the classical music, symphonies as well as chamber music. I like to listen to jazz music, a lot of jazz music, of course. And a lot of blues, a lot of spirituals. Pop music. And I think without knowing how directly it's influenced me, I think it has influenced me. I think I've taken from so many different artists that it's hard for me to pinpoint it to one particular musician. Although I've listened to pieces of music, like the *New World Symphony* of Dvorak, and because of the motifs or themes of spirituals and themes in the symphony, it's awakened something in me.

MARCIA GAUDET: I want to go back to what you said sixteen years ago. You said at that time that music helped you develop as a writer, and while writing *Miss Jane Pittman*, you played Mussorgsky's *Pictures at an Exhibition.* You also said that some of the best descriptions of things, especially dealing with blacks, have been in music. They have been described better by musicians, especially the great blues singers like Bessie Smith, Josh White, and Leadbelly. And also in jazz music—a repetition of things, understatement, playing around the note.

EJG: Right, right. Yes, I agree. Bessie Smith's "Backwater Blues," and I feel that I get the sensation, the description, and the feeling of it—of the flood of '27, as I get when I read Faulkner's "Old Man." That sharp picture that she gives in two-and-a-half lines of singing, I get a picture of what it must have been like—for the people, the water, and life at that particular time. Leadbelly singing about the prisons—at Angola or the prisons in Texas. I get a good feeling of what prison life was like. Regarding that influence in some of my work—Lightnin' Hopkins singing about "Mr. Tim Moore's Farm"—I think that influenced me in writing some of the books. When I wrote *Of Love and Dust* about a man put on the farm to work his time out, that had an influence on me. And I listened to the spirituals, and I used that kind of, those kinds of emotions when writing scenes of older women—for example, in *A Gathering of Old Men* or in *A Lesson Before Dying*, how they talked to God and the associations about God. I think that's from listening to that.

MG: Do you think the contemporary singers—and I have in mind especially B. B. King because I think you said you liked B. B. King. I'm not talking about rap music—

EJG: I don't know a thing about rap—

MG: Artists like B. B. King—do you get that same kind of feeling or influence?

EJG: I do. I think they do. I think the *early* B. B. King. The B. B. King of the fifties. You see, I've been listening to B. B. King since the fifties. Definitely. I have those records. And it's not as sophisticated as it is today. There's a young musician who's compared to B. B. King called Robert Cray. And he's just a fantastic blues singer. He sings contemporary things. The way he sings about these contemporary problems—I went through those problems as a young man in the forties. And he's young. I guess in his thirties or forties—young compared to B. B. King. So I'm very much influenced by the blues singers. Especially the rural singers, much more than the urban blues singers.

MG: I wonder about the influence of rap. The rap singers are so much a part of the mainstream culture right now—and not only an influence on young, African American culture. But it seems like an *urban* thing and so removed from the experiences of the older generations.

EJG: Right. I don't understand a thing about it. I don't understand it at all. I can't even talk about it.

DB: I think one of the interesting things about rap music is the way in which it cuts across a racial divide so that young white kids are as interested in black rap music as young black kids. And it goes both ways. Some of Eminen's strongest and most fervent fans are young black kids. And it's just a phenomenon to me that I don't understand either, but there's a kind of ability to communicate and something going on there that I think is not for our generation.

MG: But in a way the blues and jazz singers did the same thing.

DB: Yeah. That's interesting. I hadn't thought about that.

MG: It just may be the form that generation needed. And that was my other question, do you think that the great blues and jazz singers did serve that purpose—of sort of appealing very widely. They were singing often about specific black experiences, but they reached a larger audience.

EJG: Yes, I think so. Yes, I think that definitely happened. And I don't know where Elvis Presley would be today if it were not for black musicians. And the group that really made white America aware of the influence of blues—especially rural blues—was the Rolling Stones from England. They were the first white group to really come out and say, "Yes, definitely, we've been influenced by these people." By Muddy Waters and Chuck Berry and all of these black singers. These blues singers definitely influenced many of the white singers. This young man who died in a plane crash several years ago—from Texas—Stevie Ray Vaughan—a tremendous blues musician, and you can see the influence of black music on him. So it's definitely there. Go back to jazz, as you said, Benny Goodman with the Count Basie Band, how they integrated, how they worked together and made good music. Benny Goodman had people like Charlie Christian on guitar and Lionel Hampton on the xylophone. Teddy Wilson on the piano. So it's always been out there. I can understand that. That stuff that's called "hip-hop"—I can't understand. [*laughs*] I don't know what they're doing. I was at a place recently, at one of these readings, and one guy got up and asked me, "Mr. Gaines, what do you think of hip-hop music, as a writer?" What's hip-hop? I had no idea what they were talking about.

MG: And what's almost frightening to me is that I can remember—not so much with my dad because he was a musician and he loved blues and jazz but with Chuck Berry and others—when rock and roll became mainstream, and now my generation is questioning whether rap or hip-hop really is an art form.

EJG: I think of contemporary jazz—and when they came out with bebop—you know, nobody wanted to accept it. The old traditionalists didn't want to accept bebop. But then the artists and industry and all those guys stuck to it—

DB: And now we can hear it. You couldn't even hear it early on. Your ears wouldn't accept it—

EJG: Right—but it's out there. John Coltrane, when he changed music around, people didn't understand what he was doing. But John Coltrane was a genius. That was another influence on my work—listening to it—because it's really rooted in the blues. If you really listen to John Coltrane, it's really blues all the time—blues and spirituals all the time.

DB: You were mentioning Elvis Presley a while ago, and a little known fact about Elvis Presley is his love of gospel music. He would come off the stage after a performance at midnight, and at five or six in the morning, his singers, his back-up singers were still backstage. He would make them sing gospel music, and he would just go on until daybreak. And it wasn't something that happened at a stage in his career. It was all the way through. I think that he drew to a large extent from the same thing—from the blues and the spirituals.

EJG: Yeah, sure.

MG: And he didn't see that as a sort of a divide. And I wonder about that— the idea that there is sort of a break between the spirituals and blues or jazz, and even that expression—that one is much more "God's music" and the other is sort of like "the Devil's music."

EJG: I think the artist must deal with both God and the Devil. [*laughs*] I think you can't put one aside or the other. You know, like if you're going to write for certain groups, and I don't believe in writing for any specific group. So let others call blues the "sin music," and gospel is God's music, just as the minister does in *A Lesson Before Dying*. You know, when they visit Jefferson in jail and he's playing that radio and he's listening to blues, the old man— the minister—says "that sin box." Well, sometimes that sin box can help you get to heaven as well as anything else. That's what I was trying to show. But the artist himself cannot separate the religious or the blues or the spiritual. The artist cannot.

MG: Yes, I think that was always an outside judgment because the artists saw that some of their inspiration for the blues and jazz came from the deeply spiritual.

EJG: Yes, he must—he has to use both of them.

DB: The minister—and that's so beautifully drawn in your various works— has a narrower mission.

EJG: Right. He's there to save the soul, but what about the everyday life? And that's what the artist must deal with. He must deal not only with the soul but with both. That's Grant and the minister's argument. It's Reverend Moses's argument—just as the nihilist and the minister in "The Sky Is Gray."

MG: What you're saying reminds me of the ideas about the nature of religion and the sacred and profane [Emile Durkheim's concept of sacred and profane and Mircea Eliade's *The Sacred and Profane*]. It's all part of life, and you can't completely separate it.

DB: And if you start thinking that there is a separation, then you've in some way desecrated the sacred, and elevated the profane in a way. This may be a silly question, Ernie, but I've often wondered if I were a filmmaker—I remember that scene in the cafe in "The Sky Is Gray" where the man asks the woman to get up to dance and so forth, and when they make the film, of course, the filmmaker has to put a song in there for them to dance to. *And* this is just speculation, and as I said, this may be silly, but if you were consulted by the filmmaker, what are some of the possible songs that you would have had them have on the jukebox. Because I think that's an important way that you—

EJG: Oh, I don't know now if I could just come up with any song. I'm sure if I would think about it for a while, about jazz and stuff, I would come up with the right song, but I can't think of any specific song. I know it should be a sort of slow beat, but I couldn't think of a particular title. You know what happened about this particular scene. The tune that this guy played on that record was written by a friend of the director. That's the music played in the film. It was not a tune that was a traditional one that I knew about, or anyone else knew about. But it was written for this specific film.

MG: One of the things I wanted to ask you about—and again this is in relation to the idea of how art forms express things about life that we perhaps don't see in other media. And again I'm quoting you, and this was in John Lowe's book *Conversations with Ernest Gaines*. In one of the interviews there, you said, ". . . we all are naive about the true history of blacks in this country. We have Du Bois, Douglass, and Booker T. Washington, but we don't have the story of the average black who has lived to be that age" (38). How does *art* (as opposed to straight history) broaden that perspective? How does art, literature, music sort of fill in that story? Do you see art or literature or music as giving us that history that the written historical record doesn't include?

EJG: I think so because you get so much more of the experience of the everyday man, of the common man, in music—especially music, and music is so much out there that you can hear music all the time. You can hear music on the radio, on recordings, so it's always there for you. And it tells you much more about yourself than history books because so many people were not able to read the history books. And music just filled in for them. Literature, I think, was the same thing for those who had the chance, who were able to read. I think now all across the country, in eight or nine different cities, people are discussing *A Lesson Before Dying*. And wherever I go I find people, most often white people, saying, "I did not know this," or "I did not know that, and this changes my life." Someone told me about a year ago, at graduation night, "I just read your book *A Lesson Before Dying*, and it changed my life." Someone told me the same thing in Richmond, Virginia. "It changed my life." Just writing about the everyday people, and literature does that, or literature can do that. A person like Jefferson or a person like Tante Lou or a person like Miss Emma—those people are never written about in a history book. And quite often are never written about in a newspaper, and so literature can bring that to life.

MG: In some ways, that sort of unwritten history, or unwritten in the history book, that sort of thing would have been in oral tradition. In some ways, we've always had the stories in the culture about people like Tante Lou or people like Jefferson, but that often didn't leave that community. That was very local. So it was not known to those people who did not have access to the story in oral tradition. In some ways, the writer gives those stories access to a wider audience (or a wider audience access to those stories), so the writer is more important to the outsider than to the person in the community who at least might have gotten a version of those, who knew more about these. Do you think that's still true for the younger generation? Do they get those things through oral tradition?

EJG: I don't—maybe they get it through that rap. Maybe that's what they're talking about. Maybe—I almost feel that that's what they're talking about. They're communicating something out there for people to be so much impressed by it. As you said, the white kids are doing it. You go to France, you find French kids are doing it. I'm pretty sure they're doing the same thing in Japanese. [*laughs*] So, it is going on. It's something that I cannot understand, but they wouldn't understand—well, I can't say they don't understand me, now because the book is being read from the middle years in school to the university level, and I'm constantly getting letters from the students—teachers make them write the letters—but letters from the students about the book.

DB: I think one of the things that great art always has the potential to do is sort of crack us open in a way—to crack us open and to show us something that we didn't know before, and I think that person at the graduation or that woman in Richmond, you know, were saying that. Because I think we live in a time where we're not aware—that we're living in a time where there's a great need for spiritual rootedness, and I think when they pick up the book and read *A Lesson Before Dying* or "The Sky Is Gray" or one of your other stories, it puts them in touch with—that spiritual rootedness or being rooted in something that is sacred. And I think one of the things that your works do so well is to show that there is a sacredness in the everyday life.

MG: We haven't touched upon the influence of visual art, and—

DB: And you're a photographer.

MG: Yes, and we've talked about how music has influenced you. But what about the visual arts? I know that you're a really great photographer, and the photographs you took, especially at River Lake Plantation, serve as documents in a way. How do you think art, paintings and pictures and photographs—both by other artists and the things you've done—how do you see that, and what does that bring to your whole idea of art?

EJG: Well, the photographs remind me of a time, remind me of a place and of a people, that I write about. Without those photographs, I don't know that I could recall as accurately the things that I'd like to write about. And seeing the paintings by someone like van Gogh—I'm thinking about *The Potato Eaters* now, people sitting around the table. That awakened something in my mind, and I can recall that I did the same thing. There's a lamp on the table, people sitting at the table, blessing the food, eating, and the place. That brings it back to my memory—to what I saw as a child. A workman's shoes, those old muddy shoes, you know, brogans, that snaps my mind back to the past where we wore those same kind of shoes, and I've seen the people kick them off their feet and leave them out on the porch or something like that. Those kinds of things that just remind me of my own past, so I can draw from that.

MG: You've talked about *Vincent's Room [Bedroom in Arles]* and how that sort of gave you an image of the order, of arrangements—

EJG: Ah, yes, I have a picture of *Vincent's Room* in my study out there. Yes, of the minimum of things you actually need to—you can get by with so little. And I try to do that with my work. You don't have to overblow things. I mean, I'm incapable of writing using a broad stroke. I have to use a smaller pen, be very selective. I think I prefer to repeat something three times to get it over than to use a broad pen to get it over.

DB: I'm reading a book right now on Vincent van Gogh, and what you're saying reminds me of something he's saying in that book. He's says that he doesn't—he can admire the beautifully finished and the well-finished painting of the seventeenth century, but what he loves about Rembrandt is that there are parts of it that are unfinished. There are parts of it where you see the brush of the real man in there and that strikes me as sort of close to what you're saying about your stories., that they're about the little things, about the brogan that can bring you to a particular memory or about the potato eaters. And it occurred to me, too, that as you were describing *The Potato Eaters*, when he talks about that painting, he says— you were talking about blessing the food, eating the food—and he says that one of the influences for that painting was Christ at Emmaus, where Christ has to deal with a few of his followers after the Crucifixion and before he is actually ascended. So he sees his painting as a sacred painting, and I thought that was interesting that in what you said, up to this point, about the job of the artist to *marry* the sacred and the everyday, the sacred and the ordinary.

MG: You mentioned the lamp, and I'm sort of fascinated with—we called them coal oil lamps—

EJG: Right, coal oil lamps.

MG: And it's almost a nostalgic thing I have about coal oil lamps. My dad used to sell coal oil in his drugstore. When you have a drugstore in a rural area you sell lots of different things. And one of the big things that people would come to get every day was coal oil to fill the lamps. The coal oil lamps—was that something you had in your home when you were growing up?

EJG: Definitely so. I learned to read with a coal oil lamp. You see, we had no electricity on the plantation until after the war, so that was about '45 or '46, about two years before I left. But for my first twelve years, I'm pretty sure, there was no electricity, so we read by the lamp on the table or the fire in the fireplace.

MG: You know, I was thinking, too, when you were talking about the lamp on the table, and often the coal oil lamp was on the table.

EJG: Right. It was set on the mantle until you had to read or to study, and then you read like that. But when you were there just for illuminating the room, it was on the mantle. The clock would be there, too.

MG: Maybe I'm romanticizing this too much, and I'm thinking of *The Potato Eaters*, where you saw the images, you saw the objects that the light touched, and you didn't see the whole picture.

EJG: Right, the place was transformed by that light. These are kinds of things that I find in the movies as well—and I see what the camera can do. I've been influenced by all of these things. Not one thing or two things, but all of these things. I remember I used to do a lot of walking in San Francisco in the morning, and there was this old man who used to sweep the streets before we got the motorized street sweepers in San Francisco. He used to sweep the streets, and whenever I'd come back from my walk in the park, I'd see him pushing his broom. And, you know, I'd talk about baseball or football or whatever. But he would never leave a piece of paper or a piece of anything without brushing it up and moving it along to pick it up. And I thought it's a wonderful thing that this man, this street sweeper—but he's so particular about everything that he does. That little piece of trash—to be sure that it's done. I feel the same way with my writing. The little things— you be sure that they're corrected. Don't leave it there if it's not necessary. So I learned—you asked if I learned from the visual arts and from music— but I also learned from watching the everyday person, what he does, how he does something. Or watch a great athlete—see how they place themselves, how they do things so smoothly. So, writing, for me, is not just learning from novelists or short story writers, but from all the things around us.

DB: Talking about visuals, it seems to me—and I don't mean in any way to make a statement about your story—but it seems to me in so many of your stories, you get the story right out there right away. You know, like the basic parts of the story. In *A Lesson Before Dying*, right away we know what happened. And it seems like so much of the rest of your story is about drawing characters.

EJG: Yeah, right, that's what it is about. Yes, in the beginning, in the first chapter, you know what has happened and the people that are going to be involved, but the rest of it is, ah—I said one time—Oprah asked me who I was trying to reach, and I said I tried to create characters with character to improve my own character and the character of that person who might read it. So it is what happens to the characters after this tragedy has happened. And the rest of it is—portraits.

DB: When we were talking about visual art, I couldn't help but note thinking about it—one of the things you use to make a story is drawing these portraits. In that book I'm reading about van Gogh, he said the portrait was the thing. He said, "Portraits—that's what I want to do, portraits." And it reminds me of you because that's what you do. In *A Lesson Before Dying*, you know, from the beginning to the end with Miss Emma, for instance, you don't have the complete portrait until the end of the book, and there's the drawing of that portrait, the drawing of Jefferson's portrait. And it's just this beautiful collection of portraits. I felt the same way about *A Gathering of Old Men.*

EJG: Yeah, yeah. I know when I was writing *The Autobiography of Miss Jane Pittman*, I was thinking about titling it *Sketches of a Plantation*. I think what I'm possibly doing is sketching and writing letters. Writing letters is like sketching.

DB: Yeah, and you know I feel that those kinds of group portraits that Rembrandt was so famous for—I know that you're working in a completely different place and you have a different objective, but to me, *A Gathering of Old Men* is as beautiful a collection as is a seventeenth-century group portrait. I don't know who did the cover art, the dust jacket, but it seems to me that they had the idea in mind—of that old seventeenth-century Dutch masters group portrait.

EJG: Right, yes.

DB: Can you talk a little bit more about—I remember you told us one time about listening to classical music and you talked about the music, the Mussorgsky, that you were listening to when you were writing—*Miss Jane Pittman*?

EJG: Right, *Miss Jane Pittman*. I was writing about Miss Jane, and I was listening to *Pictures at an Exhibition*. The structure or frame is of this guy at an exhibition, and he was observing these pictures. And the motif would be as he moved from one picture to another, there was a motif and repetitive theme. At that particular time, I was thinking about writing *Miss Jane* from the single point of view. It wasn't really *Miss Jane Pittman* yet. It was just *Sketches of a Plantation*. That was the original idea. But in order to have a common theme to connect those sketches, well, there would be this little old lady. Just sketches and sketches, and after each book, there would be this huge ending. There are four books—the War Years, Reconstruction, the Plantation, and the Quarters—and each one almost ends up in violence. If you listen to the sketches in *Pictures at an Exhibition*, all of these characters are going through this piece of music. And at the very end, it's loud, loud Russian crazy music. "At Hell's Gate" I think it's called ["The Heroes' Gate in the Imperial City of Kiev" or sometimes called "The Great Gate of Kiev"]. But then I realized that music could only take me so far, and then without anything else, it wasn't going to work. With music, you can learn so much from it, but you could not repeat it in literature exactly as it was there. So I went over it, the sketches of the plantation that I did, the short biography of Miss Jane Pittman that I did, and I realized that I still was not getting the real character that I had to get. So I had to put all of that aside and go back and do *Miss Jane Pittman*. But I started off with that *Pictures at an Exhibition* as the first influence on what I wanted to write about.

DB: I remember, Ernie, that one of the great thrills that I had in listening to *Pictures at an Exhibition* after you talked about what you had done and what your experiences with it had been and everything was to hear the *walking* music in *Pictures at an Exhibition*, and to realize how much walking that little woman did. Because she walks, yes, and that was so exhilarating for me to realize that.

EJG: Well, I got that from—that walking stuff—so much I got from Eudora Welty's "A Worn Path." The walking and walking and walking. And that was also a good influence on my "The Sky Is Gray." The walking and walking and going back and forth.

MG: You both have commented that blues was a good influence on the form you put "The Sky Is Gray" in.

EJG: Oh, yes. "The Sky Is Gray" as well as in *Of Love and Dust*. Especially *Of Love and Dust*, the blues form that's used in Lightnin' Hopkins there. And just one verse from Lightnin' Hopkins:

> The worse thing this black man ever done
> Was move his wife and family to Mr. Tim Moore's farm.
> Mr. Tim Moore's man never stands and grin. [That's the overseer.]
> He said, "You stay out the graveyard, nigger, I'll keep you out the pen."

And so, I took that and dealt with Marcus. He would not go to the grave-yard. I mean he would not be killed, and this guy here would keep him out of the pen. And the next verse was like: "But he wake you up so early in the morning. You catch a mule by his hind leg. [to go to work]." So those two verses were really what pushed the story. And, of course, I knew all the things I could bring in because I had lived on a plantation and I had seen things that happened around me, so I could bring other things into the story—government affairs, and all that stuff.

MG: I remember you saying that in "The Sky Is Gray" indirection, "playing around the note," was an influence from the blues.

EJG: Yes, I said you don't have to do something all the time for it to be effec-tive. You don't have to see them thrown out of a store or a place where they're going to get something to eat up town. You don't have to have that happen in order to get the feeling that this was a segregated world. Some things you don't have to come to directly and scream at. You just play it smoothly, and that is even more painful for you, a reader, to see—this mother and child walking down this cold street without being able to go in to get warm or to get something to eat. It's so much more effective so that—you leave some stuff out. But what you do is get that little line that really shows it exactly—that shows enough—and you leave the other stuff out. At least I feel that way.

MG: Yes. So it's sort of like in blues, you hear the melody. They always come back to it, but they're also going around it. We're seeing all the things related.

EJG: Yeah, right. I was listening to a great solo by Lester Young—ah, playing "My Funny Valentine." And you very seldom hear "My Funny Valentine," but he's playing so much around it that you get a greater feeling for "My Funny Valentine" without really having to sing it. It's things like that I try to do when I'm writing.

DB: It seems that you also use the repetition as a formal device in a story like "The Sky Is Gray" as well with that tooth and the mother and the son. They go in and they're pushed back out. They go in and they're pushed back out.

EJG: Just like in *A Lesson Before Dying*. You don't have to see a guy going to the electric chair. You never see them pulling the thing and all that. That's been done before. You don't have to see it. You know, what I try to do is show the horror of it. Plus the exact way in which they brought the chair in and adjusted the thing, so they had the right corner, the wires in the right place, right near a window but pushed back into a corner, and all these little small details in the preparation to execute somebody. All these little things. To hear the generator from a long distance away. What I think is the most horrible thing is if you're standing up there. And as Paul says, he dropped his head, he lowered his head because he didn't want to look at the thing—directly at the thing—but he heard the noise, and that's much more powerful. That's what I try to capture with this thing.

MG: One of the interesting things about having that kind of thing, like a generator—that struck me, in fact, when we saw the play at UL this fall, is that idea of the "electric chair." The electric chair is so foreign to contemporary students, but then in talking about that, they were asking why there was a generator. Well, I'm not exactly sure, but it occurred to me that electricity was not yet the norm at that time and place. Those were sounds, like the sound of the generator, that were just totally foreign, that they would not have heard anywhere. And the idea of using this as a way of execution when electricity was not yet understood. It was not a part of the average home yet in rural Louisiana. And I think it struck me that the effect on the people witnessing it at that time was probably much greater than looking at it in terms of electricity, which is something taken for granted now. But both the sound [of the generator] and the idea of electricity were not the norm then—and then the *misuse* of it. Something that could be used for good but wasn't really available yet, and then a tremendous misuse of it.

DB: I hadn't thought about that.

EJG: Another situation of getting around the whole thing instead of coming directly on it is the seductive scene between Marcus and Louise in the first scene in *Of Love and Dust*. Marcus is trying to break into the house where they are, and all you can hear is the noise in there and the running around the room in there. That, to me, is stronger than you seeing the physical thing going on. Just hearing this noise through that door and then the silence! You don't hear any noise anymore, and you know they're in there. You know, just playing around it.

MG: I think that playing around the note and the indirection you do so beautifully—and I know you're probably not interested in what the critics are saying—but one of the big things in linguistic anthropology now is the idea of *reported speech* and what happens when the speech is reported by someone else. And I thought how much your novels use that—especially in *Of Love and Dust* but in *A Gathering of Old Men* and *A Lesson Before Dying* as well. And you've said that—that it's not that Grant has experienced it directly, but he reports what is told to him by someone else. I think someone needs to do an article on reported speech in Ernest Gaines's novels.

DB: I was reminded just a while ago when you were talking about Marcus and how a character gets created, and you talked one time about the relationship between Marcus and another important popular culture figure, Muhammad Ali. Could you say a little bit about that?

EJG: Well, when I wrote that book, I wanted for Marcus to be a sort of— with the "gab" of Muhammad Ali, and at the same time I wanted him to be somewhat like a guy I actually knew. And this guy lived in Baton Rouge, one of these Creole guys. And he was tough; this guy really was tough. And he was the kind of guy who could walk into a bar and say, "I can whip any man in the bar." He got into a fight in Baton Rouge, and two guys jumped him. And he got his knife out, and he killed one of the guys. He killed one of the guys and was sent up for seven years in Angola, but he got out in five. And his boss tried to keep him out—they thought he was defending himself, you know. And he had a chance to stay out, but he would not. He refused to stay. He said, "I'm going to pay my dues because I don't want to owe anything." So he went to Angola for five years, and he came back out. And they ran him out of Baton Rouge, ran him out of town, and so he went to Houston, Texas. But the word had gotten to Houston about this guy. He picked up a woman in Houston, and they went to San Francisco. I had known him here in Louisiana, and I used to hang around with him in San Francisco. He'd walk into a bar and say, "I'll whip any man in the bar. Everybody want to fight me?" And I'd say, "Lionel, don't start that." And he'd say, "You scared." And I'd say, "Yes, you damn right. Somebody's going to challenge you, man." So, eventually, he would be killed—someone killed him. As a matter of fact, that happened the same weekend I came down here to start filming *The Autobiography of Miss Jane Pittman*. I had seen him a couple of days before I came down here, and he said, "Boy, I sure would like to be in that picture show. I'd sure like to be in the picture show. You think you could get me a little part in it?" I said, "I don't know." So, he said, "I want to get on down there. Let's me and you get on down—drive down there." He was one of these guys working as a mechanic, and he had a bunch of old cars around the place—all together probably couldn't make one good car. But he wanted to get in one of those old Cadillacs and drive on down. I said, "I'm not going down there like that—probably couldn't get out of San Francisco." And, so I left. I got a flight out, I think, on Thursday. And Saturday, I friend of mine came by to tell me that he had been killed. Anyway, Marcus was sort of based on him, but I wanted Muhammad Ali's gift (or ability) to talk, talk, talk. I was writing *Of Love and Dust* at the same time Muhammad Ali was a young guy. I think he had just changed his name to Muhammad Ali—in the mid-sixties. That would be '66 or '67. So that was based around him. His looks and everything about him—and Lionel had his color and so on, kind of lightish brown. And his looks and clothes—the sharpest thing in the world—and that car dealer out there. So, those two guys I had in mind when I created Marcus.

MG: And Muhammad Ali had that wonderful artistic ability with words. He could have been a poet.

EJG: He was a poet; he was a poet, and he was a great fighter too. And Marcus, too, would fight anybody, day or night. And Lionel was the same.

MG: Was Proctor [in "Three Men"] based on him as well?

EJG: Well, Proctor not as much. But it's the same sort of story. Proctor, you know, he decides he's going to go up, but a Marcus is the sort who says, "I'm not going to Angola. I'm getting out of that place." This is the same sort of story because I had written "Three Men" and offered it for publication in the collection of stories, but Bill Decker, my editor said, "First, give me a novel." So, I said, "Okay"; suppose someone like Proctor would try to get out of what happened. So in the novel, I changed the thing around.

DB: I did think a moment ago when you said that about Muhammad Ali being a poet that you could make a case that Muhammad Ali taught the rappers how to rap.

MG: Yes, because he was the first to put what was always a part of the culture, especially playing the dozen and the rapping, out into the mainstream.

And both because he was already a fighter and he already had the status of a champion, he made it much more acceptable. And then the black comedians took it over. Somebody eventually will do a study tracing how we got to rap. But I think you're right. Ali did have a great influence.

EJG: Yes, and there's a group called "The Last Poets," and they work that kind of music too. And of course many, many years ago you had these groups—I don't think they called it rapping. They called it something else. But they did a lot of this.

DB: I think that what we know now as hip-hop and then rap—it was a long way in coming. The Beat poets were going there with that kind of emphasis on the performance.

EJG: Yeah, right. It's part of this whole thing.

DB: While we're talking about poetry—you know, what a remarkable piece of literature to me is Jefferson's notebook [from *A Lesson Before Dying*], and I think it's one of the great American poems in the last half of the twentieth century. And I just wondered if you could tell us a little bit about how you came to that piece—or what you wanted to do with that piece of writing. Because I think it's in some ways—probably not for you, but for us—in some ways it seems like such a brave piece of writing because the story is being told by people who have different kinds of effectiveness and facility with language. All of a sudden there's this thing that comes up in the book that's disarming because it's so pure and it's so beautiful. And I wonder what you were trying to do—if you could talk a little bit about that.

EJG: I was trying to have this person, this human person, who—within a few weeks of his death—does this thing where he identifies himself as a human being on trial. Everything is "trying" for Jefferson. He tries to say something about himself as a human being. What does he believe in; what does he think? We don't know him, I think, until he starts his diary. We don't know him until we hear him speak. We don't know a man until he speaks. He's trying to say something, to show who he is. We have these pictures of him provided by Grant, but we don't know what's inside of him. And that's what I needed to do. I didn't want any kind of soliloquy, you know, or aria to stop the walk, or when they ask if he has any final words, for him to talk for an hour, and all that stuff. So it was what I knew I had to do. And as I told students, I say it all the time, I had no idea how I would do it when I started to write the book. I had no idea there would be a diary. I had no idea there would be a radio in that story. I've used the analogy many times of getting on the train in San Francisco and going to New York. And you only know so much. You don't know everything. And the radio is one of the things that came up for me on the train trip, and the diary came up for me on that trip. Over a period of seven years. I spent seven-and-a-half years working on the book—'85 to '92. So during those seven years, the idea of the radio and the notebook came up. I suppose if I had written the novel in three years, this wouldn't have happened. I don't know what would have happened. I have no idea. But for seven years I got to stand back and think. And, during the fall, I was teaching and thinking all the time. And then I'd go back to San Francisco and write on that book. And, of course, I came up with the idea of the notebook. But the exact date I came up with it, I don't know. I knew I had to have him say something about his life—about what he believed in, about justice and about God and injustice and everyday routine stuff, you know. What is life about to him? What is meaningful to him? But he had to give us those things himself because he would not reveal himself to Grant or to Miss Emma or to anyone else. He had to give it himself. And he writes it at night when nobody is there. He scratches all over this—writes it so awkward—over the line, under the line, above the line, across the line—he's writing it without punctuation or capitalization or anything. He's just writing it down, trying to say something about his life.

DB: I remember right at the beginning—you know, Grant's been telling us about him all along—and I imagine him writing and not even being really aware of what he's doing in the notebook except trying to express himself. But at the end when he talks about telling Mr. Wiggins that the bluebird is singing, and he returns to the daybreak, which he wrote of in the second entry. That's such a jolting thing, you know, because you think that you've been carried a great distance by this journal writing. This man is about to die, and he knows that's an inevitable thing. And he's hearing birds singing and imagining that they're blue. That's just incredible to hear because the last entries turn the whole piece into a poetic testament.

MG: Yes, definitely. While Darrell was talking about the diary, I got out this other quote from *Porch Talk* where you said:

> I think art is order. I think art must be order, no matter what you do with it. I
> don't care what Picasso did with twisted faces and bodies—all that sort of thing—

I think there has to be a form of order there, or it's not art. The novel to me is art. The short story is art. And there must be order. I don't care what the chaos is. You must put in some kind of decent form. (*Porch Talk with Ernest Gaines* 16–17)

And then you go on to say that to you that's sort of imposing that order on what may seem chaotic. And I think—

EJG: I said that? That's pretty good. [*laughs*] I don't know if I can say something good as that now.

MG: Yeah, isn't that cool—and you said a few good things today too. [*laughs*] And it reminded me of this when we were talking earlier with Darrell about the diary—because you're taking something out of its normal form of written communication, and it at first appears to be chaos—and then you put this order on it, and it just becomes absolutely poetic. And I agree with Darrell. I think it is a form of poetry.

EJG: Right, yes.

DB: You know that kind of slow revelation inside the notebook where he says that he's sorry for having said what he said about Vivian. And then at the end of the story when he goes back to being aware of the outside world again and what's going on outside of his cell, there's that beautiful kind of repetition that brings it all full circle. And the pieces for me are so beautifully constructed. I think the part of the expression that affects me so much as a kind of poem is the way in which the speaker is so unaware in a way of what's being said, but there's a complete human being there. This is the pure voice of the poet speaking in that notebook.

EJG: Yes.

MG: Did you have a sense of—I would think maybe the dates—but did you have any other sense of *how* you were imposing that order on the diary other than dates?

EJG: Well, I thought the diary had to elevate the story. I thought that was the point of elevation. I think the story could not just go—he could not just go as Grant telling it. It had to be—what is that thing Joyce called it— the *epiphany*, the thing that brings everything to light. It's the thing that raises it. It's the thing that—often someone says, "I enjoyed your book." But after you read the diary, if that does not elevate you, then I don't know what else to do.

MG: That's an interesting point, because we think one of the functions of art is that it gives that uplifting—that there is a sense of being enlightened or braced up. And there is that response to the diary.

EJG: That's what I wanted the diary to be—that uplift. He's talking about dying, and "I'm gonna die" and says the bluebird is singing. He pauses for a while and says, "I hear my teeth hitting, and my heart, but I'm strong." When he comes, "I'm going to be brave." All these things—that is the uplifting in his mind. He's not going to be this coward they're going to drag. He's not going to eat a whole gallon of ice cream with a pot spoon. He's going to eat a little Dixie cup. All of these little things elevate him—to salvation, to the uplifting of the soul of that person.

MG: And I think though—I understand from my students and most other people who have talked about it—that few people can get through that diary without tears, but by the end of it, they're uplifted. By having gone through it, they survive it—

EJG: Right, yes. Once you go through it, you feel better.

DB: And that part of the novel serves in the same way or it serves the same purpose—or has the same effect as the spiritual, too, because so often the spiritual is about something that's heavy and burdensome, and then finally we sing it because we know it's going to lift us.

MG: And even if we have tears while we're singing it, we know it's going to lead to uplifting.

EJG: Right.

DB: I have just one more question, but while I was thinking of my last question, you mentioned Joyce's epiphany, and I know Joyce is an important figure for you and an important storyteller. I wondered if you could say a little bit, maybe one or two things that you learned from Joyce.

EJG: The number one thing that I suppose we all—modern and contemporary writers—learned from Joyce is the stream of consciousness. But I learned from Joyce to use—from Joyce and Faulkner—to center your work on an area, and I learned to use his stream of consciousness, too, of course. And then the one-day thing I got from Joyce's *Ulysses*. You can do almost anything you want in that one day. Joyce must have gotten it from Greek tragedy, but I definitely got it from Joyce. And I was trying to do that one-day frame with "A Long Day in November," and I was trying to do it in *A Gathering of Old Men* and in "The Sky Is Gray," how to put the story together. You know, in "The Sky Is Gray," I could have stretched out the story for weeks and months, and *A Gathering of Old Men*, I could have stretched on for months, but I narrowed it down. So that, and the concentration of your work in one locale.

DB: In a lot of ways when I look at your work and I try to see what literary traditions—I think we all work in a kind of a continuum. We try to make art, but whether we're aware of it or not, we're continuing what somebody else started, and for me, I keep seeing Joyce, you know, at the headwaters in your work.

EJG: Right, yes, and like Turgenev, I guess the small chapters and the small books. I think he was my first great influence after reading his *Fathers and Sons*—when I was writing *Catherine Carmier*. But you draw from everybody. I'm drawing from Shakespeare. When I was writing that chapter when Raoul discovers that Catherine is running away with Jackson, you know, I was thinking about *King Lear*. He was just going mad, you know. Raoul is going mad when he realizes that his daughter and his life is running away from him. Writing *In My Father's House*, I had Greek tragedy in mind—the strong man falls, and he can't get up and all this sort of thing. That's why I had such a problem writing that book. [*laughs*] You know, I'm drawing from all of these books I've read, things I've studied in college. I learned from all of that. It's not only one.

MG: Do you think that that is true in your writing now, especially in writing *The Man Who Whipped Children* [Gaines's novel in progress]? Do you think you're drawing from different influences at this stage?

EJG: Yes, I think so. I think that my voice—my particular voice—is the most dull and boring thing in the world. [*laughs*] I have to draw from other people. I have my own story to tell, but I'm constantly getting into the voices of other characters. I don't wish to reach a point where I feel I cannot learn from others. I'm going to always try to learn from others, like my brother, you know, that just lost his wife, and less than two weeks later he had to have his leg amputated. And I'd go in to cheer him up, and he was cheering *me* up all the time. My brother Lionel, you know, *he's funny.* He was telling me the funniest stories about the hospital and some of the people in the hospital.

MG: I agree that's one of the sources—in the oral tradition especially—the great storytellers like Lionel.

EJG: Yes, he is a great storyteller. And he's still telling stories. He was telling me that the doctors told him that they were afraid they would have to take his leg off. And he told the doctor, "I'd rather be up here with one leg than to be down there with two." [*laughs*]

MG: *Down* there? [*laughs*]

DB: That's great. [*laughs*]

EJG: So I told him, I said, "Man, you sure are brave." I don't know what I'd do. I'd have to think about that for a week.

DB: And he could just rattle it off.

MG: And just the way he phrased it.

EJG: His wife had just died a week or so before that. I said, Damn, I know he's always been a braver man than I, but damn! [*laughs*] What you gonna do?

MG: I love that story you told me about when he wanted to get out of the hospital—

EJG: Right, they told him he would leave on Wednesday, and he said, "They better not crawfish on me, or they gonna see a one-leg man on the highway in his wheelchair." He said, "I'm getting on out of here." [laughs] He was telling me a buddy of his the other day was having a heart attack, and they thought he had died. They covered him up with a sheet, and he said they all went out on the porch and everybody was crying and everything. And somebody decided to go back into the house, and this guy was sitting up in the bed. They asked, "You not dead?" [*laughs*] I said to Lionel, "Boy, don't you ever think of anything serious?" He had all those nurses and those doctors in that hospital laughing. He didn't care what he said. I wish I had his courage.

"What Men Dream about Doing": A Conversation with Ernest J. Gaines

Wiley Cash / 2005

From *Mississippi Quarterly* 60:2 (2007): 289–304. Reprinted by permission.

In 1948, at the age of fifteen, Ernest J. Gaines left the False River plantation on which he was born and traveled to California to search for an education unavailable to African Americans in rural Louisiana. He briefly returned to Riverlake Plantation as a young writer from San Francisco in 1963 to reacquaint himself with the land and the people, all the while gathering notes for his first novel, *Catherine Carmier.* In 1981, he began teaching creative writing at the University of Louisiana at Lafayette, just over an hour's drive south of False River. In 2000, he and his wife, Dianne, purchased a strip of riverfront property across the road from Riverlake Plantation and spent quiet weekends and vacations away from the university and the city, always returning to Lafayette and the university-owned home that will forever be known as the Gaines House.

In the fall of 2003, Gaines served his final semester as professor of creative writing. He is now *professor emeritus* and the university's permanent writer-in-residence. At the close of a teaching career that has spanned three decades and led him all over the world, it was no surprise to anyone who knew him that Gaines decided to return home and settle permanently on False River. This final return is significant for a number of reasons but primarily because it is his attempt to "reclaim" the land on which his ancestors worked as slaves and sharecroppers for generations. Since his return he has built a beautiful home and acquired the plantation cemetery that sits a mile behind the still-standing master's house. Each fall on the Saturday closest to All Saints Day, he and Mrs. Gaines host a clean-up event: the descendants of those buried in the cemetery gather to plant shrubs, pull weeds, and fight off the encroaching sugarcane. Gaines also has moved and restored the

church that once sat in the quarters and that served as the schoolhouse in
A Lesson Before Dying and *The Autobiography of Miss Jane Pittman*. It now
rests in his backyard.

I was a student in Gaines's final workshop in the fall of 2003, and I, along
with several of my classmates, developed a close relationship with him and
Mrs. Gaines. We regularly attend the cemetery cleanup and other events
they host at the new house that many now refer to as *la maison entre les
champs et la rivière* or "the house between the fields and the river." Being
there in the cemetery and on the land makes it easy for one to understand
the source of Gaines's stories. The experience is surreal but, because of his
fiction, strangely familiar.

In the following interview, conducted in April 2005 and spring of 2006,
Gaines discusses his retirement and his return to the plantation on which he
was born, and he shares the insight he has gained from witnessing the constant flux in the people and landscape of the state he has come to represent.
Understandably, the most significant of these changes came at the hands of
hurricanes Katrina and Rita. Here Gaines, as he does in his fictional repre-
sentations of rural Louisiana, laments the loss of a culture and people that
are so intrinsically bound to a place that has been forever altered.

Wiley Cash: I want to begin by discussing the two hurricanes, Katrina and
Rita, and the effect they had on you here in False River.
Ernest Gaines: We're about one hundred miles northwest of New Orleans,
so we didn't really feel any impact from Katrina. We had some rain and
some wind but no high storm or anything like that. We had blackouts and
the lights were out for about twelve hours, but that was all from Katrina
here in False River. Rita came up from the east and most of her damage was
done around the Lake Charles area. And we didn't have too many effects
then either because we're northeast of Lake Charles. We had a couple of
dry limbs fall in the cemetery during Rita, but, thankfully, none of the head-
stones were damaged.

WC: How did Katrina affect Mrs. Gaines's family home in New Orleans?
EJG: After the hurricane and flood there was two feet of water in the house.
It's a sturdy, historic home, but the floors and the walls will still have to be
taken out and renovated. Some of the furniture was damaged, and some of
it we just couldn't rescue. But some of it is in storage in New Roads, and
some of it is here in this house. We managed to save some of the stuff. The
home is in mid-town and we had quite a bit of looting, but we don't think it

was done by your regular thief coming in off the street. We had televisions and computers taken, but china and other really valuable things were taken as well, old, personal things that people would have to know were worth more than a television. These kinds of things had been in my wife's family for years, and now they're gone. The police and the fire department came through and cleared all the houses to make sure no one was in them, and it's not like they can lock up behind them when they leave. That kind of thing is just going to happen. But Dianne is a strong woman and a religious person. She wouldn't let something like this stop her. You just save what you can, and then you go on.

WC: Were you surprised at how much more coverage New Orleans got with Katrina than Lake Charles got with Rita? It seemed that the national media focused mainly on New Orleans and Katrina and only partially covered the devastation from Rita.

EJG: The media was already in New Orleans for Katrina when Rita hit, and I think that's what happens when national television focuses heavily on one place; they get burned out. They spent so much time and so much energy in New Orleans that by the time Rita came along they had already told what seemed to them as the bigger story. Katrina was a bigger storm, and it caused much more damage in New Orleans than Rita caused in Lake Charles. I suppose the media felt they had covered the bigger story as they saw it, and Lake Charles seemed like a lesser story to tell. The same thing happened in Mississippi. New Orleans got most of the attention because it is the city the world knows about.

WC: What was it like to have several national and international news agencies call you right after Katrina and ask you for a statement?

EJG: There were several places that called my agent. The Associated Press was one. *National Geographic* was another. The German paper also called and wanted a story. Several of them called and asked for a statement. I knew then that I wasn't in any kind of emotional condition to be written about in the paper. I couldn't have given them anything then.

WC: Did you feel uncomfortable, as if they were asking you to speak as a representative for the state?

EJG: I understood because I have sort of a name and all of my books are about Louisiana, and the press knows about those things. They probably wanted an African American voice or opinion, and I suppose I was the one they wanted to call on. After they'd talked to the mayor and the politicians, I guess they wanted someone from a literary field. I was listening to NPR yesterday, and they were interviewing John Scott, the famous New Orleans artist and sculptor. They were asking him the same sort of questions they probably would have asked me. They asked if New Orleans was going to come back. He said, "Yes, in some ways it is going to come back, but it will never be the same New Orleans again." I feel that same way. In his art he draws from the African American community: the music, the dance, the Mardi Gras, the places people live, the cuisine; this is what he draws from. He said that no matter what they do they aren't going to have that same sort of thing ever again; they won't have those same neighborhoods ever again. I feel that same way. I feel those interviewers wanted me to say things like that, but at that particular time, almost three months ago, I had to look at things and think about them and process them. I couldn't just get on the phone and make statements that soon after the storm.

WC: In the title essay from your new book, *Mozart and Leadbelly*, you write about Bessie Smith and William Faulkner and their portrayals of the Great Flood of 1927. How do you think Katrina and the flood she caused compare to the 1927 flood?

EJG: Other than Katrina and what she did to New Orleans, the 1927 flood had a more tremendous effect on the South than any disaster in history, and just about every blues singer who was worth his or her salt sang about the great flood of '27, just as Faulkner wrote about it in "Old Man." But Faulkner couldn't describe the flood as Bessie Smith could. She did it in twelve lines, and it took Faulkner one hundred pages. Of course they're both talking about the same flood, but one's doing it through music and the other through prose. What she does in those twelve lines Faulkner never could have done in one hundred pages and what he does in one hundred pages she could not do in twelve lines, yet they were both true.

WC: What is it about natural disasters that make them so mythical, especially as compared to man-made disasters, and why are artists like Smith and Faulkner so compelled to portray them?

EJG: Anything that is grand we seem to remember longer, and of course that is where myth comes from. I'm thinking about the *Titanic* and the *Hindenburg*. They've made movie after movie of these things and will continue to make movies about them. Anything on a grand scale we're going to remember, whether it's natural or caused by man. Look at World War II.

We're going to remember that for the rest of our lives. Great myths came out of it. They're still playing with the Civil War, and a lot of people won't let it die. I was listening to the news just yesterday about the rebel flag being flown over at LSU's football games.

WC: After living in San Francisco, can you compare the floods and the hurricanes in the South to the earthquakes in California?

EJG: No, I don't know that you can. I know that there's no comparison between the 1906 quake that just about destroyed San Francisco and the one we had in 1989. People still discuss the 1906 quake in mythical terms, and something about it is in a paper in California every week, just like the flood here is. I was in San Francisco the day after the 1989 quake, and they were still having aftershocks. But it was nothing like what I saw on television with Katrina in New Orleans. I've never seen anything like that. Even the photos I've seen of the destruction of San Francisco after the 1906 quake were nothing compared to what I've seen with Katrina.

WC: Do you think that the South, especially compared to the other regions, has a cultural disposition that causes southerners to view natural disasters in religious and biblical terms?

EJG: I don't think so. You have to understand that every part of the country has its problems. Now we see the Rockies and Colorado and all the snow they've had. The highways are shut down, and you can't go from one place to another. But it's nothing compared to the major catastrophe we had here with Katrina. Nothing compares to that. But you're going to get those catastrophes because they're a part of nature, and I think most people know that.

WC: Because many of them were forced to work in labor camps after the 1927 flood, many African Americans took part in the Great Migration to northern cities to flee, not only racism, but also economic destruction and the possibility of more natural disasters. Do you think we're seeing that again?

EJG: I listen to the radio, and I read the papers. And I know there are those who say, "I want to come back home," and others who say, "No, I will never come back home." I really don't see how they're going to find the same community life they had before because it will never be the same. Their neighbors are going to be different because many of those people didn't own homes because they were renting, and those who owned homes often didn't have insurance. There's nothing for them to come back to. Many of those who left had menial jobs, and maybe they can find those jobs someplace else. It depends on who they were. Dianne's niece, Deborah, took a job outside of Dallas with the same bank, and she doesn't have any plans to come back. But maybe she will come back if they open up a branch again in New Orleans, and she can reclaim the position she had before. A lot of these people who had professional jobs and who can find professional work elsewhere may not return. I don't feel it will ever be the same. The ambiance will not be there.

WC: What kind of city will New Orleans be when all this has passed?

EJG: I think that what's going to happen is that New Orleans is going to be a different city, a smaller city, and it's going to be predominantly white. Whereas the majority of the residents were African American before Katrina, I think it will be the reverse now. There are going to be a lot of people moving into New Orleans to make money because of the name. It was a lovely city because of its history, its architecture, its music, its cuisine, and all of those other things. I'm afraid that so much of that will be lost.

WC: Much of your fiction deals with characters who leave home and then return to find that it does not suit them anymore, not so much because it has changed but because *they* have been altered by city life or education or other factors. Did you ever feel that way when you returned here from San Francisco or Paris or even New Orleans? Did you feel that something was lost when you moved away?

EJG: A lot of things are lost, but I say all the time that my body went to California but my soul did not. I held on to this little piece of earth here. And because of the old people and because of their great faith (they're buried back there a half mile from where we sit) that was the only thing I wrote about. My ties remain here. I never did break those ties. I may not, cannot go along with the old people as I did as a child, or my characters did when they were younger, but the love for them has remained.

WC: When you returned to False River in 1963 you came back from San Francisco to gather ideas for *Catherine Carmier*. On that visit, did you notice that the younger African Americans were leaving the plantations for the cities and universities, and if so, did you try to identify that shift in *Catherine Carmier* through the tension between Jackson and the rest of the community?

EJG: The tension in *Catherine Carmier* that Jackson had toward his people came from the fact that he had gone away and been very well educated and he had come back here and the same problems were going on. The South had not changed at all. Nothing had changed at all. The people were the same. Although the land was shifting with the work, the people were moving from the plantation to sharecropping, to smaller towns, or moving away completely, the attitude was the same. The whites' attitude was the same and the blacks' attitude was the same, especially out in the rural areas. He was so alienated to that now, after those ten years, it brought on the tension between himself and the community as a whole, not only between himself and Raoul, but between himself and the community as a whole.

WC: In her essay "Rootedness: The Ancestor as Foundation" Toni Morrison discusses "discredited knowledge" and the balance between superstition and religion and the more credible, enlightening aspects of education. Do you think Jackson sees religion and the often superstitious tie to the land as "discredited knowledge," as something he can dismiss?

EJG: He saw it as something that no longer gave him that kind of satisfaction, that kind of direction to follow in his life. As a child and for these old people, yes. As a child he did. But after he'd gone away to go to school he could see that something else must direct his life and that was education, not just bluntly, blindly believing religion would carry him and help him as Aunt Charlotte did. He'd changed so much from the way he was as a child there, and he saw in them that they had not changed at all in those last ten years. The world was shifting, and they were still remaining the same people. That was the conflict there. Religion was part of their lives, and he didn't fit in there anymore. In *A Lesson Before Dying* Grant loves his aunt and Jackson loves Aunt Charlotte, but they can no longer communicate the way they did before because of that separation. But when you leave you lose parts of yourself and your relationships in that separation. I felt that loss, too, when I was taken away because I *had* to go because of the lack of education here. But only the body was taken away, and you'll find that in my characters.

WC: Did you feel that it was your job as a writer and native son of this area to chronicle it to ensure that some things about the land, people, and culture would never be lost?

EJG: No, I didn't think that at all. It was something I couldn't get away from. It wasn't a choice at all. It was something that followed me and went along with me. I felt that the old people said, "OK, go away and be educated, but you cannot *leave*. You will never forget us." I could never forget them.

WC: Was it something you felt they chose you to do?

EJG: I don't feel that I was chosen; I feel that I was lucky. I'm not so egotistical to believe that I am better than anybody else or chosen over anybody else. It was something that had to happen. I don't know how to explain it. I don't think that I've written history or described this place as is. I'm a creative writer, and I write stories about my little village. It's my view of things around me. So I never felt like I was a chronicler of this area. I've never felt that way. I try to create stories out of something that could have happened or may have happened or what men dream about doing.

WC: I was at a conference in Baton Rouge where you read "Christ Walked Down Market Street" from *Mozart and Leadbelly*. That story is very different from the stories set here in Louisiana. Did setting the story in San Francisco affect the way you wrote it?

EJG: You know how I started that story. I was teaching at the University of Houston–Downtown. Looking out of the window of my hotel I could see this guy walking by and begging for a handout. His clothes were too big for him, and he was holding them up with one hand and reaching out with the other hand. But I couldn't put that story in Houston because I didn't know enough about Houston. Also, I'd read the story "The Spinoza of Market Street" [Isaac Bashevis Singer], and I loved that title. I loved that title because we have a Market Street in San Francisco. The main street in San Francisco was called Market Street. That just stuck in my mind, this guy walking around. I'd seen people just like that on Market Street in San Francisco. I never thought I'd written a story good enough to be published that was about any place but Louisiana. That's why I wrote that story.

WC: But it's so spiritual and philosophical. Did San Francisco contribute to that?

EJG: In a way, yes. If I knew Houston as well or New Orleans as well, I could have put it in either one of those cities. It didn't have to be in San Francisco. But because there was a place in San Francisco, a Market Street, and because I'd experienced beggars on the streets in San Francisco, on Market Street in San Francisco, it was an easy thing for me to bring it there. I don't know that San Francisco as a city influenced the philosophical nature or the religious symbols. I'd never thought about that until now. I just felt that I could write it about San Francisco because I'd seen that same character on the streets there. I was always handing out coins. The last time I gave a guy a quarter he said, "Thanks, Mr. Rockefeller." I went back and said, "Give me my damn quarter back." He said, "No, no, no." I was always doing that, handing out coins.

WC: What about the conversational nature of that story? It's a first-person narrative, but it's also a conversation. How do you do that, and was it fun?
EJG: It was very simple to do. It was partly to show what kind of guy Christ was. "Sure," he'd say, "I'll buy you a drink." He'd have an interesting story to tell. I'd listen to him. I had no problem doing it. I had fun doing it. There are little tricks to it. It was no problem to write from the point-of-view of that guy telling the story.

WC: It's your favorite story?
EJG: Yes, because it's a great failure. It's not complete, and I'm not satisfied with it. And yet, I love it. I like reading it. I would like to read "Christ Walked Down Market Street" from now on. It's a fun story to read because you don't expect to see Christ in that trench coat, that pinstriped suit, that red tie, and that hat cocked to the right. I don't know how fundamentalist Christians would take it, but I like it.

WC: Are you ready to let it go?
EJG: Yes, but I still feel that it's not done. Just as I feel about *In My Father's House*. I feel that although that book ends, it is still, for me, the most unsatisfying piece of mine.

WC: You would like to think that each book has taught you something about the craft of writing and about yourself as a writer. Your current project, *The Man Who Whipped Children*, what has that taught you about writing and about this area now that you're home?
EJG: I'm afraid that I find myself repeating myself. I think I have a good story there, but I don't think it's ready to come out of me right now. I tried writing that book soon after I finished *A Lesson Before Dying*, and that was in 1993. This is 2005 so it's been twelve years. I wrote on it when we were in France in 1996. I've written on it here, but I've put it down in the last eight, nine, or ten months, maybe longer. Nothing's dragging me back. Building this house has taken a lot of my time. And we've traveled all over the country with *A Lesson Before Dying* because these different cities are reading it and inviting us there. Dianne and I have gone to about twelve different states and cities in the last couple of years.

WC: What does that feel like to go to a city and know that thousands of people have read your novel?

EJG: It's wonderful. This spring I was working in Savannah, Georgia, in a high school with about three hundred students, and they'd all read the book. They were gathered from several schools; there must have been about eight, nine schools. Big yellow school busses were driving up there, and all these kids were coming into the auditorium. It's exciting. I don't know that this has happened to any other writer in the country. I haven't heard of it. It's an exciting thing. You go there, and people from all walks of life have read the book and are talking about the book. Whether they're teachers or students or policemen or doctors or business people or politicians, they're all reading it or discussing it. It's a really exciting thing to have happen.

WC: How does it feel when someone at one of those events comes up to you in awe and says, "*You're* Ernest Gaines."

EJG: I just say, "Hi, how are you?" and I shake your hand and sign your book.

WC: Is that modesty something your aunt instilled in you?

EJG: Maybe it was my auntie. My first agent was like that. She always said, "E., don't get a swell head; don't ever get a swell head. That audience out there can use you like an orange. They'll chew the juice out of the orange and spit it aside. Just be yourself, and just be regular." And I am; I always have been. I never thought about being anything else but regular with my brothers and my friends. I love going to football games and watching things on television just like the rest of the guys. I don't know that I'm all that humble. I know there are writers out there much better than I am. There are conversationalists out there better than I am. My brother Lionel can tell greater jokes than I can.

WC: Speaking of your aunt, where do characters like Miss Jane, Jefferson's aunt, and the mother from "The Sky Is Gray" come from? Where does this strength come from with which you imbue the women in your fiction?

EJG: From my aunt I suppose. She was crippled. She never walked in her life. But she had more strength than anyone else. Morals. Courage. And I think that's where I get what little I have, from my women. I knew other people who were very strong. I had an aunt I used to travel with across Baton Rouge parish who sold cosmetics. You know that stuff that women put on their bodies: perfume, lipstick, cheap stuff. I used to travel with her a lot. She was just a good human being. I knew some good people in my family. She also used to do a lot of shopping for the old people on the plantation, and she would take me with her to go to New Roads to buy things for them. I was the guy who would take it out of the car and to the house, and then we would go to another house and do the same thing. She was just a wonderful human being. Her name was Octavia Jacques. She was just a good human being.

WG: What about James's mother in "The Sky Is Gray"? She's not very nice, but she is very dedicated, especially to him.

EJG: Something about my own mother goes into that character. She would say, "You've got to do those things because you've got to help me. If anything happens to me, you're going to have your brothers, your siblings. You've got to go out and do it." I never could kill anything, but Mama could. I don't think she would have beaten me had I not killed something, but she would have tried to shame me because I'm supposed to do those things. We used to fish together, set traps for birds, crawfish together. I remember one time we were crawfishing in a bayou and my little brother Lionel had his arm down a hole, trying to get something out of the hole. My mother said, "What are you doing?" and Lionel said, "A snake went down there, and I'm trying to get it out." He was going to try and kill it with that little crawfish pole. It was a little stick about this long with a string on it. That's how we used to fish crawfish out of the bayou. My mama hit him with it, "Bam!" "Get your hand out of there!" Lionel was always like that. He loved to kill snakes. If he had nothing else to do he would go look in the woods and find a snake and kill it. He'd get the smallest piece of stick and go up, "Bam! Bam!"

WC: When you're here the guys from False River call you E. J., and I've never heard anyone else call you that.

EJG: My name is Ernest James, and you know how Southerners are. They always use that initial. If you're not Bubba then you're something else. If you're not Bubba, you're E. J. or Junior. I was called E. J. and J. The first time a guy called me Ernie I had no idea who he was talking to. Ernie stuck the first time I went to Vallejo, California. But everybody here has always called me E. J.

WC: You said in the 1960s that you could not have lived in Louisiana and safely written the things about Louisiana that you wrote.

EJG: I suppose that would have been true had I not gone to San Francisco and studied writing and found a library. You see, I could not go to a library here when I was a child in 1948, when I left from here. There was a little library in New Roads, but I couldn't go there.

WC: And now you just read there a few months ago.

EJG: Right. They always want me to read. As a matter of fact, when they opened the new branch of the library, they invited me to read at that opening. When the old library was opened to blacks, they were apprehensive and a bit shy about going into it because they had been denied that right for so many years. They just didn't want to go in that place. So they built a brand new library, and, when they opened it up, I was the first person to come and read. They said, "*You* can bring people in here." That was the first gathering in a library of blacks and whites in this city.

WC: What did it mean to you to do that?

EJG: I was happy to see that mixture of people. I don't want to go to a place where only blacks can show up or only whites can show up. I've been to places like that. We were very proud of what we saw in Savannah and how many blacks there were involved and teaching at Armstrong. It was wonderful to see all those people mixed and they're talking. *A Lesson Before Dying* had brought them together because they'd all read and discussed it. I received a wonderful, just a wonderful letter from Beth Howells at Armstrong. She wrote us just a beautiful letter about how she felt about our being there and about the book and about how it brought people together. It makes you feel so great, that you can bring people together for just a little while and see how they get along. You wonder, "Why can't we do this all the time?" It's a great, great feeling that I had something to do with that.

WC: After coming back and living in Louisiana and being, in some ways, a representative of Louisiana, how have both you and Louisiana changed to accommodate and nurture one another?

EJG: I feel that even before I left here there were some people who wished they could communicate better and gather together and be around people, but at that time our society would not allow people to meet, like you and me. You could come to my house, but I could not go to your house and sit and talk at your dining-room table just as we're doing. So, I just hope that I can contribute something and my wife does as well, both of us together. We go all over the place, and we bring all these different people here to our place. We've had some rich people in this place; people who own big plantation homes have been right here and eaten with us. People who owned this plantation come right here and eat with us, and we take coffee in their place. As long as I'm doing something to contribute, to better relations between people, both black and white, it makes me feel wonderful.

WC: In a 1993 interview, you said the cemetery was the only part of the plantation you would love to buy. And now, twelve years later, your cemetery association owns it. You built this beautiful house, you moved the church from the quarters and restored it. What does it mean to you to be able to do that?

EJG: I feel that I did that, not for myself really, but for my ancestors. My parents and grandparents and aunts and uncles and friends. This is a memorial to them. I could have just as easily stayed at the house in Lafayette. That house was mine for the rest of my life if I wanted to stay there. But once my wife and I got the chance to buy this property we took it. We bought it and built this house. And we have a trailer down the riverbank, and we have a guesthouse over here. This is not just for me. It's for the ancestors and the future, the younger people who will come along. My brothers' children and my brothers' and sister's grandchildren will be able to come here and say, "Our people were slaves here at one time." That makes me feel good, that I can give them something for the future, as well as a memorial to the ones buried back there. When I gave that interview before, when I said that, I had no idea at that particular time that we would get this piece of property here. I had no idea at all that we would ever, ever live here. Yes, I always wanted to preserve that place as long as I could for the people buried back there because, without those people buried back there, I would not be a writer. I would not be the man I am today or a teacher or anything. I don't know what I would do or would have done had it not been for them. I know many people, both white and black, who are very proud about what we have done with the cemetery. I'm sure many of them are proud of what we've done here. Many of these people realize this, and they never ever criticize Ernie Gaines for saying he couldn't go into the library and all that because they know it's fact. They don't tell me, "Be quiet about this stuff." They know the facts. They say, "Yes, it was like that. And we're very proud that he's back." I'm not saying *every* person out there is proud. Most people I know, whites and blacks, are proud that we're here. Like the guy who came up to our table the other day in Lafayette. He said, "Are you guys solving the world's problems over there talking like that?" When I left from here, I could not have sat in there with you. I could not have sat in there at all. It makes you feel good that some things are changing. But as the French said, "The more things change, the more they remain the same." But there are things that are changing. Like yourself. You can ask me things about black religion. Forty or fifty years ago no white guy would ask those kinds of questions.

WC: Did you always know that you were going to come back here?

EJG: I knew I always wanted to, but I never knew that I would come back. Even five years ago, six years ago, I never knew that I would live here. No way. I always wanted to end up in my later years in a small southern town, a university town. I wanted to end up at a place where I could be around a school, and I wanted to be in the South. When this came up in Lafayette in 1981, we just jumped at the chance because I was close to home, and I could come any time I wanted to. Then we saw this piece of property here for sale. We were just lucky at that time. The right place at the right time and the right amount of money. We'd just gotten a MacArthur Grant and *A Lesson Before Dying* had been sold to the film, and after Oprah picked it up it shot to the bestseller list in the *New York Times*. Soon after that the property came up for sale, and we could afford to buy it at that time. We could not afford to buy it before this all happened. It just happened. That's one of the reasons that I know there is a God, and I know that it's not only for me because the old man upstairs knew that I would want it for others. I like being here because my folks never could have lived here, and they never could have come in this house unless they came in the back door with a mop and a broom and a bucket. The reason why I'm here is that I feel that I'm doing something that the old people would have been proud of. That's how I feel about this place. They would be proud. My father and my mother could have sat out there at that river at that trailer and fished there and eaten there. Of course they couldn't do any of that stuff when they left from here back in the 1940s. Others who lived here twenty or thirty years ago could not do that.

WC: You couldn't have imagined it, but now that you've done it, it makes sense.

EJG: Right. I never could have imagined these things happening. I picked cotton here, on this land, right here where we're sitting. My parents cut sugarcane here, pulled corn right here on this piece of earth, on these six acres of land. There was no way in the world they could have thought anything like this could have happened to one of us.

WC: Considering all of the success you've had, who would you be had you never left?

EJG: I don't know how I could have gotten an education had I stayed here. I don't know what would have happened to me. Maybe I could have gone away to get an education at Southern University, or high school in Baton Rouge, but I didn't have anybody in that town at that time with whom I could live. Had I gotten an education and not gone to California, I probably would have ended up teaching in an elementary school or high school or junior high school or something like that. I don't think I would have been a writer. At age fifteen you're hungry and you're young and you're ready to learn. Maybe I would have been able to go to a library here, in New Roads, when I was thirty or forty years old, but at that age, the interest, that burning desire to be a writer, would have passed me by. Maybe I would have discovered something in Baton Rouge or New Orleans. I have no idea.

WC: Do you ever think about it?

EJG: I don't think so. Once I discovered a library and started writing in San Francisco I couldn't think of anything else in the world I wanted to do. Now had I failed there I would probably have ended up teaching there, too. But I was so determined to become that writer that I couldn't afford to fail. I sacrificed everything. I gave myself ten years after leaving Stanford. I said, "I've got to prove it." And they were a tough ten years. I had no idea any of this was going to happen.

The Scribe of River Lake Plantation:
A Conversation with Ernest J. Gaines

Anne Gray Brown / 2006

From *Southern Quarterly* 44:1 (2006): 9–31. Reprinted with permission of *Southern Quarterly*, Dr. Kate Cochran, Editor.

He's your favorite uncle. You know, the one who takes you by the hand and lets you buy anything you want at the candy counter despite the "rules about sweets." He's the one who introduces you to his personal motley crew, a rag-tag bunch, drinking "shooters," slapping the table in a serious game of bid whist being played under the shade tree on a simmering August afternoon and who says, with great pride and a thousand-watt smile, "This is my niece!" He's the one who slips you a few dollars at the family gathering when no one's watching and gives you a nanosecond wink along with a sly grin, silently swearing you to secrecy. And he's the one who always has a gigantic tale that always begins, amid groans and room-exits from relatives and friends, "You know, I knew this fellow one time that . . . ," and you know instinctively that when he finishes the story, everyone will be doubled over in laughter, tears streaming down cheeks, stomachs tightly held, begging him to stop the madness. Or at least take it down a notch. Or two. Saved for the next gathering of the folks.

You claimed him against all others, knowing that you were safe in his company, that no harm would come your way, that with him as chief protector of your youthful exuberance, everything would be all right. He was your human comfort zone, and you embraced the aura of his warmth with carefree abandon.

Meeting Ernest J. Gaines was like reconnecting, after a very long absence, with your favorite uncle, the one who you'd often hear tales about at family gatherings, the one who was ever-present and elusive at the same time. The one who would walk into the room beneath the imaginary halo. You simply couldn't wait to embrace him. But you restrained yourself. After all, you knew that in due time, you'd make that connection.

To be in the presence of Ernest J. Gaines is to be in the presence of your favorite uncle. Only this uncle is a literary icon, a master of the art of storytelling. You know that you're in the sphere of a man of incredible imagination, bravery spoken, kind and generous to a fault. He gives you much reason to believe that with all the work that he's penned over the years, his work still holds a special place in the hearts of his readers, that his characters are not simply fictional constructs but are, in a sense, real people that we have all come to know, love, and respect.

It is no secret that much of Ernest J. Gaines's strength and fortitude are ancestral. He says so and gives homage to the people who came before him. He claims little credit for himself but offers an abundance of authority to *his people*. "I am what I am because of them," says Gaines. To say that he learned much from his people is an understatement. Over the years, he has mastered much, but he is quick to say that he is "still learning" the craft of writing. This writer accepts that argument. It's not kosher to disagree with an icon about the business of his craft.

He grew up on the Point Coupee Plantation in Oscar, Louisiana, where he and his wife, Dianne, currently reside, and it's where he derives his power to tell the riveting narratives that readers have all come to enjoy: the stories of Miss Jane, Jefferson, Reverend Phillip Martin, Chippo Simon, Madame Toussaint, Catherine Carmier, and a host of other characters from his eight works of fiction. While the names of the characters may be the author's invention, their tales are quite frequently reality-based, for we have all encountered a Snookum, a Mary Louise, a Copper Laurent, a Tante Lou, a Miss Merle, and a Reverend Ambrose.

If we've elected to forget that such people exist in our lives, it's because we sometimes don't wish to be reminded of where we come from, how we got there, or what took the bus so long to get to the next station. Gaines does none of this conscientious, deliberate forgetting. He embraces his ancestry proudly, wearing it like a banner across his heart. His letter "A" is prominent, representing the pride and strength of his ancestry, not an ancestry of shame, derision, and despair. Whenever he speaks of the kinfolk on the plantation and of his youthful days spent there, a look of respectful remembrance comes to bear. You can rest assured you're hearing the truth be told.

His canon of work includes the classic novel, *The Autobiography of Miss Jane Pittman*, and the best-selling novel, *A Lesson Before Dying*. Even though at this stage of his life, the author is enjoying the fruits of his labor, he is still involved in literary endeavors, recently speaking at the Rural Life Museum in Baton Rouge as well as writing an essay for *National Geographic*. "The Turtles," Gaines's first published short story, now enjoys a place of historical significance in the canon of his work. The story about a young boy on the threshold of manhood is fifty-years-old. It was first published in *Transfer* magazine [San Francisco State College] in 1956. Last year's release of *Mozart and Leadbelly*, a collection of essays and short stories, speaks to the author's continued dedication to the craft of writing and storytelling.

Over the course of his distinguished career, in addition to being a former professor and writer-in-residence at the University of Louisiana at Lafayette for over twenty years, he has racked up an abundance of honors and awards, most notably the (Louisiana) Governor's Arts Awards Lifetime Achievement Award; the National Humanities Medal Award; the (Paris) Chevalier of the Order of Arts and Letters; the MacArthur Foundation Fellow Award; the National Book Critics Circle Award; the Louisiana Humanist of the Year Award; Honorary Doctor of Letters from Brown University, Louisiana State University, Bard College, and Denison College; the Honorary Doctor of Humane Letters from Whittier College; a Guggenheim Fellowship; a National Endowment for the Arts Award; the National Governors Association Award for Lifetime Achievement to the Arts; and the Southern Book Award for Fiction. He's also a member of the American Academy of Arts and Letters. *A Lesson Before Dying* was nominated for a Pulitzer Prize in Literature.

Ernest J. Gaines is a national treasure. When we met, I called him such. A very modest gentleman, he quickly brushed aside the comment, saying, with quiet laughter, "Oh, I don't know about that." To that very demure response, I must add that not only is he a national treasure, he is also a kind and gentle man with a soulful countenance, one who continues to share his gift of imaginative brilliance with us after all these years. We thank him kindly for his presence of words. That, and, of course, always being the favorite uncle who keeps giving us the tall tales at the gathering of the people.

AGB: Writing is a process of discovery. As a writer, what are you still discovering about yourself?

EJG: I'm still discovering myself. I'm still finding out who I am, I'm still finding out my weakness, my prejudice, my strength. Through my characters, I'm finding myself. I try to create characters *with* character to better understand my own character and maybe help the character of the people who might read me. So I'm still trying to find out more about myself. I think that's what writing is all about, finding out things about oneself. At the same time, of course, you're writing to make money, if you can make money by writing. You're writing to entertain, whether you're writing a short story or mystery story or crime story, whatever you're writing, you're writing to entertain. All the time, however, you're creating characters and creating situations, and if you're sincere with your creation you are searching in ways to understand yourself better.

AGB: Is it safe to say that from your humble beginnings as the unofficial scribe on the False River plantation your career as a writer began? How did the people on the plantation come to know you as the go-to person to write their letters? Can you talk about your "appointment" to this coveted position?
EJG: My aunt raised me. She was crippled; she never did walk. She crawled across the floor all her life, and because she couldn't visit others, the people use to visit our house. They'd sit there and talk and talk and talk all the time. None of these people had ever gone to any school. No education at all. It was my aunt who told me that I should write their letters for them and read their letters for them when they received mail, which I did. They would come over there, and I'd sit on the floor by their chair. Sometimes, if it was a man that I was writing a letter for, he'd sit on the floor or on the porch, or I'd be sitting on the steps. And I'd have my little yellow pencil and write on a tablet this wide, and I'd write their letters. They would know how to *begin* the letter, but they wouldn't know how to proceed. They'd say, for instance, "Hey, Sarah, how are you? I am well. I'm hoping you are the same." And you'd sit there minutes after minutes, and they don't know what to talk about. And they'd say, "Say something about the garden," or "Say something about the field." So, I'd just say, "OK."

So you just try and put it down, and then you read it back, and then, well, they'd say, "Uh-uh, that ain' right!" [*laughs*] So I had those little pencils with those little pink erasers on top, and then you'd put it down again. But they would always call on me. They wouldn't call on my brother. I was the "chosen one" to do those kinds of things. Well, I'm the eldest of my siblings, and of course, I had to take care of my aunt who could not walk. So I started writing like that.

AGB: Long before the published stories and novels, you were the writer *then*.
EJG: I realize *now* that I was writing then, but I didn't know that at the time. I was just doing what I was supposed to do. I was just putting these things down for these people. I was asked recently what is the easiest way for me

to write my stories, and I said, "I write from the 'I' point-of-view," and I also said, "You know, I think I'm still writing those letters for those people." There's an "I" there. I'm still trying to write the letters for the old people. I think so. Because I can't think of anything else to write about, sometimes I go back there in that cemetery and just sit there and look at some of the graves and those tombs, and I think, "If it were not for them, I wouldn't be the writer I am." Well, I know I would not be a writer. They're the ones who started me off when I was very young.

AGB: How does background shape the writer's art?
EJG: You don't write in a void. I need and must have "place" to write about. I can't write about a place I don't know anything about. I can't write about northern Louisiana. I don't care about northern Louisiana. I can't write about New Orleans, although I've written an essay for *National Geographic*. But I've not written anything fictitious about New Orleans because I don't know New Orleans that well. So my background is that I need to know the indigenous things, the fields, the water, the trees, the vegetation, the people, the clothes they wear, what they eat, songs they sing, that sort of thing. For the infinity of the story you need that kind of background. Well, I do. I can't write about any other place. I can't write about Texas or New York or Hollywood. I need that background. There's so much involved in it until it becomes part of me.

AGB: What is it that younger writers can learn from mature writers in terms of structure, character development, style, and technique?
EJG: They can learn all that you have just mentioned! [*laughs*]. It's something that I learned from reading the great classic writers—by reading, say, the Faulkners, by reading the Hemingways, reading the Tolstoys, reading the Chekovs, reading Turgenev, reading Joyce. You know, reading those writers. You learn those things because much of what you think you *might* know to do this work, you soon find out. Writing is much harder than just reading. When you read something, and it comes out very easy you can bet that the writer has spent hours, a long time getting that stuff together to get that sentence right.

AGB: I know that you were influenced by Faulkner's writing. Why were you attracted to his work?
EJG: I don't know that I've been much more influenced by Faulkner any more than, say, a writer like Hemingway or Ivan Turgenev. Well, I should

take that back. Faulkner has an edge over these writers, but it was not totally Faulkner's influence over me for my style of writing. Of course, we write about the South, the Mississippi borders, Louisiana, some of the same kind of characters you'd find in Faulkner's small towns, hanging around the storefronts, working in the fields. You'd find the same sort of characters in Louisiana. Faulkner made me concentrate more on my characters.

He showed me how similar they were, white or black characters in a field. I definitely don't go along with Faulkner's philosophy, his description of the characters, yes. He's a master at capturing that southern dialogue, whether it's white or black. But it was a certain level of dialogue that Faulkner was interested in. He could get the most illiterate of black dialogue, but he was never interested in writing middle-class black or upper-class black dialogue or middle- or upper-class characters.

When it came down to writing about peasant life, life in the fields, or life in a small town among the very poor people, yes, Faulkner had that kind of influence over me. He showed me how to describe the country stores, how people stay around on the porches. I knew that, but I didn't know how to do it on paper until I saw what he had done. Another thing he did was show me how to concentrate in a single area. Well, he'd already gotten that from people like [James] Joyce. So it's come down through the years from Joyce to Faulkner to others to myself, this concentrating on one general area. I definitely learned that from Faulkner as well as from Joyce. So these are some of the things that influence me.

When it came to philosophy and when it came to my characters reacting, it was my judgment as to how my characters would react, not Faulkner's, because I don't know that Faulkner could have created a Marcus in *Of Love and Dust* and a Louise. I don't know that he could have created Miss Jane Pittman. He could have created Dilcey [*The Sound and the Fury*] but not Miss Jane Pittman. Miss Jane, he would not have created her because he never would have walked her by that white man at the very end of the story. So there are certain things, as I've told others, that Faulkner told Dilcey's story from his kitchen, Miss Jane Pittman told her story from her own kitchen, and they were two different stories, two different interpretations, told in two different ways. There were a lot of similarities, but when you get down to the nitty-gritty, there were some differences there.

I remember talking to someone who told me about the interviewing of the ex-slaves for the WPA back in the early thirties, when writers needed work, and a white writer could go up to an old person who'd been enslaved and ask questions, and that person would give a certain kind of answer.

When a black person would go to an ex-slave, someone with whom they could understand and communicate, they'd give a different kind of answer. It was a subtle kind of thing that Miss Jane was different from Dilcey. Faulkner gets Dilcey's story. I get Miss Jane's story. Faulkner got Dilcey's story in his kitchen. I get Miss Jane's story in her kitchen. Dilcey would probably have told me a different story, but I did not create Dilcey. Faulkner created Dilcey. I created Miss Jane Pittman.

AGB: Many of today's writers of color, male and female, do not write the kinds of narratives that speak to the culture of community, the importance of the land, and the integrity of its people. That's why your work is so important. Can you talk about your affection for the land, this region, and growing up here on the plantation?

EJG: I've always had a love for this place. I left here when I was fifteen years old. I had to go because I couldn't attend high school here, I could not go to a library here, and I didn't have any people in a nearby town with whom I could live and go to school. So my folks brought me to California when I was fifteen, but I left an aunt here who had raised me. And I also left other family members here, so I left a part of me here. I've told others that the body went to California, but the soul remained here in Louisiana. I left but I didn't leave. Something kept holding me back, holding me back here.

I could not write about anything except Louisiana, even though I spent most of my time in California. I could not write about anything except the land, the bayous, the rivers, the swamps. I had no interest in anything else. I could only write about the things that my people had experienced, my ancestors had experienced. See, we've lived on this particular plantation here for five generations, and I met some people when I was doing research for *A Gathering of Old Men* who knew my grandparents' grandparents on this same place. So something about it just kept me here. Although I studied creative writing at San Francisco and at Stanford and I knew the bohemian life in San Francisco, I'd been in the Army, so I knew the Army life. When it came down to writing I tried to write stories about those places, but nothing was successful.

The only success was here, and I knew that the reason why, the only thing that I could write about, truly and deeply, and put all my soul into was this subject here. And I knew that it was because I still felt connected to everything here. When I started teaching at UL in 1981, I was near this place, and I was always coming back, always coming back here and talking to the old people. And when my wife and I had a chance to buy a part of this plantation, of course we jumped at the chance and built a house here because I feel that I am still close to the people, my ancestors. They're buried about three-quarters of mile in the cemetery back here.

Now, this is False River here, the fields of False River. I picked cotton right here, on this place, where we're sitting, right here. My mother and father chopped sugarcane here, and my uncles all pulled corn around this area. This is farmland, nothing but farmland. When we bought the place, it was a field. The church school of Grant's is modeled after my church school. It was my church school, you know, six years in it. We moved the church onto this property before we built the house, during the same time. The church was moved here before the house was built. We started building on the house when we moved the church over here. It was in the quarters.

AGB: Now, in terms of the proximity to your present house, where did you live?

EJG: I lived about three hundred yards from where we are now. The Big House from where my grandmother worked for so many years is just up the road here about two hundred yards, so this is where we lived, right here. Maybe Dianne can take you back there to the church, and you can see some of the pictures back there on the wall. But anyway, we moved the church. The church was falling apart, and we asked permission, from the people who owned it on the other side of the plantation, if we could have the church and they said, "Yes." And so we moved it over here and renovated it. All of that keeps me connected to the place and to the people and to my past. When we get together, my friends now, we talk about the times when we lived here.

AGB: Describe your days here as a youngster on the plantation.

EJG: There were many hard days, many mean days. You know, that's why we had about five months of school, because we couldn't go to school when we were needed in the field. In the spring you picked potatoes and pulled onions and whatever else, and in the fall and winter you had to go into the cotton field. We were about seven or eight years old. We were very small children. So those were some terrible, terrible times for us.

There was racism and, of course, everything was segregated at that time. There's still racism, but everything was segregated at that time. I couldn't go to a place and have a decent drink of water or a sandwich or anything like that. At the same time, it seemed like the black people were much closer together. They were constantly helping each other because they knew you couldn't get help out there, so they would help you on the place. So all of that kind of stuff kept me intact with the place, not with the state of Louisiana, but with this general area, because that's where my folks had come from.

I saw some miserable days. My people suffered. Let me put it this way: I am what I am today because of them, and I cannot ever forget that. They suffered but they endured, and I survived. From their endurance, I survived. That's why I can write it in books today as I did for them, the older people, writing letters for them when I was a teenager, well, before I was a teenager, ten or twelve years old. Because of those letters, I suppose, that's why I can write books. So there's that contact, that connection. I've never tried to disconnect myself from my folks or this general area. I'm not saying the South. I'm not saying all of Louisiana. I'm saying this general area here. This place. And this kind of thing I learned from Faulkner. Write truly enough about a single place. But you cannot, of course, truly tell all the stories.

AGB: If we could shift gears a bit here, let's talk about some of your novels. There is, in many of your works, the presence of some form of (or reference to) music. For instance, Jefferson, in *A Lesson Before Dying*, is slightly transformed by the gift of a transistor radio given to him by Grant; there's the great fight scene in the club in *Of Love and Dust*; there's the slow-dance scene in the club with Grant and Vivian in *A Lesson Before Dying*; and there's Reverend Phillip Martin's daughter's piano playing in *In My Father's House*. Why does music have such a prominent place in your work?

EJG: I've always enjoyed music. I play music all the time. Usually in the morning there's a radio station here that plays three hours of classical music beginning at ten and ending at one. My wife and I both listen to it. Then, the station plays something else. But music's around all the time. Music has always been around me, both in the country as well as when I lived in San Francisco. So it just naturally comes into my writing. I think I've been influenced by African American music much more than by African American literature because I never studied a variety of fiction writing or any other writing by African American writers.

During the time I was in high school and college the American white writers or the European white writers were the writers that I studied; their work is what I was taught. But the music was always there at home. Gospel music or blues music or jazz music was always there. Even when I was a small child, music was always around me, so music has just naturally come into the work. Formal music is represented by Mozart, but the music that I grew up listening to, the music that my folks have all listened to is the music of Leadbelly, Bessie Smith, and these people. And there's the jazz music of Count Basie, Louis Armstrong, and others. No, I could not live without music. I love music.

AGB: You mention that you were influenced much more by African American music than you were by African American literature. Now, in terms of your lack of an active physical presence in the civil rights protests in California during the sixties, you were greatly criticized for not being more visible and for not being a protest writer. I believe that your work speaks to the same issues that the more vocal members of the community were visibly protesting: racism, poverty, class, and gender issues. How did you handle the criticism, and did you ever attempt to write a novel, aside from *The Autobiography of Miss Jane Pittman*, that spoke directly to the issues I've mentioned?

EJG: I could not write the novels of Baldwin or Richard Wright, although I came from the South. When I left the South, I didn't go to that mean world that Wright ended up in. I went to a small town in Vallejo, California. I went to an integrated neighborhood. My junior high school, high school, and junior college were all totally integrated. As I said earlier, I left a place I loved very much. I have protest in my stories.

If you look at the very first story that I published internationally, "The Sky Is Gray," where those people have to walk up and down the cold street in the town, if that is not protest, I don't know what protest is. Those people are cold; those people are hungry. This child is in pain; the mother is in pain. Isn't that protest? Isn't that protest? What am I supposed to do? Get thrown out of a restaurant or start a demonstration in front of the courthouse or something like that? The struggle was showing the only way I know how to work to better my conditions.

AGB: I suppose those who criticized your physical absence in the civil rights protests wanted all of the protest writers to be Stokely Carmichaels *on paper* or H. Rap Browns *on paper* or Huey P. Newtons *on paper*, and when you protested in a different forum, well, I presume that your writings were seen as short stories that did not mean much because there could be no verbal chanting of the Carmichael/Brown/Newton nature.

EJG: Take for instance the short story, "Just Like a Tree." "Just Like a Tree" is a protest story. Here's this woman from the North coming to get her aunt because of the violence that's going on down there, and the young man coming to tell her, "I know the bombing is going on, and I know they want me to stop, but I cannot stop. I must continue to protest." I was writing those stories back in the sixties. "The Sky Is Gray" was written in '62; it was published in *Negro Digest* in '63.

AGB: I remember *Negro Digest* and, as I recall, the publication was a "protest" kind of publication.

EJG: Yes! And Hoyt Fuller at that time was selling that story as a protest story. I remember when *The Autobiography of Miss Jane Pittman* first came out, one person who reviewed the book for a Chicago paper, one of these "Chicago intellectuals," said she couldn't see anything in that story until she got to the very last book of the story, the last part of the story where this little fellow, Jimmy, goes out in the protest. But she didn't see how Miss Jane had survived all those years and years and years to come to the point where she could teach this young man to go out and do those kinds of things.

This person who reviewed the book had never seen anything like it. Miss Jane was not protesting enough. I said, "Well, how do you deal with those people like that?" You know, I just continue to write. I write as well as I possibly can write. I don't care what other people think. I've never felt that I had to answer any letters or anything when they wrote criticisms of or critical things about my work. I had other things to do. But I think many of them are coming around and seeing now what I have done. At the time, no, they could not accept it. I was not "black" enough.

AGB: Yes. Yes. Look at where your work is and how it's viewed, and the canon of your work and all that. Look at the longevity of your work. You have to listen to your heart.

EJG: Yes. I think *The Autobiography of Miss Jane Pittman* has proven me right for continuing to write other stories. But I used to tell people that every time I'd heard what Bull Connor had done with his prongs and his dogs and with his hoses, I'd try and write a better paragraph that day. I'd say that I was going to write a better, stronger page today. I'm going to beat him, and this is my protest.

AGB: Even as a teenager, when I initially read *The Autobiography of Miss Jane Pittman*, I thought the story was protest writing. I didn't know at the time that there was a term, so to speak, for this kind of writing, but I remember calling it "strong storytelling." I'd always been a reader and had, as a teen, started reading Wright, Baldwin, Cleaver, and others, but when I read *The Autobiography of Miss Jane Pittman*, I felt that the storytelling format would make for its perseverance. When I was ten years old, I read Ethel Waters's autobiography, *His Eye Is on the Sparrow*, in a couple days. Even at that young age my reading interests had started to shift, and I'd started paying more attention to the writers and the writing that seemed to speak to me. Waters's autobiography was about survival.

EJG: Yes, yes. What's so great about *The Autobiography of Miss Jane Pittman* is that if anybody can survive in this mad, crazy, racist, segregated world to be one hundred ten years old and still appreciate ice cream that is what I consider heroic. Those are the heroes that I admire because those were the ones that would help me up here, to help me get to the shoulders so that I can be able to talk to you. Not many of us can survive, not many of us are willing to survive for our children to the point that we can live to be one hundred years old.

AGB: Let's talk briefly about your thematic treatment of father and son separations. The theme governs many of your short stories, from "The Sky Is Gray" to the title story in *Bloodline*, to your signature novel of father and son separation, *In My Father's House*. Why is so much of your work devoted to the theme of absent fathers?

EJG: Fathers and sons were brought here in chains and then separated on the auction block in slave-holding places. I don't think that they've made a connection since. Too often our fathers cannot help the sons. African American fathers do not send us to war. They're very seldom our judges when we're standing at trial. They're not often our doctors. They don't represent us when we're in the courtroom. We often blame him without realizing that he's never been given that opportunity to defend us. We've fought in every war that this country has ever had, beginning with the War of Independence, and yet, when it comes to defending our families, our children, our wives, some way or another the white man makes all of those decisions, and that separates father and son. You know, "I can't depend on my father to save me, and I need you to save me."

AGB: Can you discuss the thematic parallels of the closing lines in "The Turtles" and "The Sky Is Gray," where each parent tells their young son that he, the child, is a man?

EJG: You get the same thing with *A Lesson Before Dying*. Tante Lou wants Jefferson to stand up like a man. In *A Gathering of Old Men* when Charlie runs away, and he comes back and tells them all, "I'm a man now. You call me 'Mister.' It's not your old 'Charlie' anymore. I'm a man, and you'll treat me like I'm a man."

In reading so much about why young black men are in prison today, so many are fighting over their manhood in the black community, they're fighting over their woman: "You're not treating me as a man," or they're knocking this woman around because she's not treating him like a man. So much of it is our psyche: "I've got to be a man, I've got to be a man, I've got to be a man." And of course, our mothers, when we're born, it's "my little man." And we want him to be a better person than his father: "You're the man. You're the man. You're the man of the house."

In *In My Father's House*, Robert X does not kill the guy, and his younger brother kills the guy who rapes his sister. And he's "the man." He's the man of the house now. Robert X turns against his father because he feels that his father should have been there, but it's his own guilt that causes him to blame the father for not being there to protect them. So the "man stuff" is always around. I think I try and put it in my writing as much as I possibly can.

AGB: Can you talk briefly about your relationship with Dorothea "Stinker" Oppenheimer, your literary agent? How critical and brutal was she in terms of the work that you submitted to her?

EJG: I don't think she intended to be brutal. I just think that she was trying to make me a better writer. She would comment on incomplete stuff, well, it could be incomplete, but if she thought that I could do much better, then she was sure going to use that little red pencil! [*laughs*]. But she was my confidante; she was everything to me. We had an association for thirty-one years, from 1956 to 1987. She died in 1987. The first story that she read was "The Turtles."

It was published in a little literary magazine at San Francisco State, and she was just beginning her agency in San Francisco at the time. She got in touch with one of my teachers, and my teacher said to me, "There's a literary agent, a little old lady who's looking for writers. She'd like to meet you and talk to you." And she saw "The Turtles," and she said that she loved that story. She told me, "Whenever you write another story or anything like that, always send it to me." And that was the beginning.

She went to San Francisco when she was a teenager, and she'd gone to one of the better schools back east. I think it was either Vassar or Radcliffe. She was extremely well educated, and she loved music. She made me aware of classical music because I used to go to her place all the time. She lived in Pacific Heights there in San Francisco. There was this big radio, this giant radio, and she'd always play this classical music because we had all those radio stations there in San Francisco that played music all the time. I was always surrounded by music. When I'd go back home, I would play jazz or something else. But the music was there in her place, and we'd sit around and talk.

But when it came down to writing, she'd say, "E, listen, this is not up to par yet. I know you can write because I read 'The Turtles.'" Someone once told me that "The Turtles" was the *best* thing that I had ever written and after that was *The Autobiography of Miss Jane Pittman.* I said, "Come on! 'The Turtles' don't come close!" But they said, "Oh, yes! It's the best thing that you've ever done!" [*laughs*]

AGB: Why was *In My Father's House* your most difficult story to write? Were you satisfied with the ending, or were you simply exhausted, after seven years, of telling Phillip's story of redemption, assuming, in fact, that he did indeed redeem himself. Where were you trying to take Rev. Phillip Martin?

EJG: I write better in the first-person point of view, but I couldn't tell this story in the first person because I couldn't have Robert X tell his own story. I had to have someone else talk about Robert X. I had to have someone else talk about Phillip Martin. So I had to tell the story either by third person or totally from the omniscient point of view. I tried several points of view to tell the story, but none of them were successful. I finally ended up with the omniscient. I feel that it is not up to par with my other works because I have some difficulty with the omniscient point of view.

But that was not the only problem. The problem was how to have Phillip Martin redeem himself or what would Robert X end up doing: going back or making an attempt to kill his father or [figuring out] exactly what was going to happen, and I had all kinds of problems with that book. It was a book that I had to get right, after I'd finished *The Autobiography of Miss Jane Pittman.* I wanted to go further, but it seemed like this book kept getting in the way.

As I've said in interviews, as I may have said in the story, the father and son were separated during the time of slavery, and still, to this date, they have not really reconnected. And there's that difficulty there, and I was trying to resolve that. In the conflict between Phillip Martin and Robert X, there's a conflict that I'm not satisfied that I resolved. I don't know if it's possible to resolve or to be resolved. So it was a problem. I was never absolutely satisfied at all with what I did with the book, whether I'm working with the omniscient point of view or with the plot of the story. I wasn't very satisfied. After seven years, I just thought, well, I'd done as well as I could possibly ever do with this.

I'd tried rewriting it from so many different points of view. I tried writing it from Chippo Simon's point of view. I tried writing it from multiple points of view, but nothing was coming for me. So I just said, "OK, I'm going with the omniscient point of view, and I'll go as far as I can with that." And then, after seven years of it, I just said that I'd had enough of it.

AGB: Near the end of *A Lesson Before Dying*, in "Jefferson's Diary," you make an immediate shift from standard, conventional English to a phonetic rendering. To me, that transition and that chapter are the most powerful part of the novel. Can you discuss the significance of this inclusion and the importance of Jefferson's voice?

EJG: Well, before the chapter we don't know too much about him. We are getting some information through Grant, but we don't know enough about him. And I didn't want him trying to explain himself just before he was going to be executed. No final words. I didn't want that sort of stuff. So what I thought, what you give, is an entire chapter devoted to his thinking. The question was how do you do that? I said, Well, just let him tell it; let him tell the story. Let him tell it, and let him tell it in his own way. And so that's why the notebook comes into the story. I needed him to talk. I wanted him to do it in the only way that was possible for him to do it.

Jefferson has limited education and a limited vocabulary. Everything about him was limited. At one time I thought, Well—this was after I'd written the diary—I thought maybe I should have written it in a different handwriting, perhaps in a cursive handwriting. We hear about how everyone feels about Jefferson. We hear how Aunt Emma feels, we hear how Tante Lou feels, we hear how the sheriff feels, we hear how Grant feels, and we even hear how the children feel. But we never hear how Jefferson feels.

We never hear Jefferson's voice. It is the uplift of everything. Someone has said that "Jefferson's Diary" is such a sad story. I said, "No! Once you read 'Jefferson's Diary' it's uplifted your heart, if you had a heart." He's uplifted you, and he tells you how he feels. That is the turning point, that little "light" that Joyce speaks of, that epiphany. That brings light to the entire story.

You know, I've been asked if it was difficult to write that particular chapter, and I've said, "No. Once I decided how I was going to do it, it wasn't difficult at all to write it, to use the language that he would use, to write with no punctuation or capitalization." It wasn't difficult because he probably would not have known how to do that. By the time I came to writing this chapter, I'd been with him for about five years because it took me over a period of seven years to write the book, but I was only writing half that time a year.

The rest of the time I was not writing. I was teaching over at UL, and when I was not teaching over at UL at Lafayette, I was in San Francisco writing the book. So I knew his language because I'd been around him for about five years in that jail cell, and if you live around someone in a jail cell for about five years you'll learn something about them. So it was no problem writing it.

I was concerned, though, when I'd finished writing it, when I sent it to New York. I asked my editor, Ash Green, if he had a problem reading it, and he said, "No." I said, "Thank God," because I was worried that the way it was written, that people would say that they couldn't understand it, that they would say that they couldn't understand this dialect, that they didn't care for dialect, but that was the great uplift of the book. One critic said that the rest of the book is "typical Gaines," but this particular chapter is vintage. From this chapter onward, it just goes over and over and over.

Well, after that chapter, that's when the preparation for the execution takes place. But that chapter should uplift you to the rest of that book. Many people have said how they wept and wept and wept. Yes, well, I've wept there, too, at the play. I've seen the play about a dozen times in different parts of the country. It's very powerful at the very end.

AGB: Now, the opening line in *A Lesson Before Dying* is such a profound statement: "I was not there, yet I was there." Did you have to ponder long and hard to come up with such a wonderful opening line?

EJG: I don't think that I had to think too hard on that. I knew that Grant was going to tell the story, but I knew that he didn't want to be anywhere near it. He didn't want to be involved in it, directly involved in it, but he was always involved. He doesn't want to be there, but he's there.

AGB: The women in your novels, as well as your short stories, are presented as strong, independent, and, in many cases, domineering figures. How reflective are these fictional constructs to the real life women who were in your life in Pointe Coupee?

EJG: My aunt, who could not walk, raised us. She cooked for us. We had to bring everything to her. We had a little wood-burning stove for food, for meat or vegetables or whatever it was that she was cooking that day, and we had to sit it right before her. She sat on a little bench by the stove, and another little bench in front of her, she used as a table. She'd cut up the vegetables and the meat, and then she could put it over in the pot on the stove. She washed our clothes. We had to bring everything to her. We had an old washtub at that time.

We brought the water, the old washboard, the soap, and everything. She sat on the little bench there by the stove, and she would brace herself against the rim of the tub and wash the clothes on the board. Then she would rinse the clothes and the children would go out and hang the clothes on the line. She disciplined us. We had to bring our own switch and get down on our knees before her and take our punishment that way.

AGB: I'm sure she said, or, of course, you automatically knew that you shouldn't bring back the tiniest thing. You knew to bring back a switch "of substance," didn't you?

EJG: Oh, yes! [*laughs*] If you brought back a tiny switch, she'd send you back to get another one. I had a brother who'd bring back the tiniest one, and she'd say, "Go back, go back, go back!" And he'd go back two or three times to get the right size. She used to work in her garden, a little garden beside the house, and she would crawl over the floor and down the steps, across the yard right to the vegetable garden. Then she'd work in her little vegetable garden. There, she'd work. She had this little hoe, and she'd work among her vegetables, her cucumbers or tomatoes or beans or peas or okra or whatever we had in the garden at that time of the year. She would work among that. She had to put her hand to the earth. She needed to put her hand to the earth.

During the pecan season she'd crawl over the back yard with a little sack, dragging a little flour sack or a little rice sack, and she'd find pecans under the tree and bring them back inside and crack pecans and make pecan pralines. With all those obstacles, she was the strongest person I've ever known in my life, and I think, most of the women in my books are, somewhat, part of my aunt. No one was based on her, but several people have said that Miss Jane Pittman is the story of my aunt. But Miss Jane Pittman is not. Miss Jane Pittman tried to do all kinds of crazy things, but my aunt could never do those things because she was crippled. So Miss Jane is not my aunt, but Miss Jane has a lot of the fortitude and strength of my aunt, letting nothing in the world get into the way of her continuing her life.

When it was cold in the winter, I would, because I was the eldest of my siblings, get out and start a fire in the fireplace to warm the floor by the time she'd get out of bed, because her bed was right by the fireplace. I'd have the floor warm by the time she got out of bed to crawl over the floor to the kitchen. I was raised by my aunt the first fifteen-and-one-half years of my life. She was religious, although she couldn't go to church. She would sing a little song. And the minister would come by and talk to her, and the deacons would come by and talk to her. The women in my novels, I suppose, are based somewhat *around* her, not entirely, though. But her strength, I gave to them. I've known other strong black women. My mother was quite strong, I think, as was my grandmother. On that plantation there were very strong people.

AGB: Your work graciously honors the spiritual lives of your ancestors on the Pointe Coupee plantation. How strong a bearing does your ancestors' spirit have on you, not as a writer but as a man?

EJG: My aunt, who raised me, made me what I am, both as a man and as a writer. It was my aunt, more than anyone else, the way she was and the way she raised me to be. She's the great role model in my life, more than my mother or father or my stepfather or the writers I've read or the people I've met. My aunt was a real role model in my life.

AGB: Can you talk a little about the beautification ceremony that's held on the ancestral burial grounds every October here in Oscar?

EJG: Yes. It's a Beautification Day, the Saturday before Halloween. It's in the cemetery back here, about three-quarters of a mile from where we are right here. We ask the people whose ancestors are buried back there to come around and cut grass or plant flowers or wash the tombs. But we [Gaines and his wife, Dianne] keep it up, year round. We keep the cemetery up, but we just want to get a gathering of the people, a kind of gathering of the masses, the descendants here, once a year. The rest of the time we try and do it ourselves.

AGB: Are you satisfied with your journey from plantation scribe to the publication of *Mozart and Leadbelly*?

EJG: Am I satisfied? Oh, I think I've done some things, but I think I should have done more. I should have done more. I could have done more. There are so many "ifs, ifs, ifs." If I could have gone to the library when I was six years old rather than when I was sixteen years old, I could have done much more. If I'd worked harder the last twenty years than I've been working, I could have done more. I could have, and that's my only regret, that I didn't work quite as hard as I should have. Yes, I'm satisfied with some of my accomplishments, but I think they should be better.

Working from Home:
An Interview with Ernest J. Gaines

C. E. Richard and Marcia Gaudet / 2007

From Baton Rouge Area Foundation *Currents* Q4 (2007): 23–28. Reprinted by permission.

"I think it's the greatest six acres of land on earth. I wouldn't exchange it for anything else in the world," said Ernest J. Gaines, looking out the window from the office in his new home. "From here, I can look back at the church, and beyond the church to the trees back in the cemetery. You know, they've cut some of the sugarcane down, so I can see the trees in the cemetery back there now. I love this."

Six years ago, Gaines and his wife, Dianne, began building a home on the same piece of False River plantation acreage where he grew up, in the heart of the place that has served as the principal setting for most of his stories—a body of work that includes more than ten books and earned him a nomination for the Nobel Prize for Literature in 2004. "I picked cotton exactly where I'm sitting now," Gaines said.

After he retired as writer-in-residence at the University of Louisiana at Lafayette, Gaines moved back to Pointe Coupée Parish, outside Baton Rouge, and renewed his relationship with the same plot of oak-shaded earth that he and his family tilled for generations as sharecroppers. Gaines's relationship with the land now is a more equitable one; he doesn't have to wrestle cotton or corn from it the way so many of his forebears did, pleading their survival from the dirt. He owns this land.

"So, yes, that definitely brings satisfaction," he said. "To be able to have a little piece of this place where my folks worked for more than the last hundred years—and I know they never could've owned anything themselves."

Still, in the course of any conversation with him, it quickly becomes apparent that he is no less bound to this place than those who came before him.

On the Land

Earlier this year, Marcia Gaudet, from the University of Louisiana at Lafayette, drove out to visit Gaines at his home in Pointe Coupée. Along with colleagues Wiley Cash and Reggie Young, she is working on a book titled *This Louisiana Thing That Drives Me: The Legacy of Ernest J. Gaines*. Research for the book has given Gaudet a good excuse to visit the writer who has been a dear friend since he first came to UL Lafayette in 1981. Mail still arrives at the university for Gaines, so this time Gaudet arrived at his home with a stack of letters. Among them was one from Wendell Berry.

Berry and Gaines have known each other since their days together in the creative writing workshop at Stanford nearly fifty years ago. Berry, who farms family land in Henry County, Kentucky, is the author of dozens of books, most of which address the theme of people's relationship to the land and their past. Gaudet asked Gaines about the letter he'd received from his friend. In it, Wendell Berry professes a greater kinship with Ernest Gaines's work than any other living writer's.

"I think it's because we both knew the talk of old people," Berry's letter reads. "Old country people, in summer evenings." Later, Gaines caught himself laughing gently.

Gaines: Wendell gave a lecture at the Fellowship of Southern Writers in Chattanooga three or four months ago, and he used a little quote from my work, from *In My Father's House*, in his speech. But sometimes I think Wendell picks what he wants in my work. For example, in his speech he says that I—that the machine destroyed the people and ran the people away from the land. Well, if you had to pick cotton eight hours a day, in hundred-degree weather, you'd wish for a machine that could do this kind of work so you could do something else.

What happened was, yes, the machine did take their work, and the people did leave. And they went to the towns without any kind of skills that would be useful for working in the city. And so many of them ended up in prison, in poverty, in prostitution and drugs. Much of this happened, yes. However, I think it's the result of not being prepared to go to these places. The machine had come in and destroyed these things, like working in the fields, but it had not prepared the people for something else to do. You see the same thing in John Steinbeck's *The Grapes of Wrath*. The machines come in, put these people out of their houses, and put them on the road, looking for something and not finding it.

So Wendell and I do share a love of the land, of course. He and I are good friends. But, you know, Wendell is still working with horses in his fields on his farm. Big horses. I never had a big horse. When I picked cotton, I had to put that sack on my shoulder and pull. And many, many days I suppose I wished for machines to do this kind of work.

On the Writer's Education

As a writer, Gaines's relationship with his ancestral home near False River has been complicated and, at times, contradictory. "Fortunately for me, my folks took me away from here when I was fifteen and put me in school in California," he remarked. "As I've said many times before, the two greatest moves I've made was on the day I left Louisiana in '48 and on the day I came back to Louisiana in '63."

Not unlike the children in *A Lesson Before Dying*, Gaines's early schooling took place in the plantation church, where an itinerant teacher would come to deliver lessons for a few months at a time, according to the seasons of planting and harvesting. Education beyond the eighth grade was not available to black students in Pointe Coupée Parish at that time. World War II had brought his stepfather to California, so, when they were able to, Gaines's parents brought him out west to join them. There, he would go on to attend San Francisco State University and Stanford.

What brought him back to Louisiana in January 1963 was the news in fall 1962 that James Meredith had successfully challenged legal segregation in attending the University of Mississippi at Oxford; Meredith had won for himself the right to an equal education in his home state. Gaines took this as a sign that, perhaps, the South was beginning to offer black young people the kind of learning that he had left his home to find elsewhere. Then, too, he understood well that, as a writer, there was another kind of learning that he would only find back on False River.

Gaines: The young writer finds his education both in the library and in the people around him. I've talked about this in *Mozart and Leadbelly*: Mozart is a symbol for *form*, which you pick up in books of all kinds in the library; and Leadbelly is a symbol of the *source* for my work. That is, I learned both from the books I studied at San Francisco State, at Stanford, as well as from the people here, on this plantation, during my days growing up, the first fifteen years of my life. And then, later, coming back here a couple times a year. I learned as much about writing here, by just being around those people and talking to them, listening to them, listening to the music.

The white writers' novels—because I only studied white writers in college, and then many libraries really only carried the work of white writers at that time—I needed their form, their direction, in creating novels and short stories. But they couldn't give me the source I needed; that had to come from the people. I needed the Leadbellies. And I was constantly referring to the music, to the spirituals, to gospel, the blues, to jazz.

I remember, whenever I'd come back from San Francisco to Baton Rouge, I would always go to nightclubs with my uncles. On Sundays Baton Rouge was dry, so we had to leave town, go across the river to Port Allen to a joint, to drink and talk. Some of those places were pretty rough, and I saw some pretty rough things happen in them, which gave me a source for *Of Love and Dust*, as well as "Three Men" in my *Bloodline* stories. So this is a sort of education that you get as well. I experienced both the book—Mozart—and the source: Leadbelly. I needed both of them.

On the Ernest J. Gaines Award for Literary Excellence

Gaines's formation as a writer also benefited from his receipt of several important literary awards, beginning with a fellowship in Stanford University's creative writing program in 1958 under Wallace Stegner. There, he joined other young writers whose work would likewise become widely read favorites, including Ken Kesey, Wendell Berry, Tillie Olsen, Larry McMurtry, and Bill and Gloria Broder. "It was a wonderful class to be in at that time," Gaines remembered. "And there were many, many others through the years at Stanford. Stegner had that nose for picking out talent and bringing them there and giving them a year to work."

With no curriculum requirements, that fellowship provided Gaines with several vital resources: a stipend to live on, regular contact with other working writers, and the one luxury most coveted by all writers: time to work. Recognizing how important such literary awards have been in facilitating Gaines's career, the Baton Rouge Area Foundation established a $10,000 prize in his honor, to be awarded annually to promising African American fiction writers.

Gaines: I know what it means to a young writer to receive these kinds of awards. I received an award by going to Stanford, just one year after graduating from San Francisco State. And then, while I was at Stanford I started writing another novel, called *Catherine Carmier*, and I received the Jackson Award there in San Francisco for that. So, yes, I know what it means to receive those kinds of funds when you're starting out. It encourages you, and it helps you, too, when, as in my case, you don't have a lot of money to begin with. Why, when I was there at Stanford, I would work eight hours a day. I'd get up in the morning, go to breakfast, work until noon, come back from lunch, work until dinner at night, and sometimes after dinner. It always helps when someone gives you that chance to write.

But also it encourages the young writer because he finds that someone is interested and feels he's doing something worthwhile. And that's what young writers really need. It tells a writer that he's doing something worthwhile. Of course, if somebody's going to be a writer, he's going to be a writer anyway, whether you tell him that or not. But it always helps, and I had that.

On His Readers

His success with novels like *The Autobiography of Miss Jane Pittman*, *A Gathering of Old Men*, and *A Lesson Before Dying* has placed Ernest Gaines among America's most highly regarded living writers, here and abroad. Concentrated in a very particular part of Louisiana, his characters and settings strike readers as especially distinct, singular. And yet in Gaines's stories, the universal somehow manages to speak through the unique.

Gaines: My work has been translated into about twelve different languages—Japanese, Chinese, German, Russian, Slovene, Norwegian. How they understand anything I'm talking about, I don't know. But apparently they do. Readers from different parts of the world say, "Okay, yes, we recognize these characters; we believe in these characters." But I don't know what's going to happen in the future, you know. I've met students who don't want to study dialect. Asian students I've met in San Jose, California, for example, who came out said, "Listen, my folks didn't send me here to study dialect. They sent me to learn to speak proper English grammar." I don't know how long we'll be communicating with those students.

On the Company He Keeps Nowadays

Inevitably, the topic of any talk with Ernest Gaines will return again and again to his home on False River, just as he himself has throughout his work and his life. But it's not the place that has kept his imagination, and his readers, captivated through the years.

Gaines: Returning to it is the result of my love for my ancestors who worked much harder than I did and who are buried about three-quarters of a mile from where I'm sitting right now. Knowing that their spirit is here, their bones are here, their dust is here—these are the kinds of things that give me great satisfaction. I mean, if it weren't for that fact, I don't think I would care anything for this part of Louisiana any more than any other part of Louisiana or the South or the rest of the country.

So, owning this property, it's not necessarily for me. It's for them, and then for the living too; for my younger brothers and sisters and nieces and nephews. They can see this place and have pride in what I've done and in knowing what I've cared about.

I know that the old ones, the ones that are dead—I often sit on my back porch at night and think about how wonderful it would be if they were there sitting with me in rocking chairs and drinking coffee and talking. It's the sort of thing I think about often because this is where they were, right here, my grandparents' grandparents. This is what makes me proud of the place.

If Auntie [Augusteen Jefferson] could sit here with me or my stepfather who took me away from here or my Uncle George, who used to take me to those old beat-up bars in Baton Rouge—if I could, I'd just buy him a good glass of Gentleman Jack, and we could sit here and talk. Oh, I wish I could do that.

Interview with Ernest J. Gaines, Part I

Dominique Audiat / 2008

Interview conducted in Oscar, Louisiana, April 11, 2008. Published with permission.

Dominique Audiat: I would like to start with a personal comment: If I were asked to use one single word to qualify your work, I would say, "Authenticity." Your characters are so convincing that they seem alive to the reader. You said that lots of people could not believe that Jane Pittman was not a real person, and the same could be said about many other protagonists of your novels and short stories. All the details you give about their surroundings add to this feeling of authenticity, reinforced by the great sensitivity in your depiction that makes these characters seem so true. You do much more than just look at people: you see them and you perceive and transmit their deepest emotions. Stendhal, the French novelist, used a metaphor to describe the novel, which he compared to a mirror being shifted along a road. That is obviously what you did with the transcription of true events and true people in a true locale, Louisiana, through the fictional characters and settings you created. And whatever the hardships they have to endure, their lives are pervaded by pride and dignity. How would you define yourself, as a novelist?

Ernest J. Gaines: I've never been part of any "school" of writing. I write about the South because I am from the South, but I followed no school. I lived in San Francisco during the Beat Generation, but I was not interested in that school; I lived in San Francisco during the black militant demonstrations, but I didn't follow that school of militant writing either—though you may find anger and protest in my writing if you read it close enough—but I followed no school of writing. What is important to me is to tell a good story, and the reader takes from it whatever he or she wishes.

DA: You wrote *The Autobiography of Miss Jane Pittman* during the turbulent sixties, that militant period when people were saying, "Black is Beautiful." What do you think of that slogan?

EJG: I've not heard or spoken or read in print that slogan lately, but it was popular back in the sixties and in the seventies. It was a time of rebellion; demonstrations were going on. There was a feeling of pride in the African American community and that slogan was adopted to counter all the negative that had been said about black. It is different from identification fads that come and go, like hair, make-up. There was a time when young black males wore what they called "Afros"; then they had "cornrows." Now, at this point, they're shaving their heads. So, they go from one fad to another. They try to identify themselves in that way. "Black is Beautiful" is not a fad; it is different: we are proud of what we are, and we felt it was necessary to inform the world how we felt—Black is Beautiful.

I am seventy-five years old, and maybe I'm just too old to know all these things going around me today. But even when I was younger, I was very seldom joining in. I was never in: I was always outside looking in. Even when I lived here as a child, I was an outsider. I used to play ball and shoot marbles and do all things guys would do, but there were certain times when I would just be alone. I would walk from here back to the swamps, just to be alone. It was the same thing in California; I lived four miles from the ocean, and I would walk to the ocean, then back to my apartment.

I read the great writers, Greek writers, tragedians. I read Maupassant and Flaubert and Stendhal. I'm sure I've learned something from all these writers. I learned from the American writers: Faulkner, Hemingway; and I also learned from others: Chekhov, especially Tolstoy. I've learned more from my spirituals and gospel music, and blues and jazz, than I have from African American writers. The music had greater impact and impress on me than any writing. I couldn't be the writer I am today if it were not for my African American experience. That's what *Mozart and Leadbelly* is all about.

DA: How do you explain the title of this latest book you published in 2005? **EJG:** Mozart represents form, the influence of white western writers, European and American writers. That's where I got my form, where I learned how to write a novel, a short story. But Leadbelly represents source, the soul experience. Flaubert, Joyce, Hemingway, they showed me how to form the paragraph, the sentence. It's just like a house, and what you put in that house. And this is where Leadbelly comes in: jazz, spiritual, my experience with my race. I needed both in order to be the writer that I am. I believe in writing well. I believe in rewriting and rewriting and rewriting to get the form down. But you have to say something in your writing. Form is nothing if you have nothing to say.

DA: *Mozart and Leadbelly* contains the only story whose action does not take place in Louisiana, but in San Francisco, where you lived for so many years. I am talking of "Christ Walked Down Market Street." You said that in all your stories and novels no one ever escaped Louisiana, probably because your soul never left Louisiana. However, there is certainly a great part of your soul in that beautiful story which occurs in San Francisco, in that famous street you know so well.

EJG: This is one of my favorite stories, I suppose. And at the same time, I feel it's not complete.

DA: Throughout all your work, there seems to be a clear distinction between your personal relation to God and your relation with preachers. Can you say more about it?

EJG: You know, the preachers I've been writing about in my books, I would not write the same today. People were not very well-educated. They felt that they had been called to preach the gospel. Many of them were suspicious of someone who was educated because that person began to ask questions they could not answer. Those preachers, at that time, could not explain anything. They could only refer to the Bible. I believe in God, in my heart. But this is not enough for some people, as you can see in "The Sky Is Gray" with the preacher or with Grant in *A Lesson Before Dying*. Oh yes, I believe in God. Definitely.

DA: You seem to see God in all creation.

EJG: Yes, God is everywhere, in this little book, in the leaves, the flowers. I don't believe in any particular religion. I was baptized and raised as Baptist, and I attended a Catholic school for three years. I got away from both and tried to find God in another thing.

DA: It is very moving to see that little church in your garden, the church you attended when you were a child.

EJG: People who owned the plantation gave me the permission to move that church here, and it was also my school. It is constantly reminding me of the past. I still hear my people singing, praying.

DA: You talk of these strong links with your people in the essay entitled "Reconstructing Identity," published in *Mozart and Leadbelly*, in which you describe yourself as "a young man who was searching for that elusive *I*." You explain the difficulties you had to pack, going to California, probably because it was so painful to leave the ones you loved. And you evoke that piece of oak wood they gave you, which was such a heavy burden for you. What can you say about that symbol, and did you feel that, in a certain way, your folks were drawing you back, even though they crystallized all their dreams of education on you? Does that piece of wood symbolize the ties between personal identity and collective identity?

EJG: My people did not try to draw me back: they set me free. When I came to California, I had lots of freedom. I had to go to school, of course. But my folks just told me to stay out of trouble, not to hang around in the streets with the guys. That's how I spent so much of my time in libraries, reading and reading and reading, trying to discover who I was and how to write a novel, a short story—because they told me not to hang around in the streets. Much of my life was pleasant as a child in Louisiana, but very hard at the same time, going into the fields at six, seven years old, picking potatoes, pulling onions, and working all day. Education was limited to four to five months a year.

That block of wood said a lot about the place, the people. I had to move it down to give it form. The burden of carrying it represents the burden of becoming educated, the writing I had to do in the future. I had many stories to tell: how could I do those stories? I had to learn, and until I had learned to write, that block of wood would always be there. But I could only take a little piece at a time, and that would amount to a short story. You had to cut the piece off and do everything to make it smooth and beautiful. My agent, when I turned the story to her, said: "Yes, but it's not ready yet. You have to go back and cut another piece of that block, and you work on that." I took it to her, and she said, "Yes, but not yet." There were times when I thought I would not be a writer. Then, what could I do with my life? At those times, everybody wanted to be a writer. My agent was telling me, "You have so much to say, and they have very little to say. And that's why your burden is so heavy, and that's why you're so lucky." There were times—those cold, foggy nights in San Francisco—when I wondered what I was going to do. Then, I would think about my aunt who never gave up. She was crippled and never walked in her life. She was always crawling. And she raised us, and she never complained. When I thought of giving up and getting rid of that heavy burden, I thought of her. Whenever I felt sorry for myself, I thought of all the things she had to go through.

DA: You have very often talked of the importance of the past. I would like to tell you a little anecdote: I visited a large plantation last week, and I was alone with the black lady, in her sixties, in charge of the visiting tour. She was obviously very proud to show me the magnificence of the Big House, telling me the high price of furniture or mirrors in each room, the most beautiful one being the wedding room. She kept on explaining to me how wealthy were those masters who owned a thousand slaves and how gorgeous were the weddings in such a setting. I could not but think of the contrast between so many splendors and the cruel and miserable condition of the slaves, so well depicted by Margaret Walker in *Jubilee,* and I said so to that lady. She just answered that these were good masters and that, besides, it was the past. What do you think of her reaction?

EJG: You know, during the thirties, there were many ex-slaves alive, and very well-known writers wrote about those people: their biographies are kept in the Library of Congress. I talked to one of them, a black man, an African American professor, and he told me that with these ex-slaves, it depended who was the person asking the question: black or white, they would get a different answer. And at the same time, you will find people standing for their white masters. Then you will get different information, people who will say, "Well, it was different from that."

DA: You talked a lot about change too. In the short story, "Mary Louise," the protagonist has been waiting for ten years for Jackson, but he does not respond any longer to her love. And when he tells her, "It can't ever be like that again . . . Time changes people . . . Everybody changes," Mary Louise cannot understand him, and she is overcome with sorrow. It seems obvious that the ones who left, and came back for a short while, have definitely changed, while the ones who stayed home seem to be the same. You talked, too, about the courageous ones who allow things to change. You have known segregation and the civil rights struggle, the disillusions that led to the nationalist movement of the sixties. It is at that time that you wrote *The Autobiography of Miss Jane Pittman,* whose life ends at the beginning of the civil rights struggle. Your characters who make things change by breaking the rules, like Ned, Jimmy, even Tee Bob, pay all their actions at the cost of their lives. But this was forty years ago, and things have certainly changed a lot. Don't you have the impression to live in a completely different world today?

EJG: Things have changed, yes. Many of us have improved our condition. I obviously have, my sisters have . . . But at the same time, we have more African American young men in prison than we have in college. They don't have the same opportunities. Then, what has really changed?

DA: In the first draft of *Of Love and Dust* you wrote a happy end for Marcus succeeding in escaping from the plantation with Louise, the Cajun overseer's wife, after he killed that man who put so much pressure on him and treated him so badly. But your editor asked you to change it. Why did you follow his advice?

EJG: He told me, "I like the first part and I like the second part, but they don't fit together. The first part is tragic; the second part becomes farcical. It becomes funny with this guy doing all kinds of crazy things. You should go one way or the other with this story. You're not taking this murder seriously; you should take it seriously." And I said, "The state of Louisiana didn't take it seriously. They let people like this black man come out of prison any time after killing another black man, not a white, but a black." He said, "That's too bad for the state of Louisiana to act that way, but I think Marcus should pay for his crime." Then I had to rewrite that part of the book over and make the book a tragedy and not a farce. I just thought I was much more interested in the character of Marcus than I was in the result of that crime.

DA: Marcus was a rebel. But do you think it was just because of morality that your editor reacted that way, or because at that time, in 1968, people would not have accepted that a black man could get away after having killed a white man? Since you just said that when a black man had killed another black man, he could get out of prison after a few years, and then nobody seemed to be bothered about it.

EJG: It's quite possible. I never really discussed it. The reason I wanted to end *Of Love and Dust* as fast as I could was that I wanted my *Bloodline* stories to be published. And my editor had asked me to write a novel, and then he would publish them. So, I didn't care so much when he told me to change those things around. I changed them around because I wanted my short stories published.

DA: In the story "Bloodline," Copper Laurent being half white and half black cannot exist in any of these two worlds, and he becomes mad trying to keep his dignity in the world he has created in his imagination, in order to survive. But you wrote that story forty years ago, and I read in a recent issue of *Newsweek* magazine that, today, it was the chance of Barack Obama to be half-white and half-black because he knew the aspirations and fears of both communities.

EJG: We have many people in the same situation. Many of the mayors in this country, in the cities here, are African American.

DA: But Barack Obama is running for the presidency, and he has won many states. Don't you think that it is a sign of hope for the future, so many white people voting for an African American, when it would have been unimaginable not so long ago?

EJG: We hope so. We all hope so. Times have changed . . . I always felt that combination of white and black would change much in this country. Barack Obama has white ancestry, and he was raised by a white family; then he has a greater chance to be listened to. If he had been raised by a totally black family, I don't think people would recognize him today. Being in a white family, he had a better chance to get educated. He went to Harvard.

DA: In Louisiana, interracial relations are particularly complex with the coexistence of Creoles, black and white, African Americans, Americans, and Cajuns. Do they mix today, for instance in church?

EJG: My wife goes to church right here, in New Roads, to Saint Augustine, the little Catholic school I went to. It's only ten miles from our house. Most of the people there are African Americans. But they mix: you have the Creoles, you have the whites, you have the blacks; you have people who own the plantations, you have wealthy people and poor people; they all mix on Sunday. Everybody goes to the same church, depending on the area. But some of them will never break away from the past. They will continue to do the same things, attending the same church . . .

DA: In your last book, *Mozart and Leadbelly*, you wrote in the essay entitled "Miss Jane and I," "I was going farther and farther back into the past. I was trying to go back, back, back into our experiences in this country to find some kind of meaning to our present lives. No, Miss Jane is not the end of my traveling into the past—she is only another step back so that I can see some meaning in the present." Have you finished going back into the past?

EJG: I really don't know. I'm still not writing as much as I should be. I suppose I'll always write about the past, but I feel that the young just don't care as much about the past.

DA: Many years ago, a student asked you what it meant to be an American. What would you answer today?

EJG: I am an American. I am more American than most people. I have Indian blood in me, from people being here before Columbus discovered America. I know I have African blood and European blood: with these three bloods, white, black and Indian, I am more American than most others.

Interview with Ernest J. Gaines, Part II

Dominique Audiat / 2009

Interview conducted in Oscar, Louisiana, May 4, 2009. Published with permission.

DA: You have given a great number of interviews on *The Autobiography of Miss Jane Pittman*. The questions I wish to ask you today are in regards to the comparison I established between the fictive autobiography you wrote in 1968 and the true autobiography, *Dreams from My Father*, Barack Obama wrote in 1995. At first glance, the story of Jane Pittman, a woman born in slavery and with no education, seems to have nothing in common with the life of Barack Obama, the brilliant civil rights lawyer, who never experienced segregation and graduated from prestigious Harvard University. I found, however, many similarities between these stories which both deal with the African American quest for identity. I would like to know how, at the beginning of the third millenium, you would treat the recurrent themes pervading your work, as well as Obama's story.

Manhood

DA: You often talked of the difficulties for the black man to realize himself, not only in the South, but also in American society as a whole. Joe Pittman tragically illustrates that predicament, having no other alternative than to risk his life to escape the limitations imposed upon him by the white world. When Jane is scared to see her husband breaking wild horses, he quite pathetically replies, "What else can I do?" That was in the late 1800s.

Surprisingly, a century later, Barack Obama feels the same restrictions, despite the recognition of civil rights: "I had begun to see a new map of the world . . . We were always playing on the white man's court, Ray had told me, by the white man's rules." (Obama 85) At this time, he could not imagine that history would annihilate his bitter conclusion.

Are you nowadays as pessimistic about the difficulties for a black man to find his place in society, or do you think that the election of an African American to the presidency of the United States has totally reversed a situation you often talked about? Would you say that the unspoken discrimination is over?

EJG: No, it is not over. I always said that things change and things do not change. Yes, Barack Obama has been elected to the presidency, and he couldn't have been president had not many, many whites voted for him; because so many whites did, this is the reason why he is the president today. But there are areas in this country that are just as racist today as ever before. There are pockets in towns, and in the countryside as well, just as racist today.

I think the young African American male has a better chance today than he had fifty years ago, twenty years ago, or even ten years ago, because of Barack Obama being elected president. But he still must struggle. He must be much better than his white counterpart to get anywhere today. You know, in this country we have more African American young men in prison than we have in the colleges. Many have accomplished things. They are in politics, they are in business, but at the same time, we have many more in prison than we have in the university level. So, it is a constant fight. The African American male will be fighting for his manhood for a long time still to come.

To Live by the Rules

DA: It is striking to see how whites become the victims of the very rules they established to keep blacks in a lower rank. Tee Bob appears as the innocent white victim of those unwritten rules that forbid him to marry Mary Agnes LeFabre, the beautiful Creole woman he sincerely loves. He, alone, is determined to break the walls they erect between the white race and the black race. And he cannot survive the surrounding madness.

Barack Obama speaks of the same madness after his shocking discovery of racism and its implications. There is nobody he can turn to. Later on, he is upset to find out that his white grandmother, who raised him and truly loves him, may be terrified just because a black man is bothering her at a bus stop. Hoping to find some comfort in the wisdom of an elder, he is at a loss when the old African American poet of the sixties tells him that his grandmother is right to be scared, because she understands that black people have a reason to hate; and that he'd better learn to live by the rules.

Are these rules obsolete? If you wrote a novel today, would you still mention them?

EJG: Yes, you still have to live by the rules. They may be not as stringent as they were in the past, strict as they were in the past. But there are people opposed to a white male marrying an African American woman, and there are those opposed to an African American male marrying a white woman. It is not as strict as it was, forty-five, fifty years ago, but it is still there.

Now, if I wrote a book, it would depend on the character, I'm sure, whether he wants or wishes to take the chance of breaking those rules because that can ostracize him, especially for a white; if he broke those rules, he might not commit suicide, but he would be ostracized. It is possible that he couldn't get a political position or a position in his community or whatever. If the black did it, he could also be ostracized, or he could be hurt by somebody. If I were to write a book today, that is one of the things I would have in mind: "Remember, if you go out there and do this, you can be hurt, or you can be ostracized." Yes, I would have that said today. But it depends on the character, and see, how strong he is or how weak he is.

Interracial Relations

DA: Blacks and whites, in both narratives, seem to live in two different worlds, as though they were standing next to each other but at the same time totally estranged from one another. That antagonism comes to life in the episodes taking place, in each narrative, in the library, which appears as a symbol of history as it houses writings of the past. It is there that Tee Bob, in your fictive autobiography, and Barack Obama, in his true story, realize they cannot get rid of the burden of history. Tee Bob, locked in the library of his parent's house, is surrounded by books on slavery and history and by the portraits of his ancestors, staring at him, all reminding him that he must live by the rules. And he kills himself because he doesn't want to live in the world of madness created by his elders.

In a fortunately less tragic tone, it is in the library of his white girlfriend's parents that Barack Obama realizes that the woman he loves lives in a totally different world. And because he refuses to live in her world, he decides to leave her: he doesn't want to keep on being an outsider. She desperately tries to hold him back, saying she would be black if she could, but that it was impossible.

Tee Bob as well as that woman appear as the innocent white victims of rules made by their ancestors, unable to perceive the transcendence of love.

Do you believe in the expiation of the father's sins? Do children have to make amends for what their fathers did?

EJG: You know, in Tee Bob's case, Tee Bob is a child. He is not strong. He is controlled by the father, the history, his white history. And that is why finally he kills himself, or the reason why he does not seduce Mary Agnes, as he had the right to do it at that particular time. I'm saying that the right by the father and by his friend, Jimmy Caya—not by my way of thinking, of course, but by their way of thinking—he is supposed to use her: "Do not take her seriously"—and he could not, just as Mary Agnes LeFabre, tries to make up for what her father, what her people have done to her people—which you cannot do. I don't know how the sons, or anyone, can make up for the past. I don't know how you can do that. What you can do is try to do as well as you possibly can today, but not with the idea that you can make up for the past.

The Past

DA: The past occupies a great place in your work. As you said, Mary Agnes LeFabre tries to make up for the past, and that is impossible. And the past is overwhelming, her determination vanishing in a flash when her head and back hit the wall as Tee Bob tries to hold her back. I quote you, "The past and the present got all mixed up . . . Making up for the past left. She *was* the past now. She was grandma now, and he was that Creole gentleman. . . . It showed in her face. It showed in the way she laid down there on the floor. Helpless; waiting" (Gaines 206). It is that unbearable sight which makes Tee Bob run away from her.

Barack Obama talks of the importance of the past in similar terms in the introduction of his autobiography: ". . . as Faulkner reminds us, the past is never dead and buried. It isn't even past. This collective history, this past, directly teaches my own" (Obama x). And he is struck by the reaction of a black woman when the white community organizer tries to have blacks and whites cooperate: "But for someone like Angela, the past *was* the present; it determined her world with a force infinitely more real than any notion of class solidarity. It explained why . . . more Blacks hadn't climbed up the ladder into the American Dream . . . and why Angela had no patience with those who wanted to treat black people and white people exactly the same" (Obama 170).

How do you consider the past? As linked to time, following a linear course and swept away by the present, or as alive as the present?

EJG: I don't think it is over, just as Faulkner once said, "the past isn't dead." We have so much reminding us today of the past. This is the Deep South, Louisiana, where we live, and even the Civil War is probably spoken and discussed more today than say, the second or the first World War. There are all kinds of celebrations of the Civil War, brave soldiers of the Civil War, great generals of the Civil War; but this is the South telling, this is the South history; it is not the history of blacks. So that past is still here, with many. And that past of the South is what hurts Tee Bob.

Change

DA: Change is also a recurrent theme, in your novel and in Barack Obama's narrative. Jane often speaks of the change in African American life of which she has been a witness throughout more than a century, from slavery to the beginning of the civil rights struggle.

Barack Obama's life illustrates the continuity in that change, which has led him from his civil rights practice to the presidency of his country. I like his definition of law as "the conversation of a nation arguing with his conscience." He keeps insisting in his narrative on the importance of change, in prophetic tones: "I'd pronounce on the need for change. Change in the White House . . . Change in the Congress . . ." (Obama 133)

Do you think that the change that has permitted an African American to become president of the United States will definitely sweep away a part of the past?

EJG: Yes, I believe that. As I said, many young African American males will go beyond the line where they would have stopped before Barack Obama became president. So there will be changes there. But nothing happens overnight. Barack Obama is president of the United States, but he cannot perform miracles in a hundred days, or in one term. He can make some changes, but it is not fair to him for people expect too much change. You will find a lot of young men with tremendous pride in what he has accomplished in that field. They feel more opportunities for themselves. I just hope that fewer men will be going to prison and more in the universities. Before Barack Obama came along, many felt just hopeless; they felt that no matter what they did, they would not accomplish anything. Now, some feel that they can. But to expect any great changes, miracles, no, I do not expect that at all. He can do just so much, just so much, and that is what it is going to be for a while.

Fate

DA: The main characters of your novel appear driven by fate, like in Greek tragedies. Barack Obama seems to have the same interpretation of man's destiny, saying after Harold Washington's election, the African American mayor of Chicago, "Nothing seemed to change . . . I wondered if he, too, felt a prisoner of fate" (Obama 230). Later on, he expresses the same feeling about his African grandfather, "He knows that he will not survive a mocking fate" (Obama 438).

Do you think that fate is stronger than man's will? And if so, is freedom in leading one's life just an illusion?

EJG: Fate plays a part, of course, in one's life. You know, I am a writer because I always wanted to be a writer. If I had stayed here, in Louisiana, after I finished the elementary school level, I doubt that I ever would have been a writer. But I had to go to California where I was educated—to the high school, college, and university levels—and there I met other people in writing who were interested in myself, in San Francisco where I wrote my first short story in 1955. At that time, a young Jewish agent was just beginning her agency. She saw my story; she liked it. And she told me she would like to see anything that I would write because she felt I had much talent and she would like to be my representative. Now, what made me a writer was because I always wanted to be a writer. However, if I had not gone to California and if I had not met this lady who wanted to be my representative, I would not be the writer I am today. So I don't know where fate is; I don't know where just hard work is. I think it is a combination of things. I think life is a combination of things. I have known others who wanted to be writers as well, and they just did not write for different reasons. They did not have the same chance that I had.

I hate to think that man is just driven only by fate. I think it plays a great part, but depending on the definition of fate—when you say fate, what do you mean?

DA: Just like in Greek tragedies . . .

EJG: So no matter what you do, you are going to be hurt . . .

DA: Yes. For instance, in your novel, the cases of Joe Pittman, Ned, and Jimmy: they know they will be killed, but they keep on doing what they feel they have to accomplish. Whatever they do, something is pushing them in one direction.

EJG: You know, I believe in that particular time in our history, that in order for you to get anything accomplished, you had to push to the limit. And there were those obstacles—the white man was there, trying to prevent it from happening. Martin Luther King is a good example; he knew that eventually he would be killed. Malcolm X is another good example. They knew that one day they would be killed, but they had to go and keep going. As I said, I was lucky that I could escape the South, and I was lucky that I met this lady who said she would do as much as she possibly could for me. So I was driving myself, not to the levels, say, of Martin Luther King or Malcolm X or Jimmy in my novel, but I kept thinking, I will do anything in the world, anything in the world, to become a writer, because I definitely felt I owed it to my aunt who raised me and to my younger brothers and sisters.

There were some really hard days for me. Still, I felt that I had to keep going, keep going, because my aunt who had raised me never walked in her life, and no obstacles in my path would be nearly hard as it was for her. And that is why I kept going. And that is why, I suppose, my protagonist must go beyond that point that he felt he was unable to go: he can be stronger than he would think he can be, and he must keep going and keep going, keep going. Yes, I believe in that, even if it must destroy him. Joe Pittman says: "I cannot be a slave, I will ride horses, I will not be that farmer they want me to be"; Ned's case: "I will teach, and yes, they will kill me, but I will teach"; Jimmy's case: "I must be free, I must be free." Tee Bob, of course, he commits suicide because he cannot live by the traditions of his ancestors. All of my protagonists are like that. Miss Jane, you know, she tries to walk to Ohio from Louisiana. And of course she cannot do it, so she turns and comes back. I always give them a hard way to go, a hard path to travel. And I probably got that for having been raised by a lady like my aunt. I think so.

The One

DA: Jane talks earnestly of Jimmy's destiny: "People's always looking for somebody to come lead them . . . We needed him to carry part of our cross . . . Colored all over this parish wanted him to be the One" (Gaines 238).

Barack Obama appears as "The One" with his Messianic image in people's mind. A French Catholic magazine headline cover read: "Obama est-il le nouveau Messie?" ("Is Obama the New Messiah?"). Before him, nobody has ever been so qualified.

You told, me last year, you always felt that combination of white and black could change much in this country. Was it your own vision of "The One"? And how do you explain such an evolution after the usual representation in literature of the tragic mulatto torn between two worlds? Nowadays, on the contrary, it seems to be the chance of Barack Obama to be between two worlds because he can feel the aspirations of both, black and white.

EJG: I feel Barack Obama is president today because he was raised by the white world. Barack Obama would not have had the same chances if his father had been white and his mother black, and he had to live in the mother's environment. In spite of his intelligence, he would not have the same opportunities. When I said that a mixed-race person could solve the problem I think people could look at Barack Obama and see a very handsome man there, a very intelligent man out there. I think he had chances he never would have if he had lived in a black environment. He probably would never have gone to Harvard, or maybe he would have, but I sort of doubt that he would have any chance to do those things. I still feel that a person of mixed races, depending on how he is raised, has a better chance of reaching all the people, more people than the white man or the African American whose both parents are African American. He has a better chance to have people willing to communicate with him, when they will not communicate with an African American whose parents are both African American.

Of course, then, you have the tragic mulatto as well. You know, no matter what you do, you are going to have different people with different chances in the world. There are those who hate themselves, like my tragic mulatto who does not know where his place is. I have known people like that. Barack Obama, especially his grandmother showed him that there was a place for him, and he did not have to believe that he was nobody. You have that person, yes, and you have the person who dislikes you because you are a mixture of race. And you find that in all countries. I am sure you have it in France. I know, definitely, we have it in these countries where we have fought wars. We have it in Japan: a mixed child there has a hard way to go, especially with a black father . . . And you find the same thing in Vietnam, in Korea . . .

DA: But even in Africa. At the end of his book, Barack Obama speaks of his sister's compassion for their half-brother in Kenya, whose mother is a white American and who is torn between two worlds.

EJG: Like I said, Barack did not have to go through that. He had this white family who just loved him, and this is what makes all the difference. But if he had a white father and a black mother he would live in a different environment altogether, and then he could have major problems there. Because there is so much that a black mother could have given him. She could have given him love, but showing him how to fit in that world out there, how to make it in that world out there, I do not think that she would be in that position.

DA: But you know, Barack Obama keeps wondering in his autobiography, "Where do I belong?"

EJG: Yes, but he had the white world to support him. He had the grandfather and the grandmother. And the mother too.

Collective Identity

DA: I found a parallel between Jimmy's and Obama's struggle to convince their people to fight for their rights and to improve their condition. Jane Pittman remembers the indifference met by Jimmy, and Barack Obama is struck by the resignation of poor black people in Chicago: "They had lost confidence in their ability to reverse the deterioration they saw all around them" (Obama 230).

When Jimmy is discouraged by their indifference or their resignation, Jane explains to him that people are not ready yet. And many years later in Chicago, the men at the barbershop explain to Obama that the faltering of Harold Washington's first mayoral candidacy was due to "the lack of unity within the black community, the doubts that had to be overcome." And they underline: "But Harold tried again and this time people were ready" (Obama 147). This echoes Jane's fundamental remarks: "The people ain't ready for nothing yet. People and time bring forth leaders . . . Leaders don't bring forth the people. The people and time brought forth King" (Gaines 241).

What do you think brought forth Barack Obama?

EJG: People, time, and place. Place plays a big part in this. I do not know that he could have done the same thing if he was born in the South. You know, people, time, and place, and also that people were tired with Bush's administration. So all those things happened. If you had a strong Republican personality there, I do not think Barack Obama would have become president. Or someone else in the Democrats, as well: Hillary, everybody thought that she would be the Democratic president. But time, place, conditions, all of these things were playing this part in Barack Obama becoming president.

Racial Pride

DA: The evocation of Joe Louis's triumph in both narratives shows the tremendous impact on the spirit of the African American community of the victories of their heroes. Barack Obama evokes the emotion of the barber in Chicago when he told him, "The night Harold won . . . people just ran the streets. It was like the day Joe Louis knocked down Schmeling. Same feeling. People weren't just proud of Harold. They were proud of themselves" (Obama 148). Later on, Barack Obama evokes the pride arisen by his own election in the Senate.

Did you feel yourself that pride and that identification process?

EJG: Yes, I believe so. I definitely felt a pride. I do not know if it is to the extent of what Joe Louis did. But by the time Joe Louis beat Schmeling, we had no heroes out there at all; we did not have anybody. Joe Louis was the first hero that the majority of African Americans knew of. There have been other fighters, like Jack Johnson, there have been politicians out there, but they did not have Joe Louis's impact. We all need heroes. We'll create heroes if we do not have any. That is part of man's myths, to have significant figures out there.

By the time Barack Obama came along, we had many heroes: we had Muhammad Ali, Jackie Robinson, and Joe Louis, and many athletes, leaders as well, even movie stars, great entertainers. But of course, what he accomplished is something that none of us would have thought would have happened in our lifetime. So of course, we are proud, very proud, that he could reach that point. I remember his inauguration and how people were weeping, and with pride. Yes, we are all proud of him. I just hope that nothing happens to him and that he does not become discouraged because he cannot do all the things that he would like to do. Because that Republican Party, they are fighting him in every way they can. They keep him from accomplishing his mission. So I just hope that he can sustain the pressure that is on him, day in and day out.

Yes, we are proud of him. We need him, of course. As Oprah Winfrey has said, he is the One. But he is the One not only for the African Americans, but also for the country and for the world. Yes, he is that guy: He is the One. He is a real African American because his father was definitely an African and, according to the country, Kansas is the center of the country, so his mother, a white woman coming from Kansas, will definitely make him an African American.

Authenticity

DA: I suppose your choice of a history teacher, searching for authenticity, to conduct Jane's interview is not random. Before leaving Kenya, Barack Obama meets with a history teacher who tells him black Americans were prone to disappointment when visiting Africa "because they come here looking for the authentic" (Obama 433). And she underlines the different ethnic origins in meals, supposedly typically African. She talks also of the language her daughter speaks with her friends, "They take bits and pieces of everything—English, Swahili, German, Luo . . . They live in a mixed world. It's just as well I suppose. In the end, I'm less interested in a daughter who's authentically African than one who is authentically herself" (Obama 435).

Is the search for authenticity just an illusion? Is it that important to look for authenticity? And what is left of African American traditions?

EJG: While we retain some things, there are changes as well. I am afraid that even in the music, it is changing so much because we are bringing so many other cultures into our music. I found that in our church music; it does not have that purity, that authenticity I felt when I was a child growing up. Everything is changing, they are bringing in so many things, and I am maybe one of those people looking for authenticity, when I should not be looking for it. As I mentioned to you the other day, I think I have learned a lot from my ancestors, who are African, Indian, and of course European white. I know that I have this mixture and, because of the environment I was raised in, I am an African American. And that is where I'd rather be. But some people are just trying to stop history.

DA: But don't you think that even if they try to stop history, they can win some battles first, but in the long time, history is stronger, the sense of history is stronger? If you think that history has a direction, a sense.

EJG: Well, but history for whom? In order for Barack to be president, he had to accept different things. He could not accept totally his black father's history; I mean, only that, he had to mix it. And at the same time, these people who raised him, those whites who raised him, he had to take some things from them as well; it could not be one side or the other. I think that when he went back to this village of his father, he was looking for something, but I don't think he was looking to this regard, a means of living out his white side of him. I don't think he was looking for that authenticity. He could have been looking for his father's side: "my father's side, I just want to know my father's people. But I am not that African, but I am an American, and it is a combination of all these things."

Nature

DA: Jane has privileged relations with nature, talking to her tree, saying that old, old trees, like her oak tree which saw so many things, so many genera-tions, must be very wise. It is very striking to see that when Barack Obama goes to Kenya, he feels the same about baobabs. He writes: "Seeing the trees, there, in the hazy afternoon light, I understood why men believed they pos-sessed a special power—that they housed ancestral spirits and demons, that humankind first appeared under such a tree . . . They looked as if each one could tell a story" (Obama 437)

Did you know these African beliefs, or did you transpose your own feel-ings on Jane?

EJG: It was my own feelings. You know, the tree in *The Autobiography of Miss Jane Pittman* is a tree on the road near where I lived. I remember when I was a child, I used to walk by that tree, and there were always old peo-ple sitting there. In winter, it would protect them from the cold, because they would sit under the roof of the tree. And in summer, it would protect them from the heat. I have seen this many, many times: somebody had even placed pieces of cardboard and pieces of clothing there to make it comfort-able for the old people to sit. And I suppose as far they talked themselves to the tree while sitting there. I feel the nobility of the tree. So I gave Miss Jane my feeling of what I thought that the old people felt, but I didn't know anything about the African tradition about the trees.

You know, there is another thing I read somewhere, and I used it in the book: there was an Indian tribe here, who would catch fish and eat the fish and put the bones back in the river and say, "Go back, be fish again." If they can say that to the fish, I suppose these old people that I saw sitting under that tree could treat the tree in the same way. And there are of course very beautiful and strong old trees out there. Now, not very far from there was a tree called the hanging tree, where many black men were lynched. So you have both places: you have an evil place, and you have a very beautiful place—protection from the weather—whether it was hot weather or cold, rainy weather. You have this huge tree, with these long limbs, protecting you, hugging you, like a parent, or God.

The Quest for Identity

DA: You see God in nature, in creation, as you explained to me last year. Finding his place in the world has led Man to many interrogations about himself. You know, I started my dissertation in the seventies, at a time where "Black is Beautiful" was the motto of African American people searching for their identity, after it had been so long denied to them. After the "New Negro" of the Harlem Renaissance and the emergence of "Négritude" in the twenties, the Black Aesthetic Movement was pervaded by a strong feeling of Black Nationalism forty years ago. Barack Obama evokes that period, in his narrative, as totally obsolete.

Do you think that today young people feel more American than African American?

EJG: I still think they feel more African American than American, in spite of Barack being president. Every day they face some prejudices out there, every day . . . Our unemployment is more than twice the unemployment for whites, and they find they cannot get a job because of the color of their skin; they are back to that: "I am Black. I am African American. I am much more African American than American." I feel that they feel that way . . . I think in this country the whites see a color before they know the person. I can walk in their place, to a restaurant, and they will say, "Hi, Mister Gaines or Doctor Gaines or Mister Ernest." But if my brother came in, just where I am, he would not get that same reaction. This is when he comes back and says, "Well, I feel more comfortable around my own people." I fit in two worlds, really. I can fit in that American world, but I feel as comfortable in my African American world, and maybe a little bit more. And at the same time, I know that I cannot live entirely in that world, depending how you define that world . . .

DA: Barack Obama writes in his autobiography: "My identity might begin with the fact of my race, but it didn't, couldn't end here" (Obama 111).

You told me, last year, that having Indian, African, and European blood, you were more American than most people. At the beginning of our conversation, I intended to ask you what you thought would be the next American identity challenge if the racial one seemed about to be conquered. But obviously, in your opinion, the question of racial identity is still there; the racial problem has not been solved.

EJG: No, the racial problem has not been solved yet.

The Future

DA: How do you see the future? Are you hopeful?

EJG: I don't know what is going to happen. I am afraid that this world can be blown apart and I don't think we can save it, with all the bombs we have. The reason why I think Barack is the One is that he is reaching out to groups, to countries when the last administration did not believe in reaching out to them—Muslim countries; and Barack is saying to those: "I'd rather raise hands and shake hands with you. We do not need the fist." I'd be optimistic if we'd stop . . . But I do not think man is going to give up his bombs, his guns, or anything like that. And I cannot expect Barack Obama to bring all the people peace on earth. He cannot. So I am skeptical. I am not totally optimistic that things are going to really change. I hope I am wrong. I hope I am wrong . . . But I am afraid that somebody, somewhere, might push the button and start the next war. We have problems everywhere now in the world . . . problems, problems, problems . . .

DA: So you are pessimistic because of evil throughout the world.

EJG: I hate to seem so. I am more skeptical than pessimistic . . . I worry about people who are hungry, and we cannot get into the countries where people are hungry and bring them canned food because crooked leaders refuse; they'd rather fight someone else than feed their own children, their own people. So there are all these problems there, and anything can explode, anything can explode . . .

DA: If you wrote a novel today, would you construct your characters around that vision of the world, or would you still write about Louisiana?

EJG: I wish I could write about other places; I tried but I cannot . . . It depends on my characters. I would like to write a good love story, a mystery, but it would probably still be centered in Louisiana. I do not know any love story in Louisiana, or mystery, I could write about. I have written an interracial story, *Of Love and Dust.* I've written a Creole story, *Catherine Carmier.* I've written an autobiographical story, *The Autobiography of Miss Jane Pittman.* I have written a story of old men standing for the first time in their lives, *A Gathering of Old Men,* because they had never stood before. I have written an execution story, *A Lesson Before Dying.* I do not know another theme I could write about Louisiana or taking place in Louisiana. I wish I could write a story about California; I lived there so many years.

DA: You do not have the same feeling about California.

EJG: Oh no, I do not have the same feeling about place there.

DA: So, like you said before, place is very important.

EJG: Oh yes, place is very important. This place is very important. These six acres of land I have here mean everything for us. Place: I can write about this parish, Pointe Coupee Parish, that little town of New Roads, the river out there, the trees, the roads, going in different directions there, I can write about that . . . the cane fields, the corn fields, that, I can carry. But what story can I put in there? I do not know the story. I would not write a book about Doomsday. Oh no, I cannot write this kind of book where everything is blowing up . . .

DA: So, you would say, what is so important in man's destiny is time, place . . . and of course, character.

EJG: Yes, time, place, and a majestic character, a character of character. Jefferson does this in *A Lesson Before Dying*, when he is growing into a man. And *The Autobiography of Miss Jane Pittman* has to get a heroic character.

DA: You have heroic characters in each of your novels. Did you meet some in your life, or did you just create them?

EJG: I created my characters. But my aunt was a hero of sort, and other relatives whom I looked up to, both aunts, uncles, and my stepfather who took me to California and educated me there. So I knew some strong people, good people. And I have known others, in my own family . . . I have seen so many old ladies like Miss Jane: my aunt who raised me was definitely one, and another aunt—I used to travel in the parish with her—who sold cosmetics and brought groceries to the old people. I went with her to deliver the groceries.

DA: Like in your novel Jimmy, who also writes letters for old people as you did in your childhood. I noticed that you have put many autobiographical elements in the story of Jane, many true events. That is why her story seems so authentic.

Even though she never clearly mentions it, Jane is constructing her identity in the way she conducts her whole life. Barack Obama often speaks in his autobiography of the puzzle of being a black man and of his own search for identity. How do you analyze such a feeling?

EJG: I think I must have been searching for myself in my writing. I would never write an autobiography, but I think it is in the writing itself, just like you said yourself—Jimmy doing things for his people. . . . When people ask me what I am doing with my work, I try to create characters, to improve my own character and, maybe, the character of that reader who might read me. So it is always character, character, character. I cannot write a complete negative book: you must be striving to become something. And usually in my book it is a man because black males have been denied for a long time, even today . . . not as much as in the past, but in a way they are still being denied.

DA: Not women?
EJG: Not as much. Women could get away with much more than the men could from the time of slavery, even today . . .

DA: In conclusion what would you say to the African American community for the future?
EJG: Education, as number one, education, education, and education again. We have to get out of this idea that we do not have a possible chance. We just have to sacrifice more to educate our children, look after our children. There is an African saying that it takes the village to raise the child, but it takes the mother and the father in the first place to raise the child, both parents in order to raise the child. But we have large populations of a single parent, especially in the black community. . . . Education, they have to do that.

DA: Thank you for that ultimate interview on Miss Jane because I know that you have been asked so many questions about her autobiography since its publication, forty years ago.
EJG: But you know, if I had to save one novel, I would say: *Miss Jane* . . . if I had to make a choice . . . a sophist choice: "You love them all, but you can take just one of your books, just one," it would be *Miss Jane* . . .

I have never known a Miss Jane, but I have known a thousand Miss Janes . . . just seeing them walking along the road, listening to them talking in the distance, praying and singing at church, or crying . . . No one Miss Jane, but ten thousand Miss Janes . . .

Notes

1. *La Vie*, n° 3298—Nov. 2008.

Works Cited

Obama, Barack. *Dreams from My Father: A Story of Race and Inheritance.* New York: Crown Publishers, 2007 edition. [Originally published by Time Books, 1995]

The Tragedy of Brady Sims and Other Works: A Conversation with Ernest J. Gaines

Marcia Gaudet / 2017

Interview conducted in Oscar, Louisiana, November 21, 2017. Published with permission.

Ernest Gaines had done a reading from his new novel, *The Tragedy of Brady Sims*, at the University of Louisiana at Lafayette two weeks earlier. In this conversation at his home in Oscar, Louisiana, we talked about his new novel and about some of his earlier works. In the novel, Brady Sims is "the man who whipped children," the man on the plantation who had the responsibility for disciplining children. The novel focuses on Brady Sims's response to his son Jean-Pierre, whom Brady shoots and kills in the courtroom after he has been convicted of murder. The main narrator is the young black reporter who goes to the local barbershop to talk to the men who knew Brady Sims.

MG: Some of the things I'm going to ask are the same as we talked about at UL, but I wanted to get it down on record. My first question is about the time setting. When Jean-Pierre is growing up, it's in the forties. But when he comes back, it's roughly the same as *A Gathering of Old Men*. Is it the late 1960s? You mention that the post office and houses in the quarter had photos of Martin Luther King and Jack and Bobby Kennedy. You also mention Muhammad Ali.
EJG: Right. About that time. The late 1960s or early '70s.

MG: And that would also be the time when a newspaper that's predominantly white in a small town in Louisiana might hire a young black reporter.
EJG: Well, let's hope so because a lot of things were going on at that time. Problems in the South. And the publisher of the newspaper would probably

believe he could reach those people out there better than, say, someone coming in from east Texas because he would know his people better. It could have happened. I have no idea if it actually did happen here. By that time people believed they could fight for certain rights in the area. People thought they could improve the situation in the area.

MG: I think that's accurate. I think the white newspaper editor is an interesting character too.
EJG: Right. Good old Ambrose Cunningham.

MG: And that sets the setting. I also went back to reread the early chapter that you published in *Callaloo* in 2001 [Chapter 3]. I wanted to go back to that.
EJG: I don't really remember.

MG: Since then, you changed the main character's name from Antoine Olinde to Brady Sims, and when that chapter was published the title was still *The Man Who Whipped Children*.
EJG: Whenever I rewrite, I'm changing things. Same character, just a different name.

MG: Had you already decided to change the name of the main character when you sent it to your publisher.
EJG: Oh, yes. I had changed it.

MG: Why the change in title from *The Man Who Whipped Children*? The French publication just translated it to *L'homme qui fouettait les enfants* (published November 2016). And why did you change the name of the main character? Which change came first?
EJG: I don't know when I changed it. The American version was published after the French version. The name of the main character is the same as the French. Originally I wanted two novellas published together in a hardback. The American publishers wanted to publish them together, but I never did get the other novella finished. As a result, *The Tragedy of Brady Sims* was published in paperback as a single novella. I never did get "The Daughters of the Creole Lady" finished.

MG: So are you still working on "The Daughters of the Creole Lady"?
EJG: I think about it every day. It's a damn shame that I'm not working. I'm not working on it, but I think about it every day. But thinking about it is not

getting it done. I'm not doing a damn thing now as far as writing or anything else. I'm doing a lot of reading, but no writing.

MG: A lot of people would say it's remarkable that you published at eighty-four.

EJG: [*laughs*] I'll eventually get back to it. I might get back to it next week. I think about it every day. I need to figure out how to work it out because the title is "The Daughters of the Creole Lady," and the daughters have very little to do with the story. But I like the title. The girl who is the first cousin to the daughters, the story is about her. I have to figure out how to bring the daughters more into the story or change the title and just go with the first cousin as the main character. I don't know exactly how to do that. And that's the problem with me now. I love the title, so I want to stick to the title. But I think that the daughters are not involved enough. So that is the big problem, really.

MG: So you have to change the title or find one just as good.

EJG: Right, right.

MG: I hope you do get back to it. I enjoyed hearing you read the chapter from it.

EJG: Oh yeah, I'm going to do it. I'm going to do it sometime.

MG: Getting back to Brady Sims, is he basically the same character as Mathu [from *A Gathering of Old Men*] on a different plantation? Sims lives on Bergeron Plantation; Mathu lives on Marshall.

EJG: I think the biggest criticism of it is how can you take a guy that brutal and make him a hero? Well, it's a tragedy. His life is a tragedy. What happened was that the people who were raising their children went into the military or to work somewhere else at different military plants, and they left all the children with the old people who needed help to discipline the children. And all of this was on the back of Brady. He had to be the one to do it.

And the other thing I wanted was to let the black community control their children instead of having the white community doing so. They gave Brady the right to do it. That put too much pressure on one man.

MG: So it didn't have to be the parents—who had left either because of the war or the tractor, the continuing argument between Jamison and Celestin in the barbershop.

EJG: No. And the grandparents were too old. So they got Brady to help. But a person like Brady did not know how to talk to the children, to tell them you should not do this or you should not do that. He believed in corporal punishment. If you did something wrong, you were going to get whipped. And right or wrong, if someone said you did something wrong, you had to be punished.

MG: I think that's a really interesting thing because today we have a tendency to judge things that happened in the past using today's standards.
EJG: Brady believed that corporal punishment was the way to punish his son. Whipping him would not be punishment enough. And he would not let him go to Angola.

MG: Brady is someone who never wanted to rely on anybody else?
EJG: No, no way. And that's the big tragedy.

MG: And that is tragic. And his life, to him, would have been meaningless if he failed with his own son.
EJG: Yes, it would have been hypocritical. It would have been "I punished all those other children, and I can't let you get away with this. But I don't want those white people touching you. I'm not going to let you go to Angola. There's only one thing to do. And I don't want those white people to touch you."

MG: I know that in the 1940s, only white men would have been running Angola. By the late 1960s or '70s, had that changed?
EJG: Yes. I was at Angola about four or five years ago. I went to Angola for one of those rodeos. Someone had tickets to the Angola Rodeo, and I went. And most of these guys (in the rodeo and at Angola) are black, and the guards are black. That was five or six years ago.

MG: It's really hard to get tickets to the Angola Rodeo.
EJG: Yes, you have to know somebody. That's when I met Cain [Angola Warden Burl Cain]. He knew about me because he had read my book *A Lesson Before Dying*. And he invited me to his office.

MG: Did he comment about the book?
EJG: No, I don't think we talked about the book.

MG: Well, *A Lesson Before Dying* was set long before Burl Cain was at Angola.
EJG: Yeah, right.

MG: Talking about Brady Sims. As you said, it might be difficult to see someone who is so brutal as a hero. Because he can be brutal, it's hard to see him as a good man. He does good things, like giving away food, but he also has a streak of cruelty. In the 2001 excerpt, it says, "He could be evil one day, good the next, and then . . . mean as the devil." But Mapes also says, "I never knew a better man, white or black, than him." How do you see Brady Sims? Do you think he was basically a good man?

EJG: I see Brady Sims the way I see God. The worst things happen one day, and then beautiful things happen another day. I think Brady could be that kind of person.

MG: That's a wonderful analogy. He's such a powerful character.

EJG: I wish there was less blood when he goes to the jail, but I knew someone who did that. He got the boy out of jail and beat him until he bled. He told me that himself. I think he was a guy who could have shot somebody. He was tough, tougher than all the rest of us. There were two or three men in the quarter who used to whip children. But I just concentrated all of those characters into Brady, into one character.

MG: At the cemetery beautification day, I heard men talking about men they remembered in the quarter who whipped children.

EJG: Yes, because they didn't want the white man to brutalize them at Angola. If they went to Angola, they would not come out the same person. Some would come out more brutal. I knew such a man. He had killed a guy in a fight in Baton Rouge. Two or three guys had jumped him, and he killed one of them. When he got out of Angola, the law ran him out of Baton Rouge, and he went to Houston. The law ran him out of Houston, and he went to San Francisco. In San Francisco, he was killed. A woman killed him the same weekend I had come down here to Baton Rouge. I left San Francisco on a Thursday, and someone told me on Saturday that he had been killed the night before. He was a tough guy. Others came out of Angola, and they were just psychologically castrated. That brutality destroyed them.

MG: What was the inspiration for Brady Sims?

EJG: I knew someone like him, a real tough guy.

MG: It's an interesting thing because today it is illegal to use that kind of discipline. It would not be condoned. But earlier, there were times that it did seem to make a difference in a child's life (to use corporal punishment).

Do you think it was because the child, for some reason, understood it was to help them?

EJG: Oh, yes. You know, my aunt used to discipline us, and we had to go and get our own switch to be whipped with. We knew we had done something wrong. We knew it. And I knew that she loved me. But when I did something wrong, she had to discipline me. I would think that my friends felt the same way about their parents.

MG: In *The Tragedy of Brady Sims*, Mapes is a multigenerational sheriff. His father was sheriff before him . . .

EJG: Mapes was a third generation sheriff. His daddy had been sheriff, and his grandpa had been sheriff. The three of them were law officers over a hundred years.

MG: The other thing—I guess because Mapes knows both of them—how do you see Mathu (in *A Gathering of Old Men*) in relation to Brady Sims? In some ways, Mathu reminds me of Brady Sims in that he is independent, yet they're really different . . .

EJG: Oh, sure. They're the same person. Basically the same guy.

MG: Both are very independent, but do you think Mathu would ever have been as brutal as Brady?

EJG: Oh no, probably not.

MG: They have a lot in common, and both are very much respected by Mapes. But at least we don't see the kind of brutal side in Mathu that we see in Brady.

EJG: Mapes respected Mathu as a man, Brady as a man, despite his flaws.

MG: You've said that—though it's always fictionalized, always a different person—but you were inspired for Mathu by Walter Zeno. Do you see him as an inspiration for Brady Sims as well?

EJG: Some of it. Some of it.

MG: Brady seems to have had more brutal experiences himself than Mathu. He had more tragedy himself than Mathu.

EJG: Brady had much more responsibility than Mathu. Mathu mainly took care of himself. Brady was responsible for others. He had to take care of others. Mathu never had that responsibility.

MG: And we see Mathu's gentle side, as in the way he mentored Candy. There's not so much a gentle side with Brady, even though he did good things.
EJG: No, no, no.

MG: What about Brady's son, Jean-Pierre? Was he based on something you observed?
EJG: No, no, no. I just made him up.

MG: Okay, just completely fiction. He was the one who left, too. His mother took him away.
EJG: Yes. He's a tough guy. As a child, Brady was always trying to control him, and he just couldn't control him. And, of course, he went to New Orleans and California, and got involved in gangs and certain things like that.

MG: So the $20,000 or $10,000 he owes, that was because of a drug deal?
EJG: Yeah, the money he owed Too Tall Sammy was from a drug deal or gambling or something. And whether Jean-Pierre shared the money with the other guys, I don't know. I don't know, and I don't care [*laughs*]. Jean-Pierre has always been this wild guy. So he says, "I don't have any money." And whether he was lying or not, the other guys say, "Okay, we'll take you back to Too Tall Sammy. And I know you don't want to face him." So Jean-Pierre says, "But I know where money's at."

MG: Jean-Pierre doesn't actually shoot anybody.
EJG: No, but he was there. And there's a dead man . . .

MG: In *Brady Sims*, you have a different jury composition with the trial of Jean-Pierre, with one African American man and one white woman, than you had in *A Lesson Before Dying*. But you also have a very different defendant than with Jefferson in *A Lesson Before Dying*. Jean-Pierre is guilty, and that makes a big difference to his father because his father can't defend him.
EJG: Right.

MG: Mapes doesn't use the word "hero," but he says Brady was the best man he ever knew.
EJG: If I had to rewrite it, I don't think I would have Mapes say, "He was the best man I ever knew." I would not use those words. I would not. I might have him say, "He's not as brutal as everyone thinks he is." But I wouldn't put it exactly that way now. Mapes looks at him as a man who hunts, fishes,

very independent, who can defend himself, who doesn't take anything from anyone, who minds his own business. So that's what Mapes respects in a person like Brady Sims. And Mapes says, "He never caused me any problems unless someone brought him into it." Brady never initiated problems; something else happened.

MG: This brings me to my next question. It's basically the first time for you to bring characters back from earlier works—except for the mule Mr. Bascom [*laughs*]—but in *Brady Sims* you have Mapes and also Russell and Claude from *A Gathering of Old Men*. And Mapes does get his chance to be a first-person narrator. What influenced you to revive those characters? How did you decide on this instead of creating another sheriff?

EJG: Because I'd have to change the place. It's the same parish at the same time as *A Gathering of Old Men*—St. Raphael Parish—and Mapes would have been the sheriff. I would have had to create another parish. I can go to another plantation in the parish, but it's still St. Raphael Parish. Just like in *In My Father's House*.

MG: So it's easier to change to another plantation in the parish, but your fictional world is centered on St. Raphael Parish. You can't easily change to another parish.

EJG: Yes, you have many different plantations in the area, in the False River area, in this parish. There are four plantations on False River in this area because the water was a way of transportation. And the plantations used to rival one another. And each of the plantations had a baseball team, and they would rival each other on a Saturday or Sunday. They were all competitive.

MG: It's good that Mapes is a narrator. Mapes is very emotional and heartfelt, and we get to see Mapes when he shows a side he has not shown before. In fact, when he says, "Brady Sims was a hell of a man," he is very emotional.

EJG: Right. People tend to be like that. The most tough guys, the most bravado–type of man can be a different kind of person in different circumstances.

MG: He's also lost a friend, Brady Sims. And when someone dies, we do remember the good parts. He had seen a part of Brady that was the best he knew.

EJG: I had Mapes narrate because I didn't want to go back to the omniscient, and no one other person could have been there and narrated that at the time Mapes went to bring Brady in. Maybe he could have taken Russell, but I don't think Russell could have gotten inside of Mapes's mind as well. I didn't want the omniscient. I wanted to get inside Mapes's head. At least, on the day I was writing that.

MG: That's interesting to see. People are like that. They're not always the same, and we get to see a part of Mapes we'd never seen before. What about Louis Guerin, the young black reporter and the narrator. He is twenty-eight and a reporter for the local paper. He has gone to California and come back. How does he differ from earlier narrators? I was trying to compare him to other narrators, such as Grant Wiggins. And any connection to Jackson Guerin in *Catherine Carmier*?
EJG: None. They're all six feet tall and weigh 180 pounds. [*laughs*] It's a different time. He can go into Lucas Felix's barbershop, and they will talk to him.

MG: We talked earlier about the fact that whatever Brady was trying to do for his own son, he fails. Ironically, he does succeed in keeping him out of Angola, but he does it by shooting him. Is there any message there? And does it say anything about the effectiveness of corporal punishment? It's complex because he doesn't fail, but he has to do it by shooting him.
EJG: Well, that's the tragedy, that nothing is solved. Killing is final.

MG: Why does discipline work for some people and not for others?
EJG: We're all different. I'm opposed to much leniency when allowing the child to decide what is right or wrong. Many adults are opposed to corporal punishment, but adults are supposed to give the child direction.

MG: It was a tragedy for Brady because with all the things he could do, he didn't have the capacity to talk to the children or to use talk as a way of discipline or to reason with them.
EJG: With all of the people, they didn't go to school; they worked hard all their lives, strict upbringing. Even the teachers used corporal punishment at that time. In the forties and fifties, they used to whip children all the time.

MG: Into the sixties.
EJG: Yes.

MG: You dedicate the book to your nephew Wilfred—I thought that was a beautiful and touching tribute, and I understand why. Why did you choose Wilfred—for people who don't know him?

EJG: Well, it's too bad for people who don't know him. [*laughs*] He will help people all the time. Dianne and I can call him all the time, and he's willing to do anything. He's always doing something for somebody. He's always helping someone. It was Wilfred who got those tickets for me to go to Angola. And it's also dedicated to Irvin Mayfield, the musician. One of his great pieces of music is "Angola."

MG: What first gave you the idea to write *The Tragedy of Brady Sims*? You worked on that for a long time. Where did that come from?
EJG: I needed to write another book. [*laughs*] And there were people like that in the quarter.

MG: What about Sweet Sidney? I love that name. What or who inspired this character and his name?
EJG: In the barbershops, there's always a person like that. In an airport, somewhere I was travelling, someone had a shoeshine stand, and he had a name something like that. His name was "Lovie" or some name like that. I think it was in an airport. And the guy had a name something like that. And I thought that would make a great name for a character, so I put it in my story.

MG: In *Brady Sims*, though it takes place mainly in the courtroom and barbershop over a three hour time period, food is still part of the narrative (mainly in the reported speech in the barbershop stories where people tell what had happened). Why do you think that's so important in all your stories and novels, where often there's mention of food?
EJG: Louisiana is a state identified by gumbo and jambalaya and etouffee. No other state can make that claim. I love the food. It identifies our history, our culture. It identifies our background in south Louisiana. And there was always somebody who's hungry. And I guess I'm hungry when I'm writing.

MG: And there's a similarity in *The Tragedy of Brady Sims*, when the son, Jean-Pierre, goes to Stella's. And he orders a hamburger, but he looks so hungry she gives him a plate of beans and rice and a piece of chicken for the same price. The same thing happens in *In My Father's House* when the son, Robert X, goes to the cafe and orders something, and she gives him everything else she's cooked that day.
EJG: We had a place like that in New Roads. The lady, in fact, was a distant cousin of mine. She was a Gaines. She would do that. She was a young lady when she died.

MG: A son comes back, and there's the conflict of father and son. But also the women take care of the sons in the stories. But the women, in the case of the restaurants, they would take care of the young men.

EJG: My aunt Octavia was like that, the aunt I was talking about a while ago. The African American woman always has food around the place. If you're hungry, she would feed you. They had little gardens outside the house, and they always had greens and rice. And they raised chickens, so they had that to give you.

MG: What about fruit trees?

EJG: We had some fruit trees but not that many. Mainly, we ate vegetables.

MG: Is there anything you would like to add?

EJG: No, just check your questions.

MG: I do have a question about "My Uncle and the Fat Lady" [published in *Callaloo* in 2007]—because it was written and published after *Mozart and Leadbelly*, and as far as I know, no one has asked you about it in an interview. It reminds me of "My Grandpa and the Haint" because it seems that you were really having fun writing those stories. In both of the stories, the reader's sympathy is really with the women, and the men are either "disciplined" or punished?

EJG: Yeah, right. The men had no business doing what they were doing. They were wrong.

MG: Why are the women often the stronger characters, as they are here?

EJG: The men had no business doing what they were doing; they were wrong. The grandpa was wrong in what he was doing. As far as the other guy, the uncle, I knew someone somewhat like that. And I loved my aunt so much; she was a great lady. My uncle was my grandmother's brother, and I didn't like the way she was treated. I used to go around with her when she sold cosmetics and perfume and different things and all that sort of stuff to the black people. She would go to town in New Roads to shop for the old people, and she would have a list of groceries or whatever for them. She would take me along with her so I could carry the packages. I loved her. As far as the other one, I just made it up ["My Grandpa and the Haint].

MG: Both have child narrators, and clearly the child narrators admire the women much more than the men.

EJG: I don't like to see anyone hurt. And I loved my aunt, and she loved me. She didn't have any children, and my aunt always wanted me around all the time, as though I was her little boy. She would give me pralines and teacakes, and I would travel with her.

MG: So the story ["My Uncle and the Fat Lady"] was inspired by her?
EJG: Well, it was about him, my uncle. The aunt doesn't come up in the story at all, but it was inspired by my love for her. Although she knew about those things.

MG: And there really was a different standard, and both of those stories show that so beautifully. Yet the child has wisdom beyond the adults, and he sees what's going on. And the stories show some kind of justice. Thank you for talking with me today.

Additional Resources

Short Stories, Introductions, Forewords, and Short Essays by Ernest J. Gaines

"Old Jack." *Callaloo* 24.1 (Winter 2001): 69–70.

"Foreword." *Soul of the River Road: A Cookbook Celebrating Our Culinary Heritage.*
Cookbook Publishers, Inc. 2003. iv.

"Where Have You Gone, New Orleans?" *National Geographic* 210:2 (August 2006):
54–57.

"My Uncle and the Fat Lady." *Callaloo* 30:3 (2007): 684–95.

"Writing on Writing: Louisiana Bound" *Oxford American* 62 (Fall 2008): 138–42.

Introduction. *"This Louisiana Thing That Drives Me": The Legacy of Ernest J. Gaines.*
Reggie Scott Young, Marcia Gaudet, and Wiley Cash. Lafayette: U Louisiana P, 2009.
xi–xvii.

Additional Interviews and Articles with Ernest J. Gaines

Cash, Wiley. "Ernest and Me." *Garden & Gun.* October/November 2017: 134-39. Online.
http://gardenandgun.com/feature/ernest-and-me/.

Curley, Stephen, John Gorman, and Dale Taylor. "Galveston Reads: Gaines Interview
on Pelican Island, TAMUG." February 21, 2008. Online. http://galvestonreads
.blogspot.com/2008/02/gaines-interview-on-pelican-island.html.

Edwards, Bob. "Fighting Illiteracy with *A Lesson Before Dying.*" NPR's *Morning Edition.*
April 15, 2004.

Fahle, Rick. Interview with Ernest J. Gaines on *The Tragedy of Brady Sims.* PBS Book
View Now. National Book Festival, Washington, DC, September 2, 2017. Online
video. http://www.pbs.org/video/ernest-gaines-2017-national-book-festival-ytlg64/.

Fuller, R. Reese. "Going Home." In *Angola to Zydeco: Louisiana Lives.* Jackson: UP of
Mississippi, 2011. 126–39. [Originally published in *The Times of Acadiana*, May 5,
2003] http://www.reesefuller.com/articles/going-home/.

Seelye, Katherine Q. "Author Tends Land Where Ancestors Were Slaves." *New York Times* (October 20, 2010): A-18. http://www.nytimes.com/2010/10/21/us/21gaines.html.

Spencer, Melanie Warner. "Literary Legend." *Louisiana Life.* May/June 2016: 40–44. http://www.myneworleans.com/Louisiana-Life/May-June-2016/Literary-Legend/.

Urrea, Cindy. "Reflections of a Serious Writer." *Acadiana Profile* 18:5 (Nov/Dec 1997): 32–36.

Waddington, Chris. "Literary Legend Ernest Gaines Brings Soul and Stories to a New Orleans Book Festival." *The Times-Picayune* (November 25, 2012): A-1. http://www.nola .com/festivals/index.ssf/2012/11/literary_legend_ernest_gaines.html.

Film Documentaries on Ernest J. Gaines

Ernest J. Gaines: Louisiana Stories, 1992, Michael Smith and Ruth Laney, Producers (Louisiana Public Broadcasting, 55 min).

An Obsession of Mine: The Legacy of Ernest J. Gaines, 2008, Marcia Gaudet, Charles Richard, and Joseph Sanford, Producers (Pelican Pictures, 15 min).

Books about Ernest J. Gaines

Auger, Philip. *Native Sons in "No Man's Land": Re-Writing Afro-American Manhood in the Novels of James Baldwin, Alice Walker, John Edgar Wideman, and Ernest Gaines.* Garland Press, 1999.

Babb, Valerie Melissa. *Ernest Gaines.* Twayne United States Authors Series. Boston: Twayne, 1991.

Beavers, Herman. *Wrestling Angels into Song: The Fiction of Ernest J. Gaines and James Alan McPherson.* Philadelphia: University of Pennsylvania Press, 1995.

Brown, Lillie Anne, ed. *New Criticisms on the Works of Ernest J. Gaines: Man of Letters.* Special issue of *Studies in the Literary Imagination*, Georgia State University, Spring 2016.

Carmean, Karen. *Ernest J. Gaines: A Critical Companion.* Greenwood Press, 1998.

Clark, Keith. *Black Manhood in James Baldwin, Ernest J. Gaines, and August Wilson.* Champaign-Urbana: University of Illinois Press, 2002.

Clary, Françoise, ed. *Plus sur Gaines.* Paris: Atlande, 2006.

Doyle, Mary Ellen. *Voices from the Quarters: The Fiction of Ernest J. Gaines.* Baton Rouge: Louisiana State University Press, 2002.

Estes, David C., ed. *Critical Reflections on the Fiction of Ernest J. Gaines.* Athens: University of Georgia Press, 1994.

Gaudet, Marcia, and Carl Wooton. *Porch Talk with Ernest Gaines: Conversations on the Writer's Craft*. Baton Rouge: LSU Press, 1990.

Lowe, John, ed. *Conversations with Ernest Gaines*. Jackson: University Press of Mississippi, 1995.

Simpson, Anne K. *A Gathering of Gaines: The Man and the Writer*. Lafayette: Center for Louisiana Studies. 1991.

Young, Reggie Scott, Marcia Gaudet, and Wiley Cash. *"This Louisiana Thing That Drives Me": The Legacy of Ernest J. Gaines*. Lafayette: University of Louisiana Press, 2009.

Index